TOOLKIT FOR INTERMEDIATE ACCOUNTING
SIXTH CANADIAN EDITION

CONCEPTUAL FRAMEWORK FOR FINANCIAL ACCOUNTING ANALYSIS

Use this framework always. Use whenever analysing any accounting issues. It provides a useful summary of considerations.

USER ORIENTATION – NEEDS

OBJECTIVES

Provide information:
1. Useful in investment and credit decisions
2. Useful in making resource allocation decisions
3. Useful in assessing management stewardship

First level: The "why"—goals and purposes of accounting.

QUALITATIVE CHARACTERISTICS

A. Understandability
B. Relevance
  (1) Predictive value
  (2) Feedback value
  (3) Timeliness
C. Reliability
  (1) Verifiability
  (2) Representational faithfulness
  (3) Neutrality (conservatism when uncertain)
D. Comparability
E. Consistency

ELEMENTS

1. Assets
2. Liabilities
3. Equity
4. Revenues
5. Expenses
6. Gains
7. Losses

Second level: Bridge between levels 1 and 3

ASSUMPTIONS
1. Economic entity
2. Going concern
3. Monetary unit
4. Periodicity

PRINCIPLES
1. Historical cost
2. Revenue recognition
3. Matching
4. Full disclosure

CONSTRAINTS
1. Cost-benefit
2. Materiality
3. Industry practice

Third level: The "how"— implementation

Recognition and Measurement Concepts

GAAP HIERARCHY

(What is GAAP?) Per the CICA Handbook Section 1000.60-.61

GAAP is defined as:
1) Handbook recommendations in italics
2) Principles that are generally accepted by virtue of use by a significant number of entities in Canada—(incorporates specialized industry accounting)
3) Professional Judgement
   - ☐ Analogous situations in the Handbook
   - ☐ Practices in similar situations
   - ☐ Accounting Guidelines in the Handbook
   - ☐ EIC Abstracts in the Handbook
   - ☐ International Accounting Standards
   - ☐ Accounting standards from other countries
   - ☐ CICA research studies
   - ☐ Other sources, including text books and journals

AN OVERVIEW FRAMEWORK FOR CASE ANALYSIS

(see also chapter on case analysis in Study Guide for more detail and tips!)

CASE ANALYSIS FRAMEWORK

Use this framework when analysing cases.

1. Environment/Framework For Analysis

Consider:
a) stakeholders (what's at stake and what information is needed by users)
b) role (what role have you adopted for the analysis—controller, financial analyst, etc.?)
c) business environment—is the company being analysed in a recession or perhaps is it in an expanding market, etc.?
d) company—what does the company do? How do they earn revenues? Which costs must be incurred? What are the business risks? What is their financial history—have they been profitable for the past few years? Are their key ratios within acceptable industry norms—and getting better or worse?
e) constraints—GAAP, time, cost, etc.
f) overall conclusion based on above—financial reporting objective

2. Issue identification—for complex issues look at—legal form, journal entry, economic substance/intent

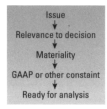

Issue
↓
Relevance to decision
↓
Materiality
↓
GAAP or other constraint
↓
Ready for analysis

3. Issue analysis

Analysis

Quantitative	Qualitative
• impact on key ratios	• incorporate GAAP definitions/criteria
• compare methods	• case specific analysis only
• depth	• look at both sides of an issue

4. Recommendation/conclusion—tie back to role and environment

Prepared by Irene Wiecek
©2002 John Wiley & Sons Canada, Ltd

SUBSEQUENT REVALUATION OF ASSETS

Below is a chart looking at main asset categories and valuation practices. Note how assets are written down to reflect lower values where there is a concern that there is a condition involving uncertainty as to potential loss. Note further that the determination of the lower amount is a function of the intent of management as to what they plan to do with the asset i.e., collect it, sell it, use it to generate revenues, etc. This "intent" gives some insight into how the lower limit is determined e.g., marketable securities that are short term are meant to be converted to cash in the short term; hence, the relevant value is marktet value. Inventories are meant to be sold and replaced and, therefore, the relevant value is often replacement cost or net realizable value.

	Asset Valuation Reference	Valuation Principle	Intent of Management
CASH	not specifically addressed in HB	historical cost/transaction value	NA
MARKETABLE SECURITIES	HB 3010.06	lower of cost and market	to sell (lower bound=market)
ACCOUNTS RECEIVABLE	HB 3020.10 HB 3020.12	lower of cost and net realizable value	to collect (lower bound=NRV)
INVENTORIES	not specifically addressed in HB 3030 except under Statement Presentation under HB 3030.11	lower of cost and market	to sell and replace (choice of replacement cost, NRV or NRV less profit margin)
LOAN RECEIVABLES	HB 3025.14	lower of cost and net realizable value (unless not measurable then FMV of security or observable market prices for loans)	• to hold to maturity (future cash flow) • to sell (future cash flow from sale) • to restructure (future cash flow) • to liquidate/foreclose (cash flows from foreclosure/ liquidation=mkt value of security)
CAPITAL ASSETS	HB 3061.38 HB 3475.08	lower of carrying value and net recoverable value	• to keep for generating future revenues (net recoverable value from future net cash flows) • to sell (future cash flows from sale)
LONG—TERM INVESTMENTS	HB 3050 does not really give a lower bound however, valuation is discussed in HB 3050.20	lower of cost and recovery amount where there is a non-temporary decline in value	• to hold onto for the long term

SUMMARY OF ACCOUNTING METHODS TO FOCUS ON

Use this chart as a study tool to identify the main methods that you should master. These methods are commonly accepted and must be learned. Brief descriptions of the methods and numeric examples are included in the Study Guide. Remember to focus on the incremental impact on net income and key ratios of using the various methods.

Revenues

- %-of-completion method
- completed-contract method
- instalment method
- cost recovery method

Receivables—bad debt estimation

- %-of–sales method—income statment method
- %-of–receivables method—balance sheet method—involves aging of AR

Inventory—costing methods

- FIFO
- LIFO
- Specific identification method
- Weighted average costing
- Standard costing

Inventory—inventory estimation method

- retail method
- gross profit method

Long—Term investments

- cost method
- equity method

Capital assets—depreciation

- straight line method
- unit of production method
- declining balance method
- sinking fund method—effective interest method

Prepared by Irene Wiecek
©2002 John Wiley & Sons Canada, Ltd

DEFINITIONS

These definitions are central to qualitative analysis of financial reporting issues. To that extent, this chart should be referred to and used when doing case analysis or analysing issues. Ideally, these concepts/criteria and definitions should be committed to memory as they form the core of intermediate accounting.

	Reference	Definition	Recognition—General Rule	Measurement General rule*
ASSETS	HB 1000.29-.31	• **future benefit** • entity **controls** access to benefit or has **risks and rewards** of ownership • **transaction or event has occurred**	• meets definition AND • **probable/likely** AND • **measurable**	• at historical cost with write down if impairment in value (see Subsequent Revaluation of Assets) • see also industry practice • at transaction cost or best estimate
LIABILITIES	HB 1000.32-.34	• **obligation**/duty to pay • little or **no discretion to avoid** • **transaction or event obligating entity has occurred**	• meet definition AND • **probable/likely AND** • **measurable**	
EQUITY	HB 1000.35-.36	• **ownership** interest in net assets	• **transaction has occurred AND** • **measurable**	• at transaction cost
REVENUES	HB 1000.37 HB 3400.03	• **increases in economic resources** (from **ordinary operations**)	• **performance/risks and rewards** of ownership passed • reasonable assurance as to **measurement** • reasonable assurance as to **collectibility**	• at transaction cost
EXPENSES	HB 1000.38	• **decreases in economic resources** (from **ordinary operations**)	• if asset **no longer has future benefit**, OR • expense (not linked to specific revenues) **occurred in period** OR, • in order to **match** with revenues	• at transaction cost or best estimate
GAINS	HB 1000.39	• **increases in net assets** from **peripheral/incidental** transactions	• when **realized**	• at transaction cost
LOSSES	HB 1000.40	• **decreases in net assets** from **peripheral/incidental** transactions	• when **likely/** measurable	• at best estimate
CONTIN-GENCIES	HB 3290	• **existing condition involving uncertainty as to possible gain or loss that will be resolved by future event**	• loss-when likely and measurable • gain-may not recognize even if likely	• at best estimate

*see also HB I508 for measurement uncertainty—must disclose nature of uncertainty and amount.

Prepared by Irene Wiecek
©2002 John Wiley & Sons Canada, Ltd

TOOLKIT FOR INTERMEDIATE ACCOUNTING
SIXTH CANADIAN EDITION

SUMMARY OF KEY RATIOS

Use this summary whenever evaluating a financial issue where financial information is given the company. You should select the key ratios relevant to the company and its environment, keeping in mind that certain ratios are more important than others in certain situations.

A Summary of Financial Ratios

RATIO	FORMULA	PURPOSE OR USE
I. Liquidity		
1. Current ratio	$\dfrac{\text{Current assets}}{\text{Current liabilities}}$	Measures short-term debt-paying ability
2. Quick or acid-test ratio	$\dfrac{\text{Cash, marketable securities, and receivables (net)}}{\text{Current liabilities}}$	Measures immediate short-term liquidity
3. Current cash debt coverage ratio	$\dfrac{\text{Net cash provided by operating activities}}{\text{Average current liabilities}}$	Measures a company's ability to pay off its current liabilities in a given year from its operations
II. Activity		
4. Receivable turnover	$\dfrac{\text{Net sales}}{\text{Average trade receivables (net)}}$	Measures liquidity of receivables
5. Inventory turnover	$\dfrac{\text{Cost of goods sold}}{\text{Average inventory}}$	Measures liquidity of inventory
6. Asset turnover	$\dfrac{\text{Net sales}}{\text{Average total assets}}$	Measures how efficiently assets are used to generate sales
III. Profitability		
7. Profit margin on sales	$\dfrac{\text{Net income}}{\text{Net sales}}$	Measures net income generated by each dollar of sales
8. Rate of return on assets	$\dfrac{\text{Net income}}{\text{Average total assets}}$	Measures overall profitability of assets
9. Rate of return on common share equity	$\dfrac{\text{Net income minus preferred dividends}}{\text{Average common shareholders' equity}}$	Measures profitability of owners' investment
10. Earnings per share	$\dfrac{\text{Net income minus preferred dividends}}{\text{Weighted shares outstanding}}$	Measures net income earned on each common share
11. Price earnings ratio	$\dfrac{\text{Market price of shares}}{\text{Earnings per share}}$	Measures the ratio of the market price per share to earnings per share
12. Payout ratio	$\dfrac{\text{Cash dividends}}{\text{Net income}}$	Measures percentage of earnings distributed in the form of cash dividends
IV. Coverage		
13. Debt to total assets	$\dfrac{\text{Total debt}}{\text{Total assets or equities}}$	Measures the percentage of total assets provided by creditors
14. Times interest earned	$\dfrac{\text{Income before interest charges and taxes}}{\text{Interest charges}}$	Measures ability to meet interest payments as they come due
15. Cash debt coverage ratio	$\dfrac{\text{Net cash provided by operating activities}}{\text{Average total liabilities}}$	Measures a company's ability to repay its total liabilities in a given year from its operations
16. Book value per share	$\dfrac{\text{Common Shareholders' equity}}{\text{Outstanding shares}}$	Measures the amount each share would receive if the company were liquidated at the amounts reported on the balance sheet

TOOLKIT FOR INTERMEDIATE ACCOUNTING
SIXTH CANADIAN EDITION

STUDY STEPS

I have incorporated this framework into each chapter to provide a consistent approach to the study of the material. Students should follow this whenever studying a new topic or attempting to analyse a new issue.

1. Understanding transaction/arrangement—business content

Tips!

- Draw a diagram that shows parties involved and details of the transactions—legal form.

- On a very basic level, know what is *given up* and what is *received by* the company.

- Attempt to prepare a rough journal entry. You may not be able to do this at this point especially since you might not have the numbers. This is useful however, at this stage as it often will draw your attention to an issue.

- Try to determine the economic substance of the transaction—consider intent.

Note: This analysis is essential when identifying and analysing complex transactions where the issue is not evident.

2. Understanding how the transaction fits into the financial reporting model and conceptual framework—analysis

Tips!

- List "recognition," "measurement," and "presentation/disclosure" down the left hand side of the page and fill in principles/concepts/definitions/criteria that you think are relevant beside each one. Use the other charts and exhibits at the front and in various chapters of the Study Guide for a complete list of principles/concepts/definitions/criteria.

- Try to identify any problems/issues that might be encountered in analysing the topic. These are usually the result of the nature of the transaction. You may have already identified these as part of Step 1 above.

- Try to identify where professional judgement will be required.

Note: This process also helps establish a framework for case analysis for more complex transactions.

3. Becoming proficient in any required calculations—skills

Tips!

- In many of the more complex areas, accountants have developed worksheets that are invaluable in doing the calculations. These must be mastered. Consider them an additional skill to carry forward in your accounting career.

- There are many methods that have been developed over the years to account for certain things such as depreciation and bad debt expense. These have been separately summarized in the TOOLKIT and also are reviewed in more detail in the main body of the Study Guide chapters.

- In order to master the calculations, you should do as many of the exercises and problems as you can. There are many problems included in the Study Guide with answers. There are numerous exercises and problems in the text, many of which have the solutions at the back of the Study Guide. These are the minimum numbers that should be done.

- When doing the exercises and problems, attempt them first without an answer since this helps you to identify your weaknesses. Afterwards, look at the answer. There is no point in doing these if you are not checking your answers.

Prepared by Irene Wiecek
©2002 John Wiley & Sons Canada, Ltd

STUDY GUIDE TO ACCOMPANY
VOLUME 1: CHAPTERS 1-13

INTERMEDIATE ACCOUNTING
SIXTH CANADIAN EDITION

Donald E. Kieso, Ph.D., C.P.A.
KPMG Peat Marwick Emeritus Professor of Accountancy
Northern Illinois University
DeKalb, Illinois

Jerry J. Weygandt, Ph.D., C.P.A.
Arthur Anderson Alumni Professor of Accounting
University of Wisconsin
Madison, Wisconsin

Terry D. Warfield, Ph.D., C.P.A.
PricewaterhouseCoopers Research Scholar
University of Wisconsin
Madison, Wisconsin

Bruce Irvine, Ph.D., CMA, FCMA
University of Saskatchewan (Emeritus)
Saskatoon, Saskatchewan

Nicola M. Young, MBA, FCA
Saint Mary's University
Halifax, Nova Scotia

Irene M. Wiecek, C.A.
University of Toronto,
Toronto, Ontario

Study Guide prepared by Irene M. Wiecek

wiley.com

Permission Acknowledgements

Extracts from Strategic Management 1 examinations published by the Certified General Accountants Association of Canada. ©1993-1996, reprinted by permission.

Excerpts reprinted, with permission from CICA Uniform Final Exams, 1995-1996, The Canadian Institute of Chartered Accountants, Toronto, Canada. Any changes to the original material are the sole responsibility of the authors and/or publisher and have not been reviewed by or endorsed by the CICA.

Extracts from CMA Exams published by the Society of Managerial Accountants. © 1994-1996, reprinted by permission.

National Library of Canada Cataloguing in Publication Data
Wiecek, Irene
        Study guide vol. 1 and vol. 2 to accompany Intermediate accounting, 6th Canadian edition

Supplement to: Kieso, Donald E. Intermediate accounting.
ISBN 0-470-83163-4 (v. 1).—ISBN 0-470-83164-2 (v. 2)

        1. Accounting—Problems, exercises, etc. I Kieso, Donald E. Intermediate accounting. II. Title.

HF5635.I573 2001 Suppl. 2   657'.044   C2001-902469-X

Production Credits
Publisher: John Horne
Editorial Manager: Karen Staudinger
Publishing Services Director: Karen Bryan
Senior Marketing Manager: Janine Daoust
New Media Editor: Elsa Passera
Publishing Services/Permissions Coordinator: Michelle Marchetti
Cover Design: Ian Koo
Cover Photo: Grant V. Faint/Image Bank
Printing and Binding: Tri-Graphic Printing Limited

Printed and Bound in Canada
10 9 8 7 6 5 4 3 2 1

John Wiley & Sons Canada, Ltd
22 Worcester Road
Etobicoke, ON
M9W 1L1

Visit our website at www.wiley.com/canada

ABOUT THE AUTHOR

Irene M. Wiecek, CA is Associate Director of the Master of Management and Professional Accounting Program (MMPA) at the Joseph L. Rotman School of Management, University of Toronto where she is also a Faculty member, lecturing primarily in Financial Reporting. She has taught in the Executive MBA, MBA, MMPA, B Com and Management Major Programs covering material from Introductory Accounting to Advanced Accounting. Currently focusing on the area of integrated learning, she is involved in redesigning the MMPA program and has developed numerous cases, which examine financial reporting, and its link to other functional area such as finance and strategy. A prolific case writer, Irene has won case competitions for writing and presenting cases as well as leading and coaching student teams. She has had several cases published in accounting journals. At the professional level, Irene is involved in an educational capacity with both the Canadian and Ontario Institute of Chartered Accountants, as well as the Society of Management Accountants. Prior to working at the University of Toronto, Irene worked for KPMG as a public accountant and as a consultant in private industry. Irene obtained her Chartered Accountancy designation in 1981.

CONTENTS

Introduction

HOW TO GET THE MOST OUT OF LEARNING FINANCIAL REPORTING

For several years, my students have been asking me for additional sources that will help them understand intermediate accounting and the use of cases in financial reporting. Students often make the following comments:

- There is too much material to cover in the text.
- The professor does not have time to go over all the material in class.
- The solutions to questions and exercises in the text are not readily available.
- There are so many questions in the text. Since we do not have time to do them all, which ones should we do?

In an effort to help students with these and other concerns related to intermediate accounting and financial reporting, I have written this book. This edition has been updated for current GAAP and has the following features:

- **Multiple choice questions** for professional exams have been included. Since many of the professional accounting bodies in Canada and the United States are now using multiple choice on professional examinations, I have included a selection of these types of question for the following exams: CA, CMA and CGA.

- **Additional cases** have been added using **real companies**—these cases emphasize qualitative analysis, as well as, quantitative analysis.

- The TOOLKIT includes summaries of **key definitions/criteria/concepts,** as well as **frameworks** for learning the material and for **case analysis.** The TOOLKIT has been designed so that students can tear off the panels/cards and bring them to class to use during discussion and analysis.

- Each chapter has been reformatted and rewritten to be consistent with the **learning frameworks** in the TOOLKIT. This will provide students with a structured approach for learning new material and for case analysis.

- I have attempted to incorporate more **diagrams** and **decision trees** to simplify the learning process.

Objectives of the Book

With this book, I am attempting to **bridge the gap** between students and the material as presented by the text and by the universities and colleges. This book is not meant to provide a shortcut; rather, it is meant to **supplement** the resources already available and to assist students in **focusing** on what is important in the course.

The emphasis is on **developing professional judgement** and **critical thinking skills** rather than on honing mechanical skills and memorization. Although **honing mechanical skills** is also important, I feel that the only way to learn the mechanical skills is for students to practise problems and calculations on their own. Therefore, solutions to selected cases, problems, and exercises from the text have been included within the book. Students should practice as many as practical for them. I have also incorporated problems of a fairly mechanical nature here, along with worked solutions.

As far as memorization goes, there are many things that must be committed to memory. However, students should not treat this as the primary objective. Rather, students should think in terms of remembering things so that they can **apply that knowledge** in real-life situations and circumstances.

Memorization is only the means to an end. Having said that, it has been my experience that students get overwhelmed with detail and are not able to internalize and carry forward key underlying principles, definitions, criteria and concepts. Therefore, I have included summaries of these in the "TOOLKIT". The TOOLKIT charts, frameworks, etc. are found as part of the cover of this book and should be separated from the book and carried around to be used whenever a case/issue is being analyzed. Eventually, the information in the TOOLKIT will be **internalized** as students use it over and over again in differing contexts. I plan to test these as study aids for students currently writing their CA and CMA exams. Hopefully, students will refer to the TOOLKIT and this book very often during the course and also afterwards in **preparing for professional exams.**

The TOOLKIT also includes a **case analysis framework,** which will help students determine parameters for case analysis and refine case-writing skills. This is a summary of the chapter that covers case analysis in detail. Again, the TOOLKIT should be used in **all** case analysis and will hopefully assist beyond the course in professional exam writing.

I am convinced that students must focus on journal entries as the first stepping stone in understanding an issue and how the issue affects the financial statements. Therefore, wherever possible, I have included journal entries. I encourage students to think in terms of debits and credits and to analyze all issues by beginning with journal entries.

HOW THE BOOK IS SET UP

The chapters in this study guide correspond directly with the textbook. Most chapters will include the following:

- **Perspective and insights** as to what makes the topic interesting and challenging from a learning perspective

- **Study steps** as outlined in the TOOLKIT—including
  1) emphasis on the **business transactions or issues** before looking at the qualitative issues and calculations
  2) an analysis of the key **recognition, measurement and disclosure** issues pertinent to the topic
  3) an **in-depth look at the calculations** and accounting methods pertinent to the topic
- **Multiple choice questions** including a selection from CA, CMA, and CGA exams
- **Quantitative problems** and worked solutions.
- **Cases** and solutions.

There is also a chapter on case analysis, as well as solutions to many exercises and problems from the text which appear at the end of each chapter.

HOW TO USE THIS BOOK

Use this book however you see fit to help you with this course. I think that it might benefit you most if you use it as follows:

- **Read** the body of the chapter before class including reviewing exhibit 1 in each chapter. Use the TOOLKIT for reference purposes. The TOOLKIT cards should be kept beside you during class, when doing problems and cases, and when reading the text and studying for tests. They have been made so that you can tear them out of the book and carry them around. Please do so! The more you use them, the more that you will internalize the material.

- After class, **work through the questions, problems, and cases** presented for each topic. It is in your best interest to attempt the answer before looking at the solution. Use the TOOLKIT when working through the case analysis and lecture notes. This will help put things in context.

- Try as many problems and exercises from the text as possible, given your time constraints, and compare your answers with the solutions provided here.

- When studying for tests, work through each chapter presented here, including the questions, problems, and cases, to refresh your memory. This should be done in conjunction with a review of class notes and the text material since not all material is covered here.

Warning! Note that different instructors/professors will have different styles and may emphasize different things. You should ensure that your study efforts mirror the emphasis placed on the material by the instructor/professor. Ask yourself after each topic: What do I think is important to know about this topic? Also, ask yourself what your instructor thinks is important to know about the topic.

PREPARING FOR PROFESSIONAL EXAMS

If you are planning on choosing accounting as a career or profession, then now is the time to start planning for completing the process. There are three professional accounting bodies in Canada: the Certified General Accountants' Association (CGA), the Society of Management Accountants (CMA) and the Canadian Institute of Chartered Accountants (CA). Each of these bodies has a certification process that involves a series of courses, exams and/or work experience.

CGA

Students enrolling in the CGA program need to have a university degree prior to accreditation. The program consists of weekly assignments, optional lectures and national examinations, plus mandatory practical experience. Those students with a university degree will receive advanced standing based on their academic qualifications and may be exempt from a large segment of the program's educational components. The web site for CGA Canada is www.cga-canada.org.

Many of the examinations have multiple choice questions, as well as, problems and cases. I have included numerous examples of the multiple choice questions in this Study Guide.

CMA

The process for becoming a CMA involves a set of entrance exams, two years' work experience and a Strategic Leadership Program. The entrance examinations are held over two days and are four hours each in duration. The Strategic Leadership Program involves classroom sessions, self-study and submission of a series of "management reports", which are similar to cases. Normally, students would require post-secondary education in order to obtain the academic credentials required in order to take the entrance examinations.

The entrance examinations are comprised of objective questions (50%), including multiple choice questions, and a case (50%). The web site for the society is www.cma-canada.org.

Where possible, I have included examples of multiple choice questions within the Study Guide.

CA

Students interested in becoming a Chartered Accountant must first obtain a university degree and complete 51 credit hours of required courses at the university level. It is possible to achieve these concurrently, i.e., with a well-planned Bachelor of Commerce degree. Students are required to write a national final set of examinations (Uniform Final

Examinations) which take three days and are three hours in duration each. Students must also fulfill a mandatory work experience requirement. Each province administers the process and in many provinces, such as Ontario, there are additional requirements such as attending the province's month-long School of Accountancy, and completing an entrance exam (the Core Knowledge Examination) and an exit examination (the End of School Examination) for the school.

The Core Knowledge Examination includes multiple choice questions. Many of the multiple choice questions included in the Study Guide are similar to those that would be on the examinations and, where possible, I have included a small number of actual questions. The website for the CICA is www.cica.ca.

A FINAL NOTE OF CAUTION

I have attempted to condense the material into something that is more manageable; however, this book is in no way meant to replace the text. Remember that the text is the key all-inclusive reference source while this guide attempts only to highlight certain aspects.

Have fun with the course and I hope that you find the book useful. I would appreciate any feedback as my objective is to assist students and professors in de-mystifying the teaching and learning of intermediate accounting.

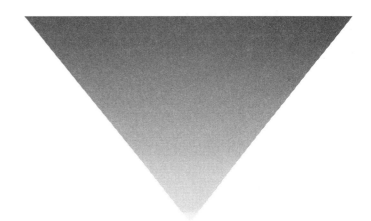

USING THE CICA HANDBOOK TO SUPPLEMENT THE COURSE MATERIAL

What is the CICA Handbook?

The CICA *Handbook* is the **authoritative source for GAAP in Canada.** It is written by the Canadian Institute of Chartered Accountants (CICA) with input from the industry and the other major professional accounting bodies in Canada. Therefore, it makes sense that students planning to become professional accountants study directly from the CICA *Handbook*. The *Handbook* is printed in hardcopy (updated periodically) and is available in electronic version through the CICA website.

Where do I get the Handbook?

The *Handbook* is available directly from the CICA. In some provinces, the provincial institutes allow students to register with the provincial institutes as **associate student members** and receive a hard copy of *CICA Handbook* at a discount. When you are hired by a public accounting firm on a full-time basis, they will often pay for your copy.

In the meantime, the university's library likely has a hard copy or a copy on diskette or CD. If you plan to become a Chartered Accountant, once you register as a full-time student, you will have access to the electronic, web-based version of the *Handbook*.

Why should I use the Handbook? Don't the text and study guide contain all I need to know?

Yes and no. The text and Study Guide do include most of what you need to do well in your course; however, as previously mentioned, students planning a career in professional accounting might want to see the material first hand in order to get used to the wording and content. When studying for professional exams, you will need to study from the *Handbook* and when practising accounting in the work place, it is the *Handbook* that will be used. Therefore, your accounting course is a good time to get your feet wet and use the *Handbook* in a supportive learning environment.

Note that some professional accounting examinations allow the *Handbook* to be used during the exam.

If I decide to incorporate the Handbook into my study plan, will it involve additional work?

Not necessarily. The information in the *Handbook* is not new and different information from the text and Study Guide. Remember that the text and Study Guide take material from the *Handbook*—not the other way around.

What can I do to incorporate the Handbook into my studies during my accounting courses?

1) When you learn a new topic, **read the related** *Handbook* **section**. There is usually a separate section for most of the chapters in the book. You may find that some of the more complex sections go beyond the text and your course, so ask your instructor whether you need to go into the additional depth. Keep it simple however; the idea is not to confuse you with added complexity, but rather to expose you to the profession's authoritative source.

2) **Learn the definitions and criteria. They are very important in any issue analysis**. Usually in each *Handbook* section, the definitions and criteria are up-front in the first few paragraphs in each section. Learn these. Note that I have included all key definitions in the TOOLKIT and in the exhibits in each of the chapters in the study guide. There are cross references to the actual section numbers in these exhibits and in the TOOLKIT.

3) Try the multiple choice questions in the Study Guide that focus on Handbook wording. As you review the answer, look in the *Handbook* to verify the wording yourself.

Your overall objective is to begin to familiarize yourself with the content, wording, and layout while you are already studying the material in the text and study guide. Remember that the core material is in your text and Study Guide and, that at this point in your career, the *Handbook* will offer you an alternate source or perspective on the topic.

GOOD LUCK!

HOW TO APPROACH CASE ANALYSIS

Case analysis is important in financial reporting and intermediate accounting. Not only does it mirror real-life decision-making, it encourages **critical thinking** and helps develop **professional judgement**. Furthermore, it allows you to test your true knowledge of journal entries and accounting theory by attempting to **apply** the latter in real-life situations. Intermediate accounting is not about memorization, calculations, and bookkeeping. Although these things are crucial building blocks, the **key skill** to be learned from the course is **problem solving** within the Canadian and global financial reporting environment.

In order to solve problems, knowledge of calculations, journal entries, and generally accepted accounting principles is important. However, a student who has mastered these has only won half the battle. You must be able to **apply the knowledge** in situations where there is **uncertainty**. It is rare in real life that someone will present you with a problem and provide all the facts needed to solve it. In many cases, identifying the problem and gathering relevant information is a large part of the task.

You must also learn to consider the **impact of the environment** on your decision-making, including the people involved such as the financial statement preparers and users. Different people think in different ways depending on their own perspectives. What is right or good for one person may not be right or good for another. For instance, assume that two people are discussing the weather. Both comment that they hope the weather will be good tomorrow. One might be thinking that she hopes it stays sunny because she has to drive to Montreal. The other might be thinking that he hopes it snows because he plans to do a lot of skiing. They both want "good weather" but each one has a completely different definition of what "good weather" is at that time. "Good" financial reporting might mean one thing to one person and a completely different thing to another.

Cases sensitize you to these things. Because this way of thinking is often different from what you are used to, you may have problems analysing cases at first. However, you will eventually catch on and find that the study of accounting is more fulfilling as a result of the use of cases. It is easier to approach this material with a completely open mind rather than trying to make it fit into a preconceived notion of accounting that may be more narrowly focused.

With cases, there is **rarely a single acceptable answer or recommendation**. There may be several, even for the same issue. The important thing is how you **support your answer** or recommendation.

What is a Case?

What makes a case, a case? Many people have different views on this. Most cases involve some sort of **"real-life"** scenario where there are one or several "issues" or "problems." You would be expected to identify the issues, analyse them, and then recommend a course of action. The cases may involve either quantitative analysis, qualitative analysis, or both.

What makes a case more challenging is the "required" information. Some cases will specify what you should do (e.g., calculate the future tax expense or identify which amortization method the company should use). Others leave the "required" section more open by requesting that you discuss the issues. In the latter, you must decide, for instance, if the future tax expense needs to be calculated in the first place or whether the choice of amortization methods is even an issue. Therein lies the challenge. What is the issue? How should the case be approached?

A successful manager should not only be able to **solve problems that have been identified** for him, but more importantly, he should be able to **identify the problems** in the first place. Therefore, in this book, many of the cases will require that the issues be identified (unstructured cases). For some of the more complicated areas, the "required" part will be more direct (structured cases).

There are also other types of cases included in this book. These are more like discussion questions that require some independent thought. These were meant primarily to "stretch the brain" and to challenge existing ideas. The following discussion deals with a scenario type case that is unstructured, since this is the most challenging.

The Case—The Challenge

Let's look at a sample case—Bronwyn Boats in Exhibit 1. I have chosen a case of moderate length and difficulty so as not to oversimplify case analysis. Read the case through to get a feel for what it involves.

This case could have been a straightforward question on revenue recognition. I could have simply asked the following question and not bothered to create a scenario: When should revenues be recognized?

The above type of **directed question** asks for **regurgitation of memorized facts** (i.e., revenues should be recognized when the risks and rewards of ownership have passed from the seller to the buyer and when measurability and collectibility is reasonably assured).

Instead, I have complicated the question by disguising it within a scenario or case. Firstly, revenue recognition must be identified as an issue and once identified, the question then becomes when should revenues be recognized in **this** scenario? The memorized knowledge must be applied to the facts of this specific situation. You must **recall revenue recognition rules** and ask yourself the following questions:

- What are the **risks and rewards** of owning/building a boat?
- When do they pass to the buyer?
- When is the **earnings process substantially complete?**

- Can revenues and costs be **measured?**
- What are the **costs** associated with these revenues?
- Are there any **collectibility** problems?

The trick here is to **identify the issue** and then to **apply knowledge** instead of merely regurgitating memorized information. That is the true test of whether you have absorbed and understood the material.

For most of you, the **initial challenge is being able to identify the issues**. Then, once that is mastered, the challenge becomes **how to analyse the issues** in a meaningful way that will result in a reasonable recommendation or conclusion.

There are many different ways to approach case analysis, but most have a similar underlying structure that may be adapted in different situations. The material below is one method of case analysis.

Understanding the Environment—Establishing a Framework for Analysis

We must first understand the environment within which the analysis takes place. A good question to ask is as follows: Is there anything about the environment or any background information that might cause us to identify different issues, or to view the issues differently, or to respond differently?

Below are some points for consideration.

1) Identify the **role** that you are playing. Usually, most cases require that you assume a role. Who are you in the case? From whose perspective will you be answering the case? As in our weather example above, different people have differing opinions and views on things.

   If your role is that of an independent advisor (e.g., a chartered accountant hired by the shareholders), you might think differently than an employee who works for the company. As an employee, you might be concerned with keeping your job and, therefore, would want to keep your boss happy by giving her what she wants. As an outside professional, hired by the shareholders, you might focus more on keeping the shareholders happy. Keeping the boss happy and keeping the shareholders happy might not result in the same course of action.

   Consideration should also be given to **ethics and legal liability**. Outside consultants who offer advice might later be sued if the advice is relied on and results in a loss to the company, shareholders, or other users. Therefore, outside consultants must assess the risk of each engagement. For higher risk engagements, they might take a more conservative position and give more conservative advice.

   Many situations involve ethical dilemmas, where the individual must make decisions that either will harm himself or harm others and a choice must be made. Sometimes, doing the right thing may result in personal loss. Humanize the analysis by thinking what you would do in the situation. For instance, accruing a large loss might result in lower net income and, hence, a lower bonus for the controller. On the other hand, not accruing the loss may mislead users.

Remember that the financial statements are a reflection of the success/failures of the company and of management in that they reveal whether management is fulfilling its stewardship function. Therefore, in preparing the statements, management might be concerned about disclosing negative items.

Tip! Put yourself in the shoes of the person whose role you are playing. Think about how you would react in a situation and what factors would influence your decision. Would you put your own needs ahead of other users?

Tip! Preparers of financial information may be biased and this must be considered in any analysis.

2) **Identify the users of the information and other stakeholders**. Who will be using the information required in the case? What will they be using it for? Also, more broadly, who will be affected by the financial reporting decisions being made and how will they be affected? This will make a difference in your analysis. Different users have different information needs and since the overall reporting objective is to provide information that is relevant to users, this user focus is critical. Again, anyone affected by the information should be considered. Chapter 1 of the text considers different stakeholders in the financial reporting environment.

Tip! For any question that requires professional judgement, always ask two questions: 1) who wants to know ?; and 2) why do they need this information i.e., what decision will they use this information for? That way you may consider tailoring the information to help the users make their decisions.

Tip! Although ideally, the main objective of financial reporting is to provide information to users that is useful for decision making, this does not always happen due to personal and corporate biases.

Tip! A good analysis will always look at the impact of the decisionmaking on the affected parties.

3) **Consider the business environment**. Is the economy in a recession or the real estate market in a slump? This will affect your analysis as the company might be more prone to bias if they are trying to stay afloat in a sinking environment. Looking at other companies in the industry will give some background on how other companies are faring in the current times

Tip! The environment will give some clues as to how information might be biased.

4) **Review the company**. What do they do? How do they earn their revenues. Which costs must be incurred to earn revenues? What are the business risks? What is the

financial history of the company, i.e., have revenues been steadily increasing over time, or decreasing? What about profits? Does the company turn a profit every year? Were the results of this year predictable? What are the key ratios that are considered to be important in the industry? How does the company's ratios compare to industry norms and its own historical ratios? All this data provides a backdrop for the analysis.

> **Insight into the way the company operates and what is important to the company helps you understand why they might find certain financial reporting issues more sensitive than others and will help in understanding what is at stake in the decision.** *Tip!*

5. **Identify constraints**. Are there any factors that will limit the possibilities? Is there a legal requirement to follow GAAP? Are there time constraints on obtaining information? Is all the required information available?, etc. Generally, if a company has shares or debt that are traded publicly, then there is a GAAP constraint.

> **If the question does not make it clear as to whether a GAAP constraint exists, then look to the main users. Normally users would want GAAP financial statements since they are more reliable and comparable.** *Tip!*

> **Acknowledging constraints up-front will help to keep you focused on the relevant analysis.** *Tip!*

6. **Based on the above, determine the overall financial reporting objective**. This is a summation of the above information. It helps to focus the analysis and conclude in a manner that is consistent with the environment. For instance, assume that your role is a chartered accountant and that you will be providing information to a bank so it can make a lending decision. Your tendency will be to offer conservative advice and disclose more information (especially about risks and potential losses), rather than less. Hopefully, this will reduce the risk of potential lawsuit should the bank suffer a loss. It will also give the bank the information needed to make a decision.

This is only one position or conclusion, and you might think that there are other overriding factors that are more important.

> **The conclusion or recommendation is a matter of judgement and there is usually no right or wrong answer, although certain cases may lean towards a certain interpretation.**

> **Once the financial reporting objective is outlined, try to be consistent in your recommendations where there are multiple issues. For example, if you conclude conservatively on the first issue, the other issues should also reflect the conservative approach unless you explain why.**

At this point, a quick review of the material in Chapter 1 of the text would be of benefit.

IDENTIFYING THE ISSUES

Once we are sensitized to the environment, and are aware of the different parties involved and their predispositions, we must tackle the next problem: identifying the issues. Just how do we identify issues? What makes an issue, an issue? This is very complex and is, ultimately, a matter of judgement. Many things must be considered.

1. **An issue is a financial reporting problem that needs resolution**. Resolution is usually not straightforward but rather is arrived at through careful analysis of relevant alternatives. In financial reporting, keep in mind that most issues will relate to how to account for something or how to present it in the financial statements. Focus on relevant issues only.

Tip! Although there might be other issues that need to be addressed in other areas such as tax or management accounting issues, try to keep focused on the financial reporting issues. Having said this, in real life, all important issues would be addressed.

Tip! For more complex issues, the issue may not be any more clear than ...How do we account for the transaction?

In cases involving complex issues, the following will help to clarify how to proceed with the analysis. 1) Draw a diagram of the exchange, including all parties involved. This will illustrate the legal form. 2) Try to answer the question: "What did the company give up and what did they get?" 3) Attempt a journal entry or at least part of one. 4) Try to identify economic substance, NB: management intent often gives a key to this.

2. **Issues may be more important or less important.** It is essential to **rank** them and tackle the more important ones first.

An issue is generally **more important if it involves large amounts**, especially those that affect the calculation of net income (or some other sensitive number on the financial statements) or a sensitive financial ratio. This is a numeric application of the concept of materiality. Which numbers/ratios are more sensitive? That depends on the situation. Net income is almost always sensitive. That is, if net income changes by a material amount, it will usually affect user decisions. Other numbers/ratios are determined to be sensitive because the users will focus on them in that particular scenario. For instance, if the company has a loan, and part of the terms of the loan are that the working capital ratio be at least 1:1, then current assets and current liabilities would be sensitive numbers and anything that affects those numbers would potentially be an issue (e.g., classification of items between current and long term).

Tip! Rank issues and deal with the most relevant and material issues first.

Tip! Look for sensitive numbers or ratios in the case. If you see a potential reporting issue that affects these numbers, then you likely have an issue.

3. **Identifying issues requires knowledge**. You cannot hope to spot an issue if you do not know GAAP. For instance, suppose a friend comes to you with the observation that his dog is shedding hair. He asks you if this is a problem. Is it? Unless you know something about dogs, and that particular breed, you will not able to answer. The shedding might be perfectly normal if it happens every year and occurs in the spring. However, if this is a breed that normally does not shed hair at all, it may mean that the dog is sick. The point is, that in order to spot a problem or an issue, you need to have specific knowledge in that area.

In the area of accounting, the specific knowledge you need to know is GAAP; the general principles, the available alternatives, the rules. Only then can you recognize if GAAP is not being followed, or advise a client how to account for something. Keep in mind that GAAP is not always legally required, or required by users of the financial information. In the latter case, you would be governed by providing the most useful information. This requires knowledge of what useful information is (see Chapter 2 on the conceptual framework). It also helps to use common sense, as well, which is part of professional judgement.

Sometimes, if you cannot figure out the issues in the case, perhaps you need to reread the technical material assigned for that or preceding weeks. After going over the material, reread the case again.

4. **Issues involve choices**. Try to see if there is more than one way to look at a problem (i.e., from different perspectives). Look carefully at the preparer of the financial information (usually management) and the users of the information. Does good financial disclosure mean the same thing to management as it does to the shareholders? Often not. In the past, companies have often held the belief that the shareholders need only be told limited amounts of information. Furthermore, management might have a tendency to disclose only things that make the company and itself look good. Shareholders, on the other hand, may think that more information is better, especially information about risks and potential losses.

If you can see differing viewpoints, there is likely an issue (i.e., one has a different idea of what the best accounting or presentation is than the other).

Look at the people in the case. Honestly attempt to put yourself in their shoes. This may sound silly, but you will find it to be one of the keys to successful case analysis. How would you feel about what's going on? How would you react? What would be important to you? After all, it could be you in the situation. If you see that the parties in the case may see things differently (remember the weather example) then there is a potential issue.

Keep your issue and alternatives basic. Most issues can be boiled down to a few simple categories:

- **Recognition**-should I recognize something on the financial statements or not
- **Measurement/valuation**-what amount should I recognize? How do I measure the transaction?

• **Presentation/disclosure/classification-**where should the item be shown, and in how much detail, if any?

> **Tip!** Most chapters in the Study Guide has an exhibit that summarizes issues by these headings.

ANALYSING THE ISSUES

Once identified, the issues must be analysed in a meaningful way such that the conclusions/recommendations are relevant, especially within the context of the environment. Points for consideration are as follows:

1) **Understand the company's business.** What does the company do? How does it earn revenues? What costs must it incur? What are the business risks? All these questions and others must be understood. It is critical that you understand the business and the environment before you can offer any advice. Therefore, spend a few minutes figuring this out. This might include drawing quick time lines of the earnings process or diagrams of the business relationships, i.e., who owns who, etc.

> **Tip!** If you do not understand the business, how do you ever hope to advise on how the business should be represented in the financial statements?

2) **Only relevant alternatives should be looked at in your analysis**. This is perhaps the most common mistake. Most students think in terms of right and wrong, black and white. When students are first introduced to case analysis, many are unable to look at an issue from more than one perspective. The tendency is to skip the assessment of the environment, skip the analysis and give the "right" answer. Resist this urge!

Once enlightened that there may be more than one way of looking at the question, students often go to the other extreme and look for alternatives or different perspectives, even where none exist. Eventually a happy medium is reached and they analyse only relevant alternatives. Be patient. Although to some of you, case analysis is intuitive, for many, this skill must be developed and it takes time.

What is a relevant alternative? A relevant alternative is one that is applicable given the reporting environment. It must make sense. There's no use suggesting an alternative if it is completely impractical or if it is impossible given the constraints. For instance, if GAAP is a constraint, do not suggest a non-GAAP approach as an alternative. It is not an option.

> **Tip!** In order to train students to look at both sides of an issue or alternatives, I encourage them to start out an analysis with the words "on the one hand.." and include "on the other hand..." at some point later in the analysis. Otherwise the temptation to only look at one alternative is too great.

> **Tip!** Looking at the issue from different perspectives is the key to identifying alternatives. Consideration should be given to the parties in the case. Imagine yourself as one party, and then as another. Would they see things differently?

Relevance is a function of the environment. Continue to ask yourself if your comment is pertinent to this specific case.

Tip!

3) **Consider qualitative and quantitative analysis**. Some cases lend themselves more to qualitative analysis, or quantitative analysis, or both. You must be sensitive to this. Cases with numbers in them may lend themselves more to quantitative analysis. However, just because numbers are provided does not automatically mean that the information is relevant. Any calculations that you do must contribute something to the overall analysis. Do not just perform numerical analysis blindly.

Whether to present numbers in the case itself is an interesting dilemma that illustrates one of the shortcomings of cases studies. In real life, you will always have numbers available to you-tons of them! You must choose which ones are relevant and then do the appropriate calculations to support or refute your analysis. You may choose to do many supporting calculations, or none at all. But usually, at a minimum, you should look at the numerical impact of the proposed alternative on net income and other sensitive financial statement numbers/ratios.

With cases, however, the author of the case cannot include all the numerical information that you would have access to in real life. He must choose selective information to include in the case and, by doing so, it might be construed that he is making a statement that these numbers should be considered in the analysis. However, keep in mind that the numbers could be a "red herring" and also that time wasted on irrelevant number crunching is time that could have been spent on productive, qualitative analysis.

Just because numbers are included in the case, does not mean that you should overemphasize quantitative analysis.

Tip!

Keep focused by asking yourself the following questions: Will these calculations support or refute my analysis? Will they help in making the final decision? Will they provide additional information to help determine what the problem is and to arrive at a solution?

Tip!

Try to strike a good balance between qualitative and quantitative analysis, assuming that quantitative analysis is warranted in the situation.

Tip!

Remember that it is easy to get bogged down in numbers. If you are doing a case on a test, allocate some time for numerical analysis and stick to it closely. If you are not finished after the allotted time, then stop anyway, even if you know that the calculations are incorrect. In a test situation, it has been my experience that it is easier to go astray on quantitative analysis than qualitative. Also, once you go off on the wrong track, it's easy to get entrenched and waste valuable time. You become unable to pull yourself away from the calculations. Therefore, the best solution is to allot time and stick to it, no matter what!

Tip!

Tip! Often some key numerical analysis opens up a deeper or more complex issue and might help explain certain things in the case. Issues may be disguised such that unless certain revealing analysis is performed, the issues will not reveal themselves and the resulting analysis may be shallow and without substance. A better answer would be expected to delve into the deeper level of analysis. This is difficult and comes with practice.

Tip! In most cases, a minimal quantitative analysis would include showing the impact of an alternative on key financial statement numbers and ratios.

4. **Incorporate technical knowledge**. You must indicate that you know the technical material (i.e., GAAP) by making reference to it in the analysis. This does not mean that you should be quoting reference sources or the CICA Handbook by section number; however, you should be making specific reference to the key underlying principles (see exhibits in each chapter of the Study Guide).

Tip! Incorporate references to GAAP in your analysis, e.g., revenues should be recognized when the goods are shipped since this represents the point at which the risks and rewards of ownership have passed. This illustrates your knowledge of GAAP in a case context.

5. Keep your analysis case-specific. Any discussions should make reference to the particulars of the case. Do not just regurgitate GAAP!

Tip! Try to start your sentences with the following "in this case....". This will force you to focus on case specific analysis.

Tip! Reread your analysis every couple of paragraphs. If any given paragraph or sentence does not have case-specific facts in it, reconsider your wording. One test to determine this is whether you could use that sentence/paragraph in another case analysis with the same issues .. without altering a word! If so, then you know that the sentence is generic and not specific to the case. Sometimes these types of sentences are unavoidable in that they are useful to set up a discussion. However, try to limit these to a minimum.

6. **Do not blindly regurgitate case facts**. Having discussed the importance of including case facts in the analysis, I will now stress the importance of not blindly regurgitating them, otherwise known as "dumping." The idea is to work selective case facts into your analysis, as opposed to just repeating case facts as a kind of introduction to the analysis.

There may only be a subtle distinction there but the former results in a much tighter, more focused analysis. For instance, in a revenue recognition question, instead of taking up space by regurgitating the company's present policy word for word, you might say the following: "At present, the company's policy of recognizing revenue before shipment is a very aggressive policy since the risks and rewards of ownership generally do not pass until goods are shipped." See how I have worked several items into that sentence. I have incorporated case-specific facts, displayed knowledge of GAAP, and made a judgemental statement or gave an opinion about the policy.

> **Try to make each sentence insightful, combining case facts and knowledge of GAAP with your analysis.**   **Tip!**

RECOMMENDATIONS/CONCLUSIONS

Recommendations should follow analysis of each individual issue. They should also be consistent with the overall financial reporting objective. For instance, if your role is the external chartered accountant providing information about a company to a bank, you may decide to offer advice that is conservative. Therefore, you would conclude, given alternatives, that revenues should be recognized later and costs recognized earlier.

> **Always reread your overall financial reporting objective or conclusion of your overview analysis before making a conclusion. This will help ensure that your conclusion is in line with your analysis of the environment.**   **Tip!**

AN EXAMPLE OF CASE ANALYSIS

BROWYN BOATS LIMITED

Assessment of the Environment Framework for analysis

With Bronwyn Boats Limited (BB), who are you? From what perspective will you be discussing the case? What is the reporting environment? Are there any constraints that will limit your analysis? These items will all affect your answer.

It would appear that you are a chartered accountant and friend of Bob's. How will that affect your analysis? As a chartered accountant, you would want to ensure that your advice is professional, unbiased, and sound. However, you would want to make sure that any advice you gave would not leave us open to future lawsuits (e.g., if someone like the bank relied on the financial statements and suffered losses).

Therefore, knowing that the bank would rely on the statements in order to advance funds to Bob, you would likely be conservative in your advice to Bob.

Would the fact that you are friends with Bob affect your answer? Perhaps. You might be tempted to give Bob the answer that he wants although this would be weighed against the above. What would you do in this situation?

What does Bob want? Does this matter? Of course it matters. He is the one who has hired you to do the job and is a friend of yours. Bob does not appear to know what he wants; however, he likely wants the statements to look good so that the bank will give him the financing he needs.

What does the bank want? Does that matter? Again, yes it does. Remember that, ideally, the objective of financial reporting is to provide information that is useful to users. The bank is the key user of these financial statements. They will use the statements to determine whether to lend money to Bob. They will, therefore, want reliable information using the accrual basis of accounting, since net income is presumably the best indicator of future profits and the ability of the company to pay off the loans.

In conclusion, you will likely be conservative in any advice given to Bob (assuming that you have decided as a professional not to let your friendship influence the advice given). GAAP will be a constraint since the bank will want reliable information. Since GAAP is a constraint, you will have to follow the accrual basis of accounting.

Identifying the Issues

The overall issue is how to prepare the financial statements since this is the first time they will be presented on an accrual basis. Remember to keep focused on financial reporting issues.

Bob has a simple operation. He generates revenues by building boats and incurs costs in the process. He obtains the contracts up-front, and then builds each boat according to the qualifications specified in the contracts. A key business risk is that the customer can refuse the boat at the end if they are not satisfied. However, Bob has never had any problems.

Therefore, the issues here would appear to be fairly straightforward: **(1) When to recognize revenues, and (2) How to treat costs associated with the revenues.**

Why are these issues? Firstly because there appears to be some choice as to when revenues could be recognized. The earnings process is not a traditional one whereby goods are produced, sold, and then shipped. Here goods are sold first, then paid for, produced, and finally delivered. Also, there is the question of whether costs can be deferred or whether they should be recognized immediately since it is not clear which costs relate directly to the revenue-generating activity.

The preceding paragraph requires knowledge of GAAP. If it is not clear to you, then read the chapter on revenue recognition.

Analysing the Issues

Revenue Recognition:
Usually for revenue recognition questions, it is wise to go over the **earnings process.** Draw a **time line** depicting the process. This helps to identify alternative points where revenues may be recognized. Keep in mind that Bob likely wants to recognize revenues earlier (more **aggressive** treatment) in order to make the statements look better. Also, remember that you would rather wait to recognize revenues since you are adopting a more **conservative** stance. Since GAAP is fairly flexible, there is some **judgement** in determining **when the revenues may be recognized** and there will be a more aggressive and a more conservative position.

You will likely present both to Bob since he will want to see the more aggressive stance and since you know that you will recommend the more conservative one. Alternatives that require waiting until cash is collected are not really relevant here since no information has been given to indicate that there are collection problems.

Make sure that your discussion is **case-specific** and try to **incorporate knowledge of GAAP.** For revenue recognition, the following concepts should be worked into the solution:

- **Risks and rewards of ownership.**
- **Critical event.**
- **Earnings process.**
- **Costs/revenues measurable.**
- **Revenues reasonably collectible.**

Ensure that the recommendation is consistent with the overview. For instance, in this case, earlier recognition is justifiable, but probably not as early as Bob would like. Therefore, the recommendation will be to conclude on the conservative side.

Costs:

The key issue is whether any costs can be deferred or treated as inventory costs. Deferral of costs will presumably help maximize net income.
Key technical knowledge to be worked into the answer is as follows:

- **Matching** principle-costs with revenues.
- **Direct costs** versus **indirect costs.**
- **Inventoriable costs** versus **period costs.**

Again, keep the discussion **case-specific** by making reference to the facts of the case whenever possible.

The recommendation will depend on the conclusion for revenue recognition since the costs must be matched with the revenues. This is not so much of an issue if the revenues are recognized bit by bit, as the boats are completed, since all costs will be recognized in the period incurred anyway along with a corresponding portion of revenues. However, if the conclusion is to wait until the boats are delivered, this would be a bigger issue since costs that vary directly with the production could be deferred.

For both costs and revenues, the answer given is only one suggested solution. Numerous others would also be acceptable, including ones with different financial reporting objectives, different alternatives, and different conclusions. That is the beauty of case analysis. As long as the answer makes sense and the position taken is defensible within the context of the case, the answer is acceptable. Work towards a defensible position!

Quantitative analysis does not really add anything to the case as there are not enough numbers given.

EXHIBIT 1

Bronwyn Boats Limited

Bronwyn Boats Limited (BB) has been in the yacht-building business for the last 20 years. Basically, Bob, the owner, builds high-priced, customized boats that take on average two years to build. His reputation is such that Bob has never had to advertise. Rather, potential customers contact him, having heard of Bob through word of mouth. Bob has never had a dissatisfied customer and prides himself on high quality workmanship.

In the past, Bob has always done his accounting on a cash basis; that is, expenses and revenues were recorded when cash changed hands. Also, Bob has never had to externally finance the boat construction since the business has always retained sufficient cash to internally finance the next boat to be built. Last year, however, Bob stripped all the excess cash from the business when he purchased his dream "cottage," a mansion on Lake Muskoka.

As a result of this, Bob found that he did not have enough cash to finance the construction of the next boat to be built and had to go to the bank for a loan. The bank told Bob that it would be happy to lend him the money as long as it could take his "cottage" as security. Also, it told Bob that it wanted GAAP financial statements (accrual based). Bob reluctantly agreed to pledge his "cottage" as security and promised GAAP financial statements.

Bob was not very worried about repayment of the loan since he had just received some very large orders. As a matter of fact, he had to hire several assistants to help him get the boats built on time. Bob also rented an additional barn in the local area so that he could work on the boats at the same time. The barn that he normally rented was not big enough to house all the boats. Bob also hired a secretary to help keep up with the filing and the paper work.

For the first time, Bob had the customer who placed the largest order sign a written contract due to the size of the boat and the expensive special materials that had to be ordered. All other agreements were verbal, although the terms of the contracts were similar except for price and delivery date. The key terms of the contract were as follows:

- Purchase price $500,000.
- Delivery date June 30, 2002 (approx 2 years).
- Downpayment of $50,000; $100,000 on June 30, 2001; rest on delivery.
- Purchaser has the right to try the boat out before last payment made; right to refuse to accept it if not satisfied.
- Bob to cover the cost of insurance while being built (Bob just included this as a cost of building the boat and passed it on to the customer anyway).

At December 31, 2000, Bob had completed about 2/3 of the work on the boat and was ahead of schedule. However, on the other boats, work was behind and they were only 10% complete.

Bob has come to you, his friend, a chartered accountant, for advice on how to prepare the financial statements.

Suggested Solution

Environment/Framework for analysis

The main **user of** these financial statements will be the banker who will provide the financing to Bob. The banker will look for the **ability to repay the loan** and a **successful business.** Bob will want to **maximize revenues and profits.** GAAP is a requirement since the bank has requested it. Bob must switch from **cash-based** to **accrual accounting.**

As a professional, you are aware that the statements will be used by the bank to make a decision as to whether a loan should be granted and, therefore, there is exposure. If the statements are overly **aggressive** and make the business look better than it really is, there is the risk that the bank will rely on the information and later suffer a loss if Bob is unable to pay. If this is the case, there is the potential for the bank to sue you.

Therefore, although you would like to help Bob get the loan, you must consider your professional obligations. Any advice that you give will be conservative, emphasizing full disclosure such that the bank has the information that it needs.

Issue Identification

The key issues are when revenues should be recognized and how to treat the related costs.

Analysis and Recommendations

Revenue Recognition:

In order to determine when the **earnings process is substantially complete (critical event)** and when the **risks and rewards of ownership pass,** the earnings process must first be identified as follows:

- Agreement/contract signed/downpayment.
- Supplies purchased.
- Construction.
- Deposits.
- Boat completed.
- Delivery.
- Purchaser tries out boat to see if satisfied.
- Final payment.

Recognize Revenues Earlier:

Earlier recognition would be supported by the following: the agreement is made up front (i.e., the boat is pre-sold); some cash is received up-front as evidence of the contract; Bob has never had a dissatisfied customer; and Bob is very experienced and is capable of finishing the boat once a customer is found.

Therefore, we might conclude that the signing of the initial agreement is really the **critical event** in the earnings process. At this point, revenues are **measurable,** being agreed to, and **costs are estimable,** given that Bob has been in business a long time and knows what it will cost. Many of the boats use special materials which Bob appears to order up-front anyway.

There is no information that would indicate **collectibility** is not reasonably assured and it appears as though Bob has always been able to collect in the past.

Recognize Later:

On the other hand, the following would support later recognition: purchaser has the right to not purchase the boat if not satisfied (really, the contract is just conditional); Bob insures the boat up to this point, indicating that he still has the **risks and rewards** of ownership; and the customer does not really indicate acceptance until the final payment.

Measurement is not necessarily estimable since the sales price may change if Bob has to alter the original plan for the boat or the purchaser is not satisfied. Costs may also not be estimable since each boat is different and Bob will not know what the price of materials is or their availability until he actually purchases them.

Recognize Revenues as the Boats are Constructed:

This is more like a **continuous earnings process** since the earnings process is made up of many **significant events.** It makes sense to recognize revenues before delivery due to the binding contracts and Bob's past reputation. A percentage of revenues and profits could be recognized as costs are incurred. Total costs are estimable since Bob has had a great deal of experience.

In this case, Bob would prefer earlier recognition to make the financial statements look better, especially since the bulk of the boats under construction are only 10% completed. The bank might not be so concerned that revenues are recognized later if they can see the contracts in order to assess cash flows. The problem is that most of the agreements are verbal and, therefore, the bank will not be able to verify them.

Given all of the above, it would seem more desirable to recognize the revenues earlier rather than later. Although this may be less conservative, it is justifiable due to Bob's track record (he has been in the business 20 years and has never had a dissatisfied customer). Likely, revenues will be recognized bit by bit based on percentage complete, since full recognition prior to the boat being built might be considered to be too aggressive. There is still **uncertainty** as to whether Bob will indeed finish the boat and that the customer will be satisfied.

Full **note disclosure** of the revenue recognition policy will be made so that the bank is aware of its impact.

Costs:

Bob must decide which costs are **period costs,** which are deferrable, and which are **inventoriable.** If the costs are inventoriable, they will be recognized when the revenue is recognized, which is more desirable than showing them as period costs, especially in years with little or no revenues.

The following costs would clearly be inventoriable since they were incurred directly in the production of the boats: payroll for assistants working on the boats, and materials used for the boats.

There are other costs that may be inventoriable. To back up a bit, the boats would be considered inventory and the Handbook states that inventory should be costed using **absorption costing,** which includes an **applicable share of overhead.** Although the latter is not clearly defined, Bob could easily consider capitalizing overhead costs that vary with production, such as rent and presumably heat, light and power for the barn. If Bob was not constructing the boats, he would not incur these costs. Therefore, there is a direct relationship.

Other costs, such as the secretary's salary are more clearly **period costs** and do not relate even indirectly to the construction of these specific boats.

In conclusion, it would be in Bob's best interest to treat any costs that vary with construction, such as direct labour, materials, and variable overhead (like the incremental rent on the barn), as inventoriable costs. These costs would be recognized on the income statement when revenues are recognized under the matching concept.

Earlier revenue recognition would require **estimation of some of these costs,** especially if the 10% complete boats were recognized as sales. This might pose some estimation problems. Recognition of revenues, bit by bit based on percentage complete makes this a non-issue since the percentage of revenues recognized would only be based on actual costs incurred to date (as a percentage of total estimated costs).

Other:

Regardless of when the revenues are recognized, Bob should consider providing the bank with information on the sales orders taken, as this will help the bank assess future cash flows.

FINANCIAL ACCOUNTING AND ACCOUNTING STANDARDS

Role of Financial Reporting

- Financial statements and financial reporting
- Accounting and capital allocation
- Stakeholders

Objective of Financial Reporting

- Management Bias
- Users' needs

Standard Setting

- Need to develop standards
- Parties involved in standard setting
- Standard setting in a political environment

Generally Accepted Accounting Principles

- GAAP Hierarchy
- Professional Judgement
- Role of Ethics

Challenges Facing Financial Reporting

chapter 1

THE CANADIAN FINANCIAL REPORTING ENVIRONMENT

PERSPECTIVE

Chapter 1 in the text sets the framework for financial reporting in Canada. It is interesting background reading with no calculations or numbers. It is, however, critical to the understanding of the book.

INSIGHTS

- ***Accounting decisions are not made in a vacuum.*** *Many things influence the decision of how to account for a particular transaction, including **who makes the decision, who uses the resulting material,** and **how similar transactions are accounted for**.*
- ***Accounting is not always black and white.*** *There are many grey areas that require professional judgement.*
- *Accounting provides information for the **efficient allocation of capital** in an economy.*
- *Standard setting is a **political process** and therefore GAAP is sometimes a compromise.*

STUDY STEPS

Understanding the Reporting Environment

STUDY STEPS

Perspective

The book adopts both a **preparer** and **user perspective** on financial statements. It acknowledges that financial statements are prepared by people, for people for decision making purposes. Financial statements should provide **useful information**.

It is not necessary to memorize lists of potential users and what their information needs are; however, an understanding of this relationship is critical. There is no need to present information in the financial statements that is not useful.

Figure out who uses the information and what decisions they use it for. ***Tip!***

For instance, an investor needs information about the past performance of a company in order to determine whether she should invest in the company. Financial statements should provide her with information about the company's profitability, whether it has paid dividends in the past, and if it can stay solvent.

GAAP, the "GAAP hierarchy" and professional judgement

Generally accepted accounting principles (GAAP) provide guidance to accountants in meeting the objective of providing useful information in most situations. GAAP act as a **constraint** to ensure that certain reporting **standards** are met. It is codified in the *CICA Handbook* (Canadian Institute of Chartered Accountants) which is prepared by professional accountants.

Since no specific rule can be phrased to suit every situation, the recommendations in the *CICA Handbook* are quite often general in nature and usually give a **basic principle.** For instance, in determining when revenue should be recognized from sale of goods, the *Handbook* suggests recognition when the risks and rewards of ownership have passed. This is a general statement that applies to numerous situations even though it requires some interpretation. A **basic principle** is preferable to having a **rule** such as "all revenue must be recognized when goods are shipped". While the latter is easy to follow and very clear, it may result in inappropriate accounting (e.g., what if the goods are shipped on consignment?).

Therefore, although GAAP provides guidance, it is often of a general nature, requiring **interpretation,** which in turn requires **professional judgement**. The recommendations in the *Handbook* do not fit every situation, and there may be situations that are not covered specifically. In the latter case, *Handbook* Section 1000 suggests looking at financial statements of other companies (especially if it is in a specialized industry, like banking) to see what the generally accepted practice is. Alternatively, it suggests the use of professional judgement by applying basic principles and concepts (such as historical cost and matching principles) by looking at analogous situations.

CICAHANDBOOK According to Section 1000 of the *CICA Handbook*, GAAP is defined as follows:

    (a) recommendations in *CICA Handbook;*

    (b) if not covered in (a), then look to generally accepted practice within the industry; i.e., look at financial statements of other companies in the same industry to see how they account for it;

    (c) use of professional judgement—use textbooks, professional journals, GAAP in other countries, consultation with other accountants, first principles, CICA Emerging Issues Committee Abstracts and other matters dealt with in the *Handbook*, etc.

This is loosely referred to as the "**GAAP hierarchy**".

Tip!   When attempting to analyse any financial reporting issue, use the GAAP hierarchy.

Bias in Reporting and Ethical Considerations

Another key thing to remember is that financial statements are prepared by people, often the management of the company. Therefore, there are **behavioural aspects** to financial reporting. People are not perfect and often act in a self-serving manner. For instance, if a manager knows that his performance will be evaluated by the shareholders based on how well the company has done, he might be motivated to make the financial statements look better than they really are.

> **Consider the motivations of those who are involved in preparing financial statements. They might not always be pure.** *Tip!*

Reporting bias defeats the whole purpose of financial reporting since in the case above, the manager's real performance might be obscured and the shareholders may make an incorrect decision based on the information presented. Where GAAP is a constraint, this problem may not be as severe, since the manager will have to follow GAAP (i.e., GAAP will constrain his choices). But to the extent that GAAP requires judgement, there will always be some leeway. Many companies require that an outside auditor review the financial statements for fairness. This alleviates some of the problem since the auditor is unbiased. External auditors often review financial statements to ensure that the information is presented fairly in accordance with GAAP.

> **Auditors add value because they perform an objective review of the financial statements.** *Tip!*

Any good analysis of financial reporting issues should consider the issues from an ethical viewpoint. Who is affected (stakeholders) and how are they affected? In an ethical conflict, there is usually no correct answer and therefore, the compromise solution that is best for most stakeholders should be selected.

MULTIPLE CHOICE QUESTIONS

1) The essential characteristics of accounting involve:
   a) Identification and measurement of financial information relating to an economic entity.
   b) Identification, measurement and communication of financial information about an economic entity to interested persons.
   c) Identification, measurement and communication of financial information about an economic entity to management.
   d) Identification and communication of financial information about an economic entity to management.

2) Major financial statements involve:
   a) Balance sheet, income statements, statement of cash flows, statement of shareholders' equity and notes.
   b) Balance sheet, income statement and cash flow statement.
   c) Balance sheet and income statement.
   d) Balance sheet, income statement and notes.

3) Explain how the process of capital allocation in an economy is enhanced by the process of accounting:
   a) Accounting provides useful information to only those investors/creditors who are authorized to have access to it.
   b) Accounting provides useful information to all interested parties looking to provide loans to a company.
   c) Accounting facilitates the optimal flow of funds within an economy by providing useful, decision-relevant information.
   d) Impartial accountants prepare accounting information.

4) Explain the meaning of stakeholder within the context of financial reporting.
   a) A stakeholder is someone who has something at stake when a decision is being made.
   b) A stakeholder includes only parties external to the company.
   c) A stakeholder includes only those parties who own or work for a company.
   d) A stakeholder has no vested interest in the decision being made.

5) Identify the objective of financial reporting.
   a) To communicate useful information to users in assessing stewardship or making resource allocation decisions.
   b) To communicate useful information in assessing stewardship.
   c) To communicate useful information in making resource allocation decisions.
   d) To capture useful information.

6) Which of the following statements best describes the notion of management bias within the context of financial reporting.
   a) Management bias involves management consciously misstating the financial statement for personal gain.
   b) Management bias results in financial statements that are not neutral and therefore not useful.
   c) Management bias is unavoidable.
   d) Management bias involves management consciously misstating the financial statements so that the company can raise funds in capital markets.

7) Should preparers of financial information consider user needs?
   a) Yes. The objective of financial statement includes providing useful information to users.
   b) No. Financial information should stand on its own without considering who will be using it.
   c) No. It is impossible to cater to the needs of all investors since there are so many with varied needs.
   d) Yes but only if the users pay for the information.

8) Why do we need accounting standards?
   a) Accounting standards help ensure that income taxes are correctly calculated.
   b) Accounting standards help ensure comparability and consistency.
   c) Accounting standards are required by law.
   d) Accounting standards dictate the right and wrong ways to handle financial accounting problems.

9) Explain the meaning of GAAP.
   a) GAAP is comprised of specific rules for every situation.
   b) GAAP is comprised of general principles that may be adapted to many different situations.

c) GAAP includes only those rules and principles included in the *CICA Handbook*.
d) GAAP is inflexible.

10) Explain the significance of professional judgement in applying GAAP.
   a) The use of professional judgement does not exist in GAAP since it erodes the concept of comparability.
   b) Professional judgement allows management to contradict the *CICA Handbook*.
   c) Professional judgement is rarely used in applying GAAP.
   d) Professional judgement is fairly pervasive in Canada since GAAP consists of general principles that need to be interpreted.

SOLUTIONS TO MULTIPLE CHOICE QUESTIONS

1) b) Accounting involves identification, measurement and communication of relevant information to all interested decision makers—be they internal or external.

2) a) All these statements including explanatory notes are considered major financial statements.

3) c) The free flow of useful information to any interested parties facilitates decision-making and allows those with funds to make better decisions as to where to place those funds. However, because the company who is looking to raise capital prepares the information, the information is not always impartial.

4) a) Stakeholders are interested parties who have something to gain or lose i.e., an auditor stands to lose his reputation, an investor stands to increase his investment etc.

5) a) Financial reporting aims to provide information that is useful in both capital allocation and stewardship assessment.

6) b) Biased information, by definition is not useful. Management bias is avoidable with the proper control environment and transparent financial reporting.

7) a) There is no need to prepare financial information unless it meets the needs of users—whether they pay for it or not. Most financial information caters to the main categories of users such as investors and creditors.

8) b) Accounting standards help ensure comparability and consistency. They do not always dictate the right way to handle every transaction as in Canada, they are comprised of general principles that are open to interpretation. Taxable income is based on rules determined by CCRA not necessarily the CICA.

9) b) GAAP is quite flexible because the accounting profession in Canada recognizes that no rule can be phrased to deal with every situation.

10) d) The use of professional judgement is necessary and allows flexibility. However, if there is already a principle articulating a specific accounting treatment in the *CICA Handbook*, the latter would take precedence.

SELECTED SOLUTIONS FROM THE TEXTBOOK

CASE 1-1

(a) Financial accounting is the process that culminates in the preparation of financial reports relative to the enterprise as a whole for use by parties both internal and external to the enterprise. In contrast, managerial accounting is the process of identification, measurement, accumulation, analysis, preparation, interpretation, and communication of financial information used by the management to plan, evaluate, and control within an organization and to assure appropriate use of, and accountability for, its resources.

(b) The financial statements most frequently provided are the balance sheet, the income statement, the statement of cash flows, and the statement of owners' or shareholders' equity.

(c) Financial statements are the principal means through which financial information is communicated to those outside an enterprise. As indicated in (b), there are four major financial statements. However, some financial information is better provided, or can be provided only, by means of financial reporting other than formal financial statements. Financial reporting (other than financial statements and related notes) may take various forms. Examples include the company president's letter or supplementary schedules in the corporate annual reports, prospectuses, reports filed with government agencies, news releases, management's forecasts, and descriptions of an enterprise's social or environmental impact.

CASE 1-6

The stakeholders in the T. Eaton Company (Eaton's) include investors, current and prospective, creditors, suppliers, management, employees of the company and others.

The investors, current and prospective, faced the loss of a significant portion of the capital portion of their investment. They also lost any past unrealized gains. Creditors and suppliers had significant balances owing from Eaton's and faced a significant increase in the risk of their balance receivable due to lack of investor confidence. This lack of confidence indicated that investment funds would not be available to complete the restructuring and reverse the trend of losses. It also signified that the collectibility of the principal as well as interest accruing was in jeopardy. Employees and management faced the loss of jobs and the potential loss of their pension plan if the trend of losses could not be reversed to avert bankruptcy.

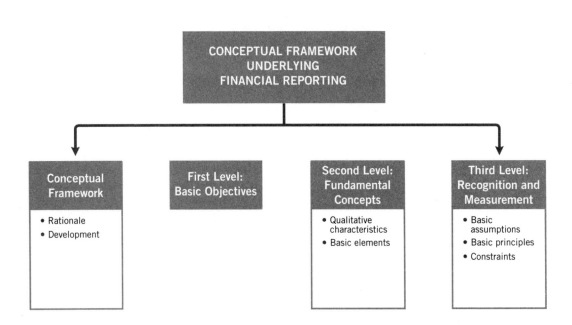

chapter 2

CONCEPTUAL FRAMEWORK UNDERLYING FINANCIAL REPORTING

PERSPECTIVE: CONCEPTUAL FRAMEWORK

This material is referred to as "first principles" and forms the cornerstone of accounting theory. This chapter also presents a framework within which accounting decisions are made.

INSIGHTS

This material is essential in any financial reporting issues analysis. You will find that these definitions and principles continually come up in discussions of many different issues.

STUDY STEPS

1. Understanding the Importance of a Conceptual Framework

A conceptual framework establishes the following:

–   The objectives of good financial reporting (i.e., to provide useful information to users).

–   What useful information means.

–   What basic things should be included (i.e., assets, liabilities, etc.).

–   How transactions and balances should be measured and when they should be recognized.

It ensures consistent, comparable financial statements and acts as a model to allow for the development of future GAAP that is consistent. The conceptual framework encompasses first principles as an integral part of the decision-making process.

2. Becoming Proficient in Using the Conceptual Framework in Analysis of Financial Reporting Issues

- **memorize the "triangle" diagram on the conceptual framework** and the **definitions** spreadsheet in the TOOLKIT.

- more importantly, **learn how to use the principles, concepts and definitions in financial reporting issue analysis.** Memorizing the framework is only a "means to an end," the "end" being that you develop sufficient professional judgement to be able to make an acceptable accounting decision within the context of the framework. With no framework, it is very difficult to make sound accounting decisions.

  - This is the first stage of solid case analysis. Many students are not able to identify issues in cases. The primary problem is that they don't know what they are looking for. If you are looking to see whether a transaction should be recorded or not, the definitions and principles in the conceptual framework will often give you the key. Liabilities are defined as financial statement elements that evidence an obligation or duty to another party that may not be avoided. If you know this definition, you can look for situations where a company might have a duty or obligation that they can't avoid.

  - You must practise applying these definitions and principles in case scenarios in order to cement your understanding of them. Therefore, one or two cases have been included at the end of each of the chapters in the Study Guide for practice purposes. It might also be useful at this point to review the chapter on case analysis included in the Study Guide.

Tip!   Internalizing this material is probably the single most important factor in learning to analyse financial reporting issues.

MULTIPLE CHOICE QUESTIONS

1) The value of a conceptual framework lies in the fact that:
   a) It provides the correct answer for every financial reporting problem.
   b) It reduces the use of professional judgement and therefore management bias.
   c) It does not allow choice.
   d) It provides an established and accepted body of concepts and objectives that may be applied to any situation.

2) The main components of the conceptual framework consist of the following:
   a) Goals and purposes, qualitative characteristics of useful information and elements.
   b) Goals and purposes, qualitative characteristics of useful information, elements and finally measurement and recognition concepts.
   c) Qualitative characteristics of useful information and elements.
   d) Goals and purposes and elements of financial statements.

3) The main decisions being made by external users of financial statements involves:
   a) Resource allocation.
   b) Stewardship assessment.
   c) Both a. and b.
   d) Neither a. nor b.

4) Identify the traits that make information useful.
   a) Comparability and consistency
   b) Reliability and relevance
   c) Understandability
   d) All of the above

5) Is it necessary for financial statement elements to be articulated in the conceptual framework?
   a) Yes, in order to provide some commonality between financial statements—especially for comparability.
   b) No, since this information is common knowledge and involves little interpretation.
   c) Yes, since this information is common knowledge and involve little interpretation.
   d) No, since too much information in the conceptual framework will result in information overload.

6) Which of the following is true regarding the going concern assumption?
   a) It assumes that a company will be in business forever.
   b) It supports the use of the historical cost principle.
   c) It assumes that a company has a finite life.
   d) It assumes that the company will liquidate its assets in the near term.

7) Which of the following best describes the periodicity assumption?
   a) The life span of the business is the only relevant period to consider in financial reporting.
   b) It is relevant to divide the lifespan of the business into smaller units so that the company may report to users on a more frequent basis.
   c) Dividing the lifespan of a business into smaller units creates too many allocation problems and therefore, the periodicity assumption precludes its use.
   d) The only relevant reporting period is the fiscal year.

8) Which of the following scenarios involves the materiality constraint?
   a) A company switches from the straight-line method of amortization to the double-declining balance method.
   b) In order to ensure that the financial statements are as accurate as possible, the company does not issue them until they have been checked and double-checked.
   c) A company, unsure about how much to accrue for warranty costs, accrues a higher amount, thus throwing the company into a net loss position.
   d) A company presents income from leased assets separately so that users can calculate return on leased assets.

9) Sometimes, it is not always possible to incorporate all the concepts or ideas in the conceptual framework since some are in conflict with each other. Identify the conflicting concepts in the following scenario. It normally takes three months for the company to finalize its year-end numbers. By the time the auditor has audited the financial statements, it is five months into the next year.
   a) Cost/benefit versus timeliness.
   b) Materiality versus reliability.
   c) Reliability versus timeliness.
   d) Timeliness versus consistency.

10) Identify which concepts are in conflict in the following scenario. Unsure as to whether to book revenues now or when greater certainty exists with respect to collectibility, the company decides to recognize revenues in the period that the goods are delivered.
   a) Revenue recognition versus conservatism.
   b) Revenue recognition versus materiality.
   c) Matching versus revenue recognition.
   d) Full disclosure versus revenue recognition.

SOLUTIONS TO MULTIPLE CHOICE QUESTIONS

1) d) The conceptual framework improves consistency and comparability yet still allows professional judgement to be used.
2) b) All of these form the basis of the conceptual framework.
3) c) Although many users have many differing needs, most users are concerned with resource allocation decisions and assessing management stewardship.
4) d) Information must be understandable, relevant, reliable, comparable and consistent to be useful.
5) a) It is important to define what main items should be included in the financial statements i.e., assets, liabilities etc so that all statements are comparable. Likewise, it is important to define what is included in each element to further enhance comparability.

6) b) The going concern assumption assumes that the company will continue to operate in order to sell its assets in the ordinary course of business in order to repay its liabilities. It therefore supports the measurement of assets at historical cost and does not require that the assets be revalued to liquidation value.

7) b) Users need timely information—whether it be daily, monthly, quarterly or annually.

8) c) Since the warranty costs will erase any net income and cause the company to be in a loss position, this event will affect users decisions. a) considers consistency, b) deals with reliability and c) deals with relevance.

9) c) The longer the company takes to ensure that the numbers are accurate, the more reliable they will be. They lose relevance however, the less timely they are.

10) a) The revenue recognition principle dictates that revenues be recognized when earned which is often when the risks and rewards of ownership pass. This, along with accrual accounting would dictate earlier recognition. However, conservatism dictates that when the accountant is unsure as to how to handle a transaction, the option that does not overstate income is the more conservative choice and should be selected.

SELECTED SOLUTIONS FROM THE TEXTBOOK

EXERCISE 2-3

1. Gains, losses.

2. Liabilities.

3. Equity, (also possible would be revenues and gains).

4. Equity.

5. Assets.

6. Expenses

7. Revenues.

8. Equity

9. Revenues.

10. Equity.

EXERCISE 2-5

1. Historical cost principle.

2. Conservatism.

3. Full disclosure principle.

4. Matching principle.

5. Materiality.

6. Industry practices.

7. Economic entity assumption.

8. Full disclosure principle.

9. Revenue recognition principle.

10. Full disclosure principle.

11. Full disclosure principle.

12. Economic entity assumption.

13. Periodicity assumption.

14. Matching principle.

15. Historical cost principle.

16. Conservatism.

17. Matching principle.

Case 2-3

(Note: There are a multitude of answers possible here. The suggestions below are intended to serve as examples.)

(a) 1. Forecasts of future operating results and projections of future cash flows may be highly relevant to some decision-makers. However, they would not be as reliable as historical cost information about past transactions.

2. Proposed new accounting methods may be more relevant to many decision makers than existing methods. However, if adopted, they would impair consistency and make trend comparisons of an enterprise's results over time difficult or impossible.

3. There presently exists much diversity among acceptable accounting methods and procedures. In order to facilitate comparability between enterprises, the use of only one accepted accounting method for a particular type of transaction could be required. However, consistency would be impaired for those firms changing to the new required methods.

4. Occasionally, relevant information is exceedingly complex. Judgement is required in determining the optimum trade-off between relevance and understandability. Information about the impact of general and specific price changes may be highly relevant but not understandable by all users.

(b) Although trade-offs result in the sacrifice of some desirable quality of information, the overall result should be information that is more useful for decision-making.

Case 2-4

1. From the facts it is difficult to determine whether to agree or disagree. Consistency, of course, is violated in this situation, although its violation may not be material. Furthermore, that the corporation changed accounting policies regarding the treatment of small tools cannot be judged good or bad, but would depend on the circumstances. In this case, it seems that the result will be approximately the same whether the corporation capitalizes and expenses or simply expenses each period, since the purchases are fairly uniform. Perhaps from a cost standpoint (expediency),

it might be best to continue the present policy rather than become involved in detailed amortization schedules, assuming that purchases remain fairly uniform. On the other hand, the president may believe there is a significant unrecorded asset that should be shown on the balance sheet. If such is the case, capitalization and subsequent amortization might be much more appropriate.

2. Disagree. At the present time, accountants do not recognize price level or current value adjustments in the accounts. Hence it is misleading to deviate from the cost principle because conjecture or opinion can take place. It also should be noted that amortization is not so much a matter of valuation as it is a means of cost allocation. Assets are not amortized on the basis of a decline in their fair market value, but are amortized on the basis of a systematic charge of expired cost against revenues. Another argument to support this opinion is to debate where the credit would go in the case of recording such an increase. Likely the temptation would be to record a revenue which would be violating another principle, the revenue recognition principle.

3. Agree. The full disclosure principle recognizes that reasonable condensation and summarization of the details of a corporation's operations and financial position are essential to readability and comprehension. Thus, in determining what is full disclosure, the accountant makes decisions on the basis of whether omission will cause a misleading inference by the reader of the financial statements. Only the total amount of cash is generally presented on a balance sheet, unless some special circumstance is involved such as a possible restriction on the use of the cash. In most cases, however, the company's presentation would be considered appropriate and in accordance with the full disclosure principle. Showing the additional detail on the balance sheet would not be relevant to the reader.

4. Disagree. The historical cost principle indicates that assets and liabilities are accounted for on the basis of cost. If we were to select sales value, for example, we would have an extremely difficult time in attempting to establish an appraisal value for the given item without selling it. It should further be noted that the revenue recognition principle provides the answer to when revenue should be recognized. Revenue should be recognized when (1) realized or realizable and (2) earned. In this case, the revenue was not earned because the critical event "sale of the land" had not occurred. In addition the development costs of subdividing the land should be included in inventory cost of the lots and appear on the balance sheet, and not as expenses of the period.

5. From the facts it is difficult to determine whether to agree or disagree with the president. It should be noted that the president's approach is not a violation of any principle. Consistency requires that accounting entities give accountable events the same accounting treatment from period to period for a given business enterprise. It says nothing concerning consistency of accounting principles among business enterprises. From a comparability viewpoint, it might be useful to report the information on a LIFO basis, but as indicated above, there is no requirement to do so.

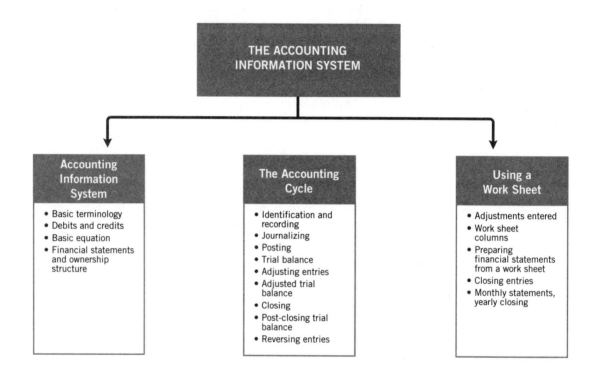

THE ACCOUNTING INFORMATION SYSTEM

Accounting Information System

- Basic terminology
- Debits and credits
- Basic equation
- Financial statements and ownership structure

The Accounting Cycle

- Identification and recording
- Journalizing
- Posting
- Trial balance
- Adjusting entries
- Adjusted trial balance
- Closing
- Post-closing trial balance
- Reversing entries

Using a Work Sheet

- Adjustments entered
- Work sheet columns
- Preparing financial statements from a work sheet
- Closing entries
- Monthly statements, yearly closing

chapter 3

THE ACCOUNTING INFORMATION SYSTEM

PERSPECTIVE

The material covered in the text reviews the accounting cycle and bookkeeping. Much of the material is a basic review from prior accounting courses.

INSIGHTS

- *The material is a review of debits and credits (basic bookkeeping).*

- *The ability to capture information completely and accurately is an essential and fundamental skill.*

- *There are no complex calculations nor complex judgement issues.*

- *The accounting equation is a simple technique that allows you to evaluate quickly the impact of a transaction on the financial statements.*

STUDY STEPS

STUDY STEPS

---

1. Understanding the Importance of Debits and Credits and the Accounting Cycle

---

Do not underestimate the importance of being able to journalize a transaction and prepare financial statements. Many students struggle through intermediate accounting without being able to master it because they do not have the fundamental bookkeeping skills.

> **Debits and credits are a fundamental building block in understanding financial reporting.**
>
> ***Tip!***

The best approach to this material is to read the chapter in the text and to attempt as many problems as possible and to verify answers against the solutions provided. This will reinforce the mechanics involved, the importance of balancing and the dual-entry bookkeeping system. Again, it would normally be assumed that this material would have been covered in an previous course and, therefore, you should be proficient in this area. If you have not taken introductory accounting recently, a review of this material would be beneficial.

The following points recap the key points in the text:

- The accounting cycle involves **capturing data, journalizing** and **posting** it to the general ledger, taking a **trial balance,** making **adjustments** to the trial balance, **summarizing and classifying** accounts for inclusion into financial statements, and **closing** income statement accounts.

- Adjustments to the trial balance are usually made at month-end, when financial statements are prepared. They involve **corrections** to accounts (often due to reconciliations with external information or subledgers), **accruals,** and **entries to adjust the value** of assets and liabilities to ensure that they are properly valued.

- The preparation of financial statements requires **grouping** trial balance accounts into similar accounts. This reduces the amount of information that is presented since too much detail on the statements makes them difficult to interpret. This step requires significant **professional judgement:** some companies like to provide more detail and some less. **Materiality** is another consideration. That is, if an account is considered to be so insignificant that it would not affect decisions made by users, the amount is not shown separately.

- GAAP requires the use of **accrual accounting** for the balance sheet and income statement since it provides more useful information to users. Under the accrual method, transactions are generally booked as soon as they can be estimated with any degree of reliability. Therefore, information is more complete and timely. It does introduce a measure of subjectivity, however.

---

2. Becoming proficient in using a work sheet and the accounting equation.

The accounting equation is a simple formula that encapsulates the relationships between financial statement elements.

Tip! Use the accounting equation to review the incremental impact of a transaction on the financial statements.

The work sheet is a mechanism for capturing unadjusted information and required adjustments to produce complete and accurate information.

Tip! Study the material in the text and complete as many exercises as possible using a worksheet. Mechanical proficiency is very important.

MULTIPLE CHOICE QUESTIONS

1) The difference between permanent and temporary accounts is as follows:
    a) Permanent accounts are never closed out while temporary accounts are closed out every month.
    b) Permanent accounts are never closed out while temporary accounts are closed out every year.
    c) Permanent accounts are T accounts and temporary accounts are not.
    d) Permanent accounts relate to income statement accounts and temporary accounts relate to balance sheet accounts.

2) Double entry accounting refers to the following:
    a) The process of booking transactions once to the general journal and once to the general ledger.
    b) The process of keeping one set of books for tax purposes and one for financial statement purposes.
    c) The process of recording journal entries that have both a debit and a credit.
    d) The process of using T accounts.

3) The basic sequence in the accounting cycle in the proper order are:
    a) Identification, measurement, posting, journalization, statement preparation, closing.
    b) Identification, measurement, journalization, posting, statement preparation, closing.
    c) Identification, journalization,measurement, posting, statement preparation, closing.
    d) Identification, journalization, measurement, posting, closing statment preparation.

4) John Chu Limited just purchased a car that will be used for its sales person. In order to capture this event, the company should record the transaction in the following manner:
    a) Prepare a journal entry and generate a journal and unadjusted trail balance.
    b) Prepare the journal entry and post to a journal/database.
    c) Prepare the journal entry but do not post until month end.
    d) Prepare the journal entry and also prepare financial statements.

5) Adjusting journal entries are primarily used:
    a) To achieve proper matching between revenues and expenses.
    b) To achieve proper matching between assets and liabilities.
    c) To close out temporary accounts.
    d) To create temporary accounts.

6) Income Summary account is used:
    a) Only at year end when the accounts are being closed out.
    b) Every month end.
    c) When adjusting entries are prepared.
    d) At the beginning of the year.

7) The difference between perpetual and periodic inventory methods is:
    a) Perpetual requires that a sub ledger be kept of all inventory purchases and sales.
    b) Periodic requires that a sub ledger be kept of all inventory purchases and sales.
    c) Nonexistent.
    d) Periodic is more costly.

8) The primary purpose of a 10-column work sheet is:
   a) To ensure that the trial balance balances.
   b) To capture the trial balance, adjustments and sort the information into financial statements.
   c) To replace the financial statements.
   d) To close out the books.

SOLUTIONS TO MULTIPLE CHOICE QUESTIONS

1) b) Temporary accounts generally relate to income statement accounts and are closed out to retained earnings annually.

2) c) All journal entries must include debits and credits that are equal such that the journal entry balances.

3) b) Transactions must be identified and measured prior to being journalized and posted. The books are closed after the financial statements are prepared.

4) b) A journal entry must be prepared to capture the transaction. The journal entry must then be posted either to a journal or into a database. The company would not generate a trial balance or financial statement until the end of a reporting period.

5) a) Adjusting entries are needed primarily to ensure revenues are recorded when earned and costs accrued when incurred.

6) a) The income summary account is used only at year end when the temporary accounts are being closed out.

7) a) The perpetual inventory method is a method that tracks all transactions for various different inventory products. It is more costly since each transaction is captured and must be posted to the correct inventory sub account. With computers, the cost has decreased substantially.

8) b) The work sheet is a handy mechanism for capturing the general ledger information and transforming it into the financial statements.

SHORT PROBLEMS

1)   *Purpose:* To review classification of trial balance accounts in financial statements.

Below is the adjusted trial balance of Tempest Limited for the month ended March 31, 2002, which happens to be their year end.

Rent expense
Salary expense
Accrued payroll
Cash
Capital assets
Accumulated amortization
Allowance for bad debt
Revenues
Unearned profits on instalment sales
Accounts receivable

Accounts payable
Shareholders' equity
Cost of goods sold
Selling and administration expense
Retained earnings
Inventory
Dividends

The software that assembles the information is new and has mixed up the order of the accounts.

Required

(a) Reorder the accounts in the proper order.
(b) Note whether each account should be on the income statement or the balance sheet. Note also whether the account is normally a debit or credit.

2) **Purpose:** To review the preparation of financial statements from trial balance.

Brochu Limited (BL) has the following trial balance at December 31, 2002, which is year end.

Cash	$ 6,000
Accounts Receivable	50,000
Allowance for Doubtful Accounts	(2,345)
Inventory	67,000
Prepaids	3,560
Machinery	123,000
Accumulated Amortization	(97,000)
Land	10,000
Accounts Payable	(70,000)
Long-term Debt	(45,000)
Common Shares	(10,000)
Retained Earnings	(25,909)
Sales	(234,000)
Cost of Goods Sold	177,909
Selling, General and Administration	47,888
Miscellaneous	(1,103)

Other information:

- Interest of 10% has not yet been accrued on the debt. It was last paid on November 30.

- The prepaid represents rent for the period December 15, 2002 to January 14, 2003.

- It is estimated that the bad debt allowance should be adjusted to 5% of accounts receivable.

- Accrued wages of $3,222 have not yet been booked.

- Income taxes are calculated at 45%.

Required

Prepare a work sheet showing adjustment, adjusted trial balance, and financial statements.

SOLUTIONS TO SHORT PROBLEMS

1)

(a)   Cash
        Accounts receivable
        Allowance for bad debt
        Inventory
        Capital assets
        Accumulated amortization
        Accounts payable
        Accrued payroll
        Unearned profits on instalment sales
        Shareholders' equity
        Retained earnings
        Dividends
        Revenues
        Cost of goods sold
        Selling and administration expense
        Rent expense
        Salary expense

(b)		Balance Sheet	Income Statement
	Cash	x dr.	
	Accounts receivable	x dr.	
	Allowance for bad debt	x cr.	
	Inventory	x dr.	
	Capital assets	x dr.	
	Accumulated amortization	x cr.	
	Accounts payable	x cr.	
	Accrued payroll	x cr.	
	Unearned profits on instalment sales	x cr.	
	Shareholders' equity	x cr.	
	Retained earnings	x cr.	
	Dividends	x dr.	
	Revenues		x cr.
	Cost of goods sold		x dr.
	Selling and administration expense		x dr.
	Rent expense		x dr.
	Salary expense		x dr.

2)

	Unadjusted Trial Balance	Adjustments	Adjusted Trial Balance	Income Statement	Balance Sheet
Cash	$ 6,000		$ 6,000		$ 6,000
AR	50,000		50,000		50,000
ADA	(2,345)	(155) (3)	(2,500)		(2,500)
Inventory	67,000		67,000		67,000
Prepaids	3,560	(1,899) (2)	1,661		1,661
Machinery	123,000		123,000		123,000
AA	(97,000)		(97,000)		(97,000)
Land	10,000		10,000		10,000
AP	(70,000)	(375) (1)	(73,597)		(73,597)
		(3,222) (4)			
LTD	(45,000)		(45,000)		(45,000)
CS	(10,000)		(10,000)		(10,000)
RE	(25,909)		(25,909)		(25,909)
Sales	(234,000)		(234,000)	$(234,000)	
COS	177,909		177,909	177,909	
SGA	47,888	375 (1)			
		1,899 (2)			
		155 (3)			
		3,222 (4)	53,539	53,539	
Miscellaneous	(1,103)	_____	(1,103)	(1,103)	_____
Net income before taxes				(3,655)	
Income taxes @ 45%					
Income tax expense				1,645	
Taxes payable					(1,645)
Net income	_____	_____	_____	2,010	(2,010)
	0	0	0	0	0

(1) accrued interest $45,000 x 10% /12
(2) rent expense $3,560/30 days x 16
(3) allowance for doubtful accounts $50,000 x 5% = $2,500; $2,500—2,345
(4) accrued wages

The format used in (2) is slightly different from the text in that all of the columns add up to zero. The text separates debits and credits into different columns and then ensures that they balance with each other. The end result is the same. The important point is that each column (or set of columns) balances.

Tip!

SELECTED SOLUTIONS FROM THE TEXTBOOK

EXERCISE 3-1

			Debit	Credit
Apr. 1	Cash		32,000	
	Equipment		14,000	
		Ben Crusher, Capital		46,000
2	No entry—not a transaction.			
3	Supplies		700	
		Accounts Payable		700
7	Rent Expense		600	
		Cash		600
11	Accounts Receivable		1,100	
		Service Revenue		1,100
12	Cash		3,200	
		Unearned Service Revenue		3,200
17	Cash		2,300	
		Service Revenue		2,300
21	Insurance Expense		110	
		Cash		110
30	Salaries Expense		1,160	
		Cash		1,160
30	Supplies Expense		120	
		Supplies		120
30	Equipment		6,100	
		Ben Crusher, Capital		6,100

EXERCISE 3-4

ANTOINE WATTEAU INC.
Trial Balance
June 30, 2002

	Debit	Credit
Cash ($2,870 + $180 − $65 − $65)	$ 2,920	
Accounts Receivable ($3,231 − $180)	3,051	
Supplies ($800 − $500)	300	
Equipment ($3,800 + $500)	4,300	
Accounts Payable ($2,666 − $206 − $260)		$ 2,200
Unearned Service Revenue ($1,200 − $325)		875
Common Shares		6,000
Retained Earnings ($3,000 − $575)		2,425
Service Revenue ($2,380 + $801 + $325)		3,506
Wages Expense ($3,400 + $670 − $575)	3,495	
Office Expense	940	
	$15,006	$15,006

Exercise 3-10

(a) 1. Insurance Expense ($4,500 × 3/12)   1,125
         Prepaid Insurance   1,125

   2. Supplies Expense ($2,600 − $450)   2,150
         Supplies   2,150

   3. Amortization Expense—Cottages   1,080
         Accumulated Amortization—Cottages   1,080
            ($120,000 − $12,000 = $108,000;
            $108,000 × 4% = $4,320 per year;
            $4,320 × 1/4 = $1,080)

       Amortization Expense—Furniture   360
         Accumulated Amortization—Furniture   360
            ($16,000 − $1,600 = $14,400;
            $14,400 × 10% = $1,440;
            $1,440 × 1/4 = $360)

   4. Unearned Rent Revenue   3,800
         Rent Revenue   3,800

   5. Salaries Expense   375
         Salaries Payable   375

   6. Accounts Receivable   800
         Rent Revenue   800

   7. Interest Expense   1,200
         Interest Payable   1,200
            [($60,000 × 8%) × 1/4]

GRECO RESORT LIMITED
Adjusted Trial Balance
August 31, 2001

	Debit	Credit
Cash	$ 19,600	
Accounts Receivable	800	
Prepaid Insurance ($4,500 − $1,125)	3,375	
Supplies ($2,600 − $2,150)	450	
Land	20,000	
Cottages	120,000	
Accumulated Amortization—Cottages		$ 1,080
Furniture	16,000	
Accumulated Amortization—Furniture		360
Accounts Payable		4,500
Unearned Rent Revenue ($4,600 − $3,800)		800
Salaries Payable		375
Interest Payable		1,200
Loan Payable		260,000
Common Shares		91,000
Retained Earnings		9,000

Dividends	5,000	
Rent Revenue ($76,200 + $3,800 + $800)		80,800
Salaries Expense ($44,800 + $375)	45,175	
Utilities Expense	9,200	
Repair Expense	3,600	
Insurance Expense	1,125	
Supplies Expense	2,150	
Amortization Expense—Cottages	1,080	
Amortization Expense—Furniture	360	
Interest Expense	1,200	
	$249,115	$249,115

PROBLEM 3-4

(a)

PARSONS LIMITED
Income Statement
For the Year Ended December 31, 2001

Revenues		
Service revenue		$42,000
Expenses		
Salaries expense	$36,000	
Utilities expense	3,700	
Repair expense	3,200	
Amortization expense	2,800	
Insurance expense	1,200	
Total expenses		46,900
Net loss		$ (4,900)

PARSONS LIMITED
Statement of Retained Earnings
For the Year Ended December 31, 2002

Revenues	
Retained Earnings, January 1	$6,800
Less: Net loss	4,900
Retained Earnings, December 31	$1,900

PARSONS LIMITED
Balance Sheet
December 31, 2002

Assets

Current assets		
Cash		$ 8,200
Accounts receivable		7,500
Prepaid insurance		1,800
Total current assets		17,500
Property, plant, and equipment		
Equipment	$28,000	
Less: Accumulated amortization	8,600	19,400
Total assets		$36,900

Liabilities and Shareholders' Equity

Current liabilities		
Accounts payable		$12,000
Salaries payable		3,000
Total current liabilities		15,000
Shareholders' equity		
Common shares	$20,000	
Retained earnings	1,900	21,900
Total liabilities and shareholders' equity		$36,900

(b)

General Journal

Date	Account Titles and Explanation	Ref.	Debit	Credit
Dec. 31	Service Revenue	400	42,000	
	Income Summary	350		42,000
31	Income Summary	350	46,900	
	Repair Expense	622		3,200
	Amortization Expense	711		2,800
	Insurance Expense	722		1,200
	Salaries Expense	726		36,000
	Utilities Expense	732		3,700
31	Retained Earnings	301	4,900	
	Income Summary	350		4,900

(c)

Common Shares			No. 301
	12/31	Bal.	20,000

Repair Expense			No. 622
12/31 Bal. 3,200	12/31		3,200

Amortization Expense			No. 711
12/31 Bal. 2,800	12/31		2,800

Retained Earnings			No. 306
12/31 4,900	1/1	Bal.	6,800
	12/31	Bal.	1,900

Insurance Expense			No. 722
12/31 Bal. 1,200	12/31		1,200

Income Summary			No. 350
12/31 46,900	12/31		42,000
	12/31		4,900
46,900			46,900

Salaries Expense			No. 722
12/31 Bal. 36,000	12/31		36,000

Service Revenue			No. 400
12/31 42,000	12/13	Bal.	42,000

Utilities Expense			No. 732
12/31 Bal. 3,700	12/31		3,700

PARSONS LIMITED
Post-Closing Trial Balance
December 31, 2002

	Debit	Credit
Cash	$ 8,200	
Accounts Receivable	7,500	
Prepaid Insurance	1,800	
Equipment	28,000	
Accumulated Amortization		$ 8,600
Accounts Payable		12,000
Salaries Payable		3,000
Common Shares		20,000
Retained Earnings		1,900
	$45,500	$45,500

PROBLEM 3-7

(a)

RUSCH DEPARTMENT STORE INCORPORATED
Income Statement
For the Year Ended December 31, 2002

Sales revenue			
Sales			$628,000
Less: Sales returns and allowances			8,000
Net sales			620,000
Cost of goods sold			412,700
Gross profit			207,300
Operating expenses			
Selling expenses			
Sales salaries expense	$76,000		
Sales commissions expense	14,500		
Amortization expense-equipment	13,300		
Utilities expense	6,600		
($11,000 × 60%)			
Insurance expense	4,320		
($7,200 × 60%)			
Total selling expenses		$114,720	
Administrative expenses			
Office salaries expense	32,000		
Amort. expense-building	10,400		
Property tax expense	4,800		
Utilities expense	4,400		
($11,000 × 40%)			
Insurance expense	2,880		
($7,200 × 40%)			
Total admin. expenses		54,480	
Total oper. expenses			$169,200
Income from operations			38,100
Other revenues and gains			
Interest revenue		4,000	
Other expenses and losses			
Interest expense		11,000	7,000
Net income			$ 31,100

RUSCH DEPARTMENT STORE INCORPORATED
Statement of Retained Earnings
For the Year Ended December 31, 2002

Retained Earnings, January 1	$16,600
Add: Net income	31,100
	47,700
Less: Dividends	28,000
Retained Earnings, December 31	$19,700

RUSCH DEPARTMENT STORE INCORPORATED
Balance Sheet
December 31, 2002

Assets

Current assets			
Cash			$ 23,000
Accounts receivable			50,300
Merchandise inventory			75,000
Prepaid insurance			2,400
Total current assets			150,700
Property, plant, and equipment			
Building	$190,000		
Less: Accumulated amortization—			
building	52,500	$137,500	
Equipment	110,000		
Less: Accumulated amortization—			
equipment	42,900	67,100	204,600
Total assets			$355,300

Liabilities and Shareholders' Equity

Current liabilities			
Accounts payable			$ 79,300
Mortgage payable due next year			20,000
Property taxes payable			4,800
Sales commissions payable			3,500
Interest payable			8,000
Total current liabilities			115,600
Long-term liabilities			
Mortgage payable			60,000
Total liabilities			175,600
Shareholders' equity			
Common Shares	$160,000		
Retained Earnings	19,700		179,700
Total liabilities and shareholders' equity			$355,300

(b)	Amortization Expense-Building	10,400	
	Accumulated Amortization—Building		10,400
	Amortization Expense—Equipment	13,300	
	Accumulated Amortization—Equipment		13,300
	Insurance Expense	7,200	
	Prepaid Insurance		7,200
	Interest Expense	8,000	
	Interest Payable		8,000
	Property Tax Expense	4,800	
	Property Taxes Payable		4,800
	Sales Commissions Expense	3,500	
	Sales Commissions Payable		3,500
(c)	Sales	628,000	
	Interest Revenue	4,000	
	Income Summary		632,000
	Income Summary	600,900	
	Sales Returns and Allowances		8,000
	Cost of Goods Sold		412,700
	Office Salaries Expense		32,000
	Sales Salaries Expense		76,000
	Sales Commissions Expense		14,500
	Property Taxes Expense		4,800
	Utilities Expense		11,000
	Amortization Expense—Building		10,400
	Amortization Expense—Equipment		13,300
	Insurance Expense		7,200
	Interest Expense		11,000
	Income Summary	31,100	
	Retained Earnings		31,100
	Retained Earnings	28,000	
	Dividends		28,000

INCOME STATEMENT AND RELATED INFORMATION

Income Statement

- Usefulness
- Limitations
- Quality of earnings

Format of the Income Statement

- Elements
- Single-step
- Multiple-step
- Intermediate components
- Condensed income statements

Reporting Irregular Items

- Discontinued operations
- Extraordinary items
- Unusual gains and losses
- Changes in accounting principle
- Changes in estimates

Special Reporting Issues

- Intraperiod tax allocation
- Earnings per share
- Retained earnings statement

chapter 4

REPORTING FINANCIAL PERFORMANCE

PERSPECTIVE

This chapter gives an overview of the income statement and the statement of retained earnings. Much of the remaining material in the text focuses on the impact of transactions on net income and the income statement. Therefore, it is essential to examine the income statement first.

INSIGHTS

- *Certain information is more important than other on the income statement, i.e., revenues, net income, and earnings per share. Therefore, accounting issues that affect these numbers are very important.*

- *Within the income statement, net income from continuing operations (versus discontinued items or extraordinary items) is more important to many users since it provides the best indicator of future income.*

- *Quality of earnings analysis assesses the quality of the information presented and recognizes that not all information presented is of equal utility in decision making.*

STUDY STEPS

Understanding the Importance of the Income Statement in Financial Decision Making

> **Income statements tell a story about the company. Before looking at any financial reporting issues, briefly review the income statement to see if revenues and profits are increasing/decreasing and at what rate. Focus also on EPS: if these are decreasing, there may be some motivation to try to prop them up, perhaps by recognizing revenues more aggressively or by expense deferral.**
>
> ***Tip!***

Tip! Even before looking at the trends noted in the above tip, determine what the main (and ancillary) business of the company is. Where do they make their money and how? What are their major expenses? This will also give some insight into financial reporting issues that may be material. Many issues revolve around identifying the earnings process of the company and whether or not it is complete.

Tip! A quick quality of earnings assessment will also give some insight into the company i.e., are the earnings managed? Do they have predictive value?

Presentation

There are numerous approaches for presenting net income. Below is a summary.

- single-step income statement
  - group all revenues together and then deduct all expenses.

- multiple-step income statement
  - revenues and expenses grouped by operating versus non operating as well as different functions

- condensed income statement
  - very brief presentation of revenues and expenses. Usually supported by more detailed supplementary schedules

Tip! How information is presented on the income statement is often largely a matter of professional judgement. Be sensitive to what is required disclosure and whether a company is providing additional information or the bare minimum.

Required disclosures

CICA Handbook Section 1520 requires at least a distinction between recurring, normal operating activities and nonrecurring, non-operating activities. Also, there are certain minimum disclosure requirements such as revenues, income from leases, government assistance, and others.

The *Handbook* also adopts the **all-inclusive approach** with a few exceptions (for example, error corrections) that would be booked through the statement of retained earnings. In practice, larger companies give a minimum level of detail and use a multiple-step approach. Remember that the **required** disclosures in the *Handbook* may also be disclosed in the notes.

Discontinued operations

Discontinued operations are required to be separately accounted for on the income statement according to *Handbook* Section 3475, as are extraordinary items (Section 3480). The reason for this is to identify and isolate the effects of **nonrecurring, atypical income and losses.** By doing this, the user of the financial statements can focus on **recurring operating activities** as a means of predicting future income.

> **Definition:**
> Discontinued operations are **the operations of a business segment that has been sold, abandoned, shut down or otherwise disposed of or that is the subject of a formal plan of disposal**.

The operations should be a separate **business segment**. The date that a plan is put in place to discontinue the operations is called the **measurement date**. At this point, any gains or losses on eventual disposition of the operations should be estimated and a) accrued if a loss, and b) not accrued if a gain. A gain would be recognized when realized. The operating profit or loss up to the measurement date would be disclosed separately as would the estimated net loss on disposition, including any future estimated operating losses.

> **Tip!** When determining whether you are dealing with a discontinued operation, look to see if it is a separate business segment and if there is a formal plan to dispose of the operation if not sold.

> **Tip!** Activities, assets and results of operations should be distinguishable from other activities, assets and results of operations relating to the rest of the company

> **Tip!** The key date is the measurement date at which point the estimated loss is measured and accrued.

> **Tip!** The measurement date is when a formal plan is put in place to dispose of the operation or when the operation is sold or shut down.

> **Tip!** A separate business segment might be indicated by product or service produced or different distribution channels/customers—in short, different business risks/business model.

Extraordinary items

> Criteria:
> - **atypical**—i.e., result from items/risks that are not typical of the business or business environment.
> - **infrequent**—i.e., must not occur frequently (note that frequent is a matter of professional judgement).
> - must not be a result of a **management decision.**
>
> NB: All three criteria must be met.

Components of the income statement and respective predictive value for users

> Components of income statement
> Net income from continuing operations ⟶ **recurring**—good for predicting future profits and dividends
>
> Discontinued operations and ⟶ **nonrecurring** by definition—the EI are extraordinary items **atypical** and **infrequent** and the DO are **discontinued**

> **Tip!** Since recurring income or net income from continuing operations is a key number, care should be taken to ensure that items grouped as discontinued or extraordinary do indeed belong there.

Income taxes—intraperiod allocation

Net income from continuing operations is shown after income taxes and any items shown after that line on the income statement (discontinued operations, extraordinary items) should be shown net of taxes.

Earnings per share

Earnings per share is either shown on the face of the statement or in the notes and shows how much each voting common share has earned during the period.

> **Tip!** This is a very high profile number and therefore a key consideration in financial statement analysis. Always look at the impact on EPS when analysing an issue.

The statement of retained earnings

The statement of retained earnings shows the changes in retained earnings during the year, with the most common changes being net income and dividends. There are a few other things that affect retained earnings such as corrections of prior errors and changes in accounting policies. Note that most transactions are reported through the income statement unless it is a correction of an error, a change in accounting policy or a capital transaction.

> **Tip!** Very few things are booked directly to retained earnings. Usually this would include dividends, corrections of prior period errors and retroactive adjustments due to changes in accounting policy.

MULTIPLE CHOICE QUESTIONS

1) Which of the following statements is most true regarding the income satement?
   a) The income statement is accurate and very reliable as it is based on accrual accounting and is prepared by knowledgeable people (management).
   b) Care must be taken when reviewing an income statement of a company since it many be subject to bias.
   c) All income statements have the same information value as they have standard presentations and must adhere to the disclosure required by GAAP.
   d) The income statement is of little value when the cash flow statement is also prepared for the company.

2) Which of the following is most true?
   a) The single-step format has more detail than the multiple-step.
   b) The multiple-step has more detail than the single-step.
   c) The multiple-step income statement presents information in such as way as to show additional relationships between revenues and expenses.
   d) The single-step method is most widely used by public companies.

3) Revenues and gains are generally reported separately on the income statement for the following reasons:
   a) More information and detail is always better than less.
   b) Users need to know how much a company is earning from its main or ordinary operations.
   c) Gains (and losses) are generally extraordinary items and are therefore required by the *Handbook* to be disclosed separately.
   d) In order to adhere to the materiality concept.

4) The following is a list of income statement components. Which of these items is not required to be disclosed by the *CICA Handbook*?
   a) Income or loss before discontinued operations and extraordinary items.
   b) Results from discontinued operations.
   c) Net income or loss for the period.
   d) Cost of goods sold.

5) Extraordinary items are defined as follows:
   a) Atypical, infrequent and do not result from decisions or determinations by management.
   b) Atypical or infrequent or do not result from decisions or determinations by management.
   c) Unusual and no result from decisions or determinations by management.
   d) Unusual and infrequent.

6) Discontinued operations are defined as follows:
   a) Operations of an enterprise that have been disposed of or shut down.
   b) Separate business segments, which have been disposed of or shut down.
   c) A separate business or part of a separate business segment which has been disposed of, shut down, or is the subject of a formal plan.
   d) A separate business segment, which has been disposed of, shut down or is the subject of a formal plan of disposal.

7) Items such as inventory write-downs are generally not considered to be extraordinary since they arise from mangement decisions. However, inventory write-downs would be shown separately on the income statement under the following conditions:
   a) The write-down is considered to be typical of the business, frequent and is material.
   b) The write-down is considered to be atypical or infrequent and material.
   c) The write-down is considered to be atypical, infrequent and immaterial.
   d) The write-down is considered to be atypical or infrequent and immateral.

8) Which of the following would not be classified as discontinued operations?
   a) An oil and gas company abandons a coal mine.
   b) A wholesale and retail company makes a formal plan to get rid of its retail operations.
   c) A car manufacturer sells off as factory that specializes in a certain type of vehicle. These vehicles will now be produced by the company in a larger, more technically advanced plant.
   d) A chemical manufacturing company closes its urea-formaldehyde operations due to a large number of lawsuits resulting from customer illnesses relating to use of the product.

9) Intraperiod tax allocation is best described as follows:
   a) Allocation of taxes between years.
   b) Allocation of taxes between income statement line items.
   c) Allocation of taxes between the income statement and balance sheet.
   d) Allocation of taxes between the income statement and notes.

10) Basic and diluted EPS are required to be presented as follows:
   a) On the face of the income statement.
   b) In the notes.
   c) On the cash flow statement.
   d) Either in the notes or on the income statement.

SOLUTIONS TO MULTIPLE CHOICE QUESTIONS

1) b) The income statement, while providing good information for predicting future cash flows and assessing management stewardship, has many limitations including the fact that the information may be biased.

2) c) Both types of presentations may contain significant amounts of detail. Furthermore, if they are presented as a condensed statement, the amount of information decreases significantly. Therefore neither a nor b are correct.

3) b) Gains are often nonrecurring and, by definition, do not arise from ordinary activities of the business. Gains are not always extraordinary, however, nor are they always material. Furthermore, more information is not always better than less. Although users appreciate a certain amount of detail, there comes a point where too much detail may obscure more important information.

4) d) Cost of good sold is desirable in terms of disclosure, however it is not required under *CICA Handbook* Section 1520.

5) a) All three criteria must be met for the item to be classified as an extraordinary item (*CICA Handbook* Section 3450.02).

6) d) The key components are separate business segment (not just part of one) and either disposed of or shut down or a formal plan exists to do either.

7) b) This is the better answer since the write-down need not be both infrequent and atypical—rather one or the other. It must also be material to qualify for separate presentation. Write-downs that are typical and frequent need not be separately presented since they form part of the normal ongoing operations of the company.

8) c) In this case, the line of vehicles is one of many other lines of vehicles produced by the company and will be produced in the new facility. This is merely a disposition of the facility and not the operations.

9) b) Intraperiod allocation allocates taxes between income from continuing operations, discontinued operations and extraordinary operations. These items are shown net of tax on the income statement. NB Interperiod allocation, allocates between periods.

10) a) Basic and diluted EPS must be shown on the face of the income statement (*CICA Handbook* Section 3500.60). Where extraordinary items or discontinued operations exist, the EPS related to these line items may be shown either on the income statement or in the notes.

SHORT PROBLEMS

1) Purpose: To illustrate accounting for discontinued operations and the preparation of a multiple-step income statement.

Below is information that relates to the operations of Raja Limited (RL) for the year ended December 31, 2002:

Raja Limited
Summary information of operations:
December 31, 2002.

	Continuing Operations	Discontinued Operations
Sales	$199,000	$99,000
Operating Expenses	143,000	123,000
Income taxes	28,000	(12,000)
Extraordinary gain (net of taxes)	10,000	

Additional information:
A formal plan to dispose of the operations was made on December 31, 2002. It was estimated that the operations would be sold at a loss of $39,000. This had not yet been booked. In addition to the above, it was estimated that the operations would lose an additional $12,000 in operating losses prior to the sale and that RL would incur $5,000 in severance pay. These amounts were not included in the $39,000 above and had not yet been booked.

The extraordinary item was not related to the discontinued operations. Assume taxes of 50%.

Required

Prepare the income statement for RL for the year ended December 31, 2002.

2) Purpose: To illustrate the difference in accounting for discontinued operations where there is an estimated gain on disposal. (Assume the same information as in 1, except that the estimated loss on disposition of $39,000 is a gain).

Required

Calculate the loss from discontinued operations as it would appear on the income statement.

SOLUTIONS TO SHORT PROBLEMS

1)

RAJA LIMITED
Income Statement
For the period ended December 31, 2002

Continuing operations	
Sales	$ 199,000
Expenses	143,000
Net income from continuing operations	
before taxes	56,000
Income taxes	28,000
Net income from continuing operations	28,000
Discontinued operations (note y)	
Loss from discontinued operations	
(net of tax recovery of $12,000)	12,000
Estimated loss on disposition	
(net of tax recovery of $28,000)	28,000[1]
Net loss from discontinued operations	40,000
Extraordinary gain (net of taxes) (note x)	10,000
Net loss	2,000

[1] ($ 39,000 + 12,000 + 5,000) $\times$ 0.5

The references to notes x and y would appear on the real financial statements and the notes would provide additional detail about the discontinued operations and the extraordinary item. They would also have to include earnings per share calculations since they were not presented here. In addition, comparatives would be shown and the prior year's income statement would be reclassified for the discontinued operation.

2) Even though the gain has not been yet realized, it would be netted against the loss from disposition as follows:

Gain	$ (39,000)
Additional losses	12,000
	5,000
	$ (22,000)

Therefore, only $22,000 of the gain would not be recognized and the only loss from discontinued operations shown on the income statement would be the actual operating loss of $12,000 incurred to date.

CASES

1) NBTEL INC.-WWW.NBTEL.NB.CA

Statements of income

(Thousands of dollars)

For the years ended December 31	1999	1998
Revenues		
Local service	$237,515	$225,599
Long-distance service	179,349	192,376
Wirless service	62,668	54,939
Other revenues *(Note 4)*	43,370	45,648
Total revenues	$522,902	$518,562
Expenses		
Cost of revenues	59,273	64,550
Amortization	104,820	107,213
Other operating expenses *(Note 2)*	276,712	241,301
Total operating expenses	$440,805	$413,064
Operating income	82,097	105,498
Other income (expense)	(2,183)	3,217
Income before debt expenses, equity investments and income taxes	79,914	108,715
Interest and other debt expenses *(Note 17)*	34,271	27,406
Restructuring of subsidiary assets *(Note 16)*	—	6,899
Income before equity investments and income taxes	45,643	74,410
Share in earnings of equity investments	—	(911)
Income before income taxes	$ 45,643	$ 73,499
Income taxes *(Note 11)*	21,973	35,086
Net income	$ 23,670	$ 38,413

See accompanying notes to the financial statements

Statements of retained earnings

(Thousands of dollars)
For the years ended December 31

	1999	1998
Balance, beginning of year	**$110,038**	$119,352
Net income	**23,670**	38,413
Dividends	**(80,516)**	(47,727)
Charges pertaining to amalgamation *(Note 10)*	**(22,774)**	—
Balance, end of year	**$ 30,418**	$110,038

See accompanying notes to the financial statements

REQUIRED:

NB—you may need to review the notes to the financial statements and/or annual report for this company to answer these questions—see the company website.

a) What approach does the company use to present its income statement?

b) What are the primary or ordinary activities? What are the secondary or non-operating activities? Consider the telecommunications business, i.e., what a telecommunications company does and how it makes money. What are the business risks?

c) Are there any unusual/extraordinary/discontinued activities? Comment on how they are accounted for.

d) In your opinion, is this income statement informative? For your answer, adopt the role of a financial analyst explaining both the good points (if any) and bad points (if any) of the income statement information.

2) PETRO CANADA—WWW.PETRO-CANADA.COM

CONSOLIDATED STATEMENT OF EARNINGS
(stated in millions of Canadian dollars)

For the years ended December 31,	2000	1999	1998
REVENUE			
Operating	$ 9 372	$ 6 095	$ 4 951
Investment and other income (Note 5)	149	52	65
	9 521	6 147	5 016
EXPENSES			
Crude oil and product purchases	5 537	3 436	2 413
Producing, refining and marketing	1 288	1 236	1 309
General and administrative (Note 6)	277	221	265
Exploration	171	78	95
Depreciation, depletion and amortization	584	558	530
Taxes other than income taxes	54	55	63
Interest	144	141	122
	8 055	5 725	4 797
EARNINGS BEFORE INCOME TAXES	1 466	422	219
PROVISION FOR INCOME TAXES (Note 7)			
Current	363	147	166
Future	210	42	(42)
	573	189	124
NET EARNINGS	$ 893	$ 233	$ 95
EARNINGS PER SHARE (dollars) (Note 8)	$ 3.28	$ 0.86	$ 0.35

CONSOLIDATED STATEMENT OF RETAINED EARNINGS
(stated in millions of Canadian dollars)

For the years ended December 31,	2000	1999	1998
RETAINED EARNINGS AT BEGINNING OF YEAR, as previously reported	$ 288	$ 147	$ 139
Adjustment for the cumulative effect of change in accounting policy on prior periods (Note 3)	(175)	—	—
RETAINED EARNINGS AT BEGINNING OF YEAR, as restated	113	147	139
Net earnings	893	233	95
Dividends on common and variable voting shares	(109)	(92)	(87)
RETAINED EARNINGS AT END OF YEAR	$ 897	$ 288	$ 147

REQUIRED:

NB—you may need to review the notes to the financial statements and/or annual report for this company to answer these questions—see the company website.

a) What approach does the company use to present its income statement?

b) What are the primary or ordinary activities? What are the secondary or non-operating activities? Consider the oil and gas business, i.e., what an oil and gas company does and how it makes money. What are the business risks?

c) Are there any unusual/extraordinary/discontinued activities? Comment on how they are accounted for.

d) In your opinion, is this income statement informative? For your answer, adopt the role of a financial analyst explaining both the good points (if any) and bad points (if any) of the income statement information.

SOLUTIONS TO CASES

1) NBTEL INC.

a) The company uses a combination of the two approaches—ultilizing a single step approach by listing and grouping revenues versus expenses yet segregating operating income from other income/expenses

b) The primary activities of NBTel are providing local and long distance services. These comprise 45% and 34% of total 1999 reveues respectively. Other non-operating activites appear to be very minor and are not itemized on the income statement.

   NBTel's business has been influenced over the last five years by increasing competition in areas which were formerly regulated monopolies. For the period January 1998 to December 2001, the CRTC had capped the rates that companies such as NBTel could charge its customers.

   NBTel was subsequently amalgamated with other communications companies to become part of Aliant Inc.

c) The only unusual item is a restructuring charge of $6.9 million in 1998. It is given separate line item treatment and included pre-tax in continuing operations. This is likely due to the fact that it does not meet the definition of discontinued operations or extraordinary items.

By putting this item on a separate line, the company is giving it sufficient prominence so that users can judge the impact of the item from both a feedback and predictive perspective.

d) The income statement gives a fair bit of detail and is therefore very useful. It allows analysts to see the respective contributions that the various types of phone services make to revenues and whether these types of revenues are increasing or decreasing over time.

It might be helpful if "Other operating expenses" were presented in more detail since they comprise 63% of total operating expenses. Note that the detail is available however the readers must refer to the notes.

2) PETRO-CANADA

a) Petro-Canada uses the single-step approach since all revenues are listed followed by all expenses.

b) Primary activities involve purchasing and extracting crude oil and gas and producing, refining and marketing it along with related byproducts.

Large amounts of funds are required in the oil and gas exploration and development industry and fluctuating market prices affect a company's ability to extract oil and gas profitably. Minor income is generated through investments.

c) There do not appear to be any unusual or extraordinary items.

d) This income statement, although simplistic (and therefore easy to follow) is quite informative. The main activites of the company are clearly identified (i.e., purchase crude oil, produce, refine and market it). By showing three years, it is very easy to see the trends. Clearly, the price of crude oil fluctuates significantly and the company must be able to pass this on to the customer in order to stay profitable.

It might be more helpful to show a more detailed breakdown of "Operating revenues". If this relates only to sales of product, perhaps the description should state this. If the company sells different products, it might be useful to see how much each product line contributes to revenues.

SELECTED SOLUTIONS FROM THE TEXTBOOK

EXERCISE 4-7

(a)

Multiple-Step Form
WHITNEY SHOE CORP.
Income Statement
For the Year Ended December 31, 2002

Net Sales			$980,000
Cost of Goods Sold			496,000
Gross profit			484,000
Operating Expenses			
Selling expenses			
Wages and salaries	$114,800		
Materials and supplies	17,600		
Amortization expense	45,500*	$177,900	
Administrative expenses			
Wages and salaries	135,900		
Amortization expense	19,500**		
Other administrative expenses	51,700	207,100	385,000
Income from operations			99,000
Other Revenues and Gains			
Rental revenue			29,000
			128,000
Other Expenses and Losses			
Interest expense			18,000
Income before income tax			$110,000
Income tax			37,400
Net income			$ 72,600
Earnings per share			$3.63***

* (70% × $65,000) = $45,500
** (30% × $65,000) = $19,500
*** ($72,600 ÷ 20,000) = $3.63

(b)

Single-Step Form
WHITNEY SHOE CORP.
Income Statement
For the Year Ended December 31, 2002

Revenues	
Net sales	$ 980,000
Rental revenue	29,000
Total revenue	$1,009,000
Expenses	
Cost of goods sold	496,000
Selling expenses	177,900
Administrative expenses	207,100
Interest expense	18,000
Total expenses	899,000
Income before taxes	110,000
Income taxes	37,400
Net income	$ 72,600
Earnings per share	$3.63

(c) Single-step:
1. Simplicity and conciseness.
2. Probably better understood by user.
3. Emphasis on total costs and expenses and net income.
4. Does not imply priority of one expense over another.

Multiple-step:
1. Provides more information through segregation of operating and non-operating items.
2. Expenses are matched with related revenue.

Exercise 4-12
(a)

ZAMBRANO CORPORATION
Retired Earnings Statement
For the Year Ended December 31, 2002

Balance, January 1, as reported	$225,000*
Correction for amortization error	
(net of $10,000 tax)	(15,000)
Retroactive adjustment for change in inventory	
method (net of $14,000 tax)	(21,000)
Balance, January 1, as adjusted	189,000
Add net income	144,000**
	333,000
Deduct dividends declared	100,000
Balance, December 31	$233,000

*($40,000 + $125,000 + $160,000) − ($50,000 + $50,000)
**[$240,000 − (40% × $240,000)]

(b) Total retained earnings would still be reported as $233,000. An appropriation does not affect total retained earnings; it merely labels part of the retained earnings as being unavailable for dividend distribution. Retained earnings would be reported as follows:

Retained earnings:
Appropriated	$ 70,000
Unappropriated	163,000
Total	$233,000

PROBLEM 4-2

BLIGE CORPORATION
Income Statement
For the Year Ended December 31, 2002

Revenues		
Net sales*		$ 968,000
Gain on sale of land		30,000
Rent revenue		18,000
Total revenues		$1,016,000
Expenses		
Cost of goods sold**		585,000
Selling expenses		232,000
Administrative expenses		99,000
Total expenses		916,000
Income before taxes		100,000
Income taxes		38,500
Net income		$ 61,500
Earnings per share		$2.05

*($1,000,000 − $14,500 − $17,500)

**Cost of goods sold:		
Merchandise inventory, January 1		$ 89,000
Purchases	$610,000	
Less purchase discounts	10,000	
Net purchases	600,000	
Add freight-in	20,000	620,000
Merchandise available for sale		709,000
Less merchandise inventory, December 31		124,000
Cost of goods sold		$585,000

BLIGE CORPORATION
Retained Earnings Statement
For the Year Ended December 31, 2002

Retained earnings at beginning of the year	$260,000
Plus net income	61,500
	321,500
Less cash dividends declared	45,000
Retained earnings at end of the year	$276,500

PROBLEM 4-4

(a)

REID CORPORATION
Income Statement
For the Year Ended June 30, 2002

Sales Revenue			
Sales			$1,678,500
Less: Sales discounts		$ 31,150	
Sales returns		62,300	93,450
Net sales			1,585,050
Cost of Goods Sold			896,770
Gross profit			688,280
Operating Expenses			
Selling expenses			
Sales commissions	$97,600		
Sales salaries	56,260		
Travel expense	28,930		
Entertainment expense	14,820		
Freight-out	21,400		
Telephone and Internet	9,030		
Amortization of sales equipment	4,980		
Building expense	6,200		
Bad debt expense	4,850		
Miscellaneous selling expense	4,715	248,785	
Administrative Expenses			
Real estate and other local taxes	7,320		
Building expense	9,130		
Amortization of office			
furniture and equipment	7,250		
Office supplies used	3,450		
Telephone and Internet	2,820		
Miscellaneous office expenses	6,000	35,970	284,755
Income from operations			403,525
Other Revenues and Gains			
Dividend revenue			38,000
			441,525
Other Expenses and Losses			
Bond interest expense			18,000
Income before taxes			423,525
Income taxes			133,000
Net income			$ 290,525
Earnings per share*			$3.52

* ($290,525 − $9,000 of preferred dividends ÷ 80,000 shares)

REID CORPORATION
Retained Earnings Statement
For the Year Ended June 30, 2002

Retained earnings, July 1, 2001, as reported	$337,000*	
Correction of amortization understatement (net of tax)	17,700	
Balance July 1, 2001 adjusted		$319,300
Add: Net income		290,525
		609,825
Deduct:		
Dividends declared on preferred shares	9,000	
Dividends declared on common shares	32,000	
Appropriation for bond retirement	50,000	91,000
Unappropriated retained earnings, June 30, 2002		$518,825

*($287,000 + $50,000)

(b)

REID CORPORATION
Income Statement
For the Year Ended June 30, 2002

Revenues	
Net sales	$1,585,050
Dividends revenue	38,000
Total revenues	1,623,050
Expenses	
Cost of goods sold	896,770
Selling expenses	248,785
Administrative expenses	35,970
Bond interest expense	18,000
Total expenses	1,199,525
Income before taxes	423,525
Income taxes	133,000
Net income	$290,525
Earnings per share	$3.52

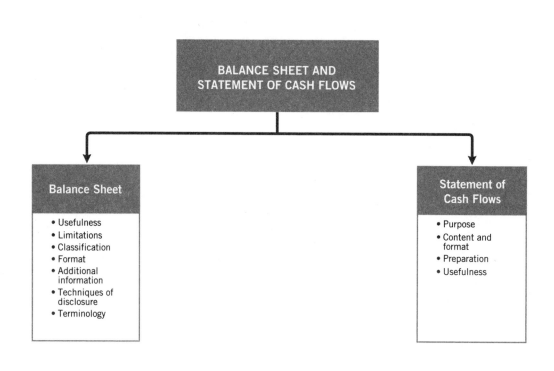

chapter 5

FINANCIAL POSITION AND CASH FLOWS

PERSPECTIVE

Chapter 5 examines the statement of financial position (balance sheet) and the statement of cash flows and their usefulness in providing information. Like Chapter 4, this information is presented at an early stage to supply background information. Subsequent chapters focus on specific elements of the financial statements and deals with how these elements should be valued and presented on the balance sheet and in the statement of cash flows. Therefore, it is important to get an overview of the statements themselves before these issues are dealt with. What is included on these statements and why? This will be covered here and it will be discussed within the context of the conceptual framework.

INSIGHTS

- *As with the income statement, certain information is generally considered to be more important on the balance sheet and statement of changes in financial position.*

- *On the balance sheet, working capital is important, as is the amount of debt, especially as it relates to the amount of equity. These elements help focus on the liquidity, solvency, and financial flexibility of the company.*

- *On the statement of cash flows (changes in financial position), cash flow from operating activities is the most important number since it shows whether or not a company is generating cash or using cash in its core operating activities. Companies cannot continue to operate in the longer term if they are not generating cash from their core activities.*

STUDY STEPS

Understanding the Usefulness and Limitations of the Balance Sheet and Cash Flow Statement

STUDY STEPS

The balance sheet

The balance sheet gives information about liquidity and financial flexibility among other things. Liquidity is important since it shows the company's ability to continue to operate. Financial flexibility is important since it shows the company's ability (or inability) to adapt financially to changing situations. For instance, a highly levered company (i.e., with significant debt) with fixed debt repayment commitments is not as flexible, and may be more exposed in hard times since it must come up with the payments or presumably, in the worst scenario, go bankrupt.

Tip! Key balance sheet ratios are the current ratio (liquidity) and debt to equity (or total assets) ratio (solvency).

Importance of note disclosures to supplement the numbers

Like all statements, the balance sheet does not tell the whole story and therefore must be supplemented by note disclosures. For instance, a balance sheet might show long-term debt of $10 million. While this is useful information, it is insufficient for users for decision making because it does not answer such questions as: When is it due? What is the interest rate? Is it secured by the assets of the company?, and so on. Therefore, the notes include additional information about the balances on the balance sheet and also additional information about things that are not included on the balance sheet, such as contingencies, commitments, subsequent events, and others. The notes should be referred to on the face of the balance sheet in order to direct the user's attention to them.

Tip! The notes are an integral part of the financial statements and the statements should never be read without reading the notes.

Tip! The notes often give essential information such as estimates in the balance sheet, how assets are valued, items that are not in the balance sheet due to inability to measure, etc.

The classified balance sheet

Most balance sheets are classified between assets and liabilities that are current and those that are non-current. A time frame of one year (or the operating cycle of the company) is used to distinguish between current and non-current. This classification allows users to assess the liquidity of the company.

Assets are generally listed in order of liquidity with cash being first. In specialized industries, this might not always be the case.

The cash flow statement

This statement looks at where a company gets its cash from and what it spends it on. It also classifies these sources and uses of cash between operating, investing, and financing activities.

One of the more important numbers on the statement is "cash used in or provided from operations." This is important because, over the long run, a company's operations need to generate cash in order to keep the company solvent. A company whose operations are generating cash is a healthy company since the excess cash can be used for expansion, paying down debt, or paying dividends.

"Cash used in or provided from operations" is calculated by converting the income statement from an accrual basis to a cash basis. The mechanics of preparing this statement are covered in Chapter 23.

> **When performing any financial statement analysis, always look at cash from operating activities as a first step. This is a critical number and shows whether a company can generate cash from its main activities. If it cannot, then it will likely not survive long!** *Tip!*

Ratio analysis

The appendix to this chapter looks at ratio analysis briefly. There are several common ratios identified in the appendix that you should familiarize yourself with. When determining how to account for an issue, always consider the impact of the alternatives on key ratios. Note that certain industries focus more on certain ratios due to the nature of the industry e.g., the retail industry looks at gross profit as a key indicator of performance due to the importance of pricing, controlling inventory and sourcing. The real estate industry might focus more on debt to equity or total assets ratio as this is a capital intensive industry (requires lots of financing to acquire and develop properties) and the risk that these companies may not be able to repay their often substantial debt is significant.

It is important to identify the important ratios in the case of the specific company being analysed and then to benchmark against something such as an industry average or prior years.

> **There are many different ratios and many different ways of calculating these ratios. It is not important to memorize every one and every calculation. A few basic ratios are all you need to do a basic financial analysis.** *Tip!*

> **When looking at ratios calculated by analysts and companies, ensure that you understand how they have calculated the ratios. Ratios may be manipulated as well as earnings.** *Tip!*

> **In order to help identify important ratios in the industry, start with the business. What are the risks? i.e., risk of insolvency as in the real estate industry? i.e., sourcing, inventory costs and pricing issues as in the retail industry. Companies will often highlight key ratios in their annual report.** *Tip!*

> **To benchmark, look for other companies in the same industry as identified by the securities commissions *www.sedar.com*. Go to the website and search for companies by industry. The companies will likely not be exactly the same but will provide you with a rough basis for comparison.** *Tip!*

> **Another benchmarking technique is to do a trend analysis from year to year.** *Tip!*

MULTIPLE CHOICE QUESTIONS

1) The balance sheet, although providing significant useful information to users has significant drawbacks including:
   a) Valuation, use of estimates and lack of completeness.
   b) Valuation and lack of completeness.
   c) Lack of completeness.
   d) Use of estimates.

2) The balance sheet suffers from many limitations. The following is a list of possible limitations. Identify which one is not a true limitation.
   a) Because of the historical cost principle, the statements do not always reflect the most relevant values of assets.
   b) While appearing to be quite exact, the statement is really inexact, owing to the numerous estimates and judgements involved in preparing the statement.
   c) Although all measurable assets of the company are shown on the balance sheet, a problem arises since certain assets that contribute significantly to the process, such as goodwill, are omitted due to the inability to measure.
   d) The balance sheet only looks at material balances and therefore, does not provide sufficient information for decision-making.

3) Below is a list of cash balances. Which one of these balances would not be included in current assets?
   a) petty cash held by the various operating units of the company
   b) cash restricted for the repayment of long-term debt in two years
   c) cash restricted for meeting minimum payment on delivery of inventory before year end
   d) cash being saved in case of an emergency

4) Which of the following liabilities on the balance sheet would not be included in the current liabilities classification on the balance sheet?
   a) bank overdraft
   b) current portion of long-term debt
   c) current portion of long-term debt that is expected to be refinanced with another long-term issue
   d) unearned revenues

5) Albert Limited is being sued by Benny Limited. The lawyers feel that it is likely that Benny will be successful and will likely settle for between $150,000 and $250,000. In this case, the lawyers don't have any insight into the exact amount of the loss within that range. How much should be accrued in the financial statements of Albert?
   a) $150,000
   b) $250,000
   c) $200,000
   d) $0 due to the fact that the range is too large and no estimate is better than another

6) Assume the same facts as 5 above. What should Benny accrue?
   a) $150,000
   b) $250,000
   c) $200,000
   d) $0

7) The day before Jamie Limited's year end, an employee named John, slipped and fractured his wrist on a slick of oil that had leaked out from a piece of equipment in the factory. By year end, John had not indicated that he would sue the company. The day after year end and before the financial statements were issued, John hired a lawyer and sued the company for a material amount of money. The company's lawyers thought that it was probable that the company would lose the case; however, at this point, they could not determine the possible loss. Jamie Limited was fully insured and all losses would be covered by the insurance company. What amount would be accrued in the year-end financial statements?
a) $0 since the lawsuit happened in the following year.
b) $0 since the loss stems from the pre-year-end event but is not measurable.
c) $0 since John had not indicated at year end that he would sue.
d) $0 since all losses will be covered by the insurance company.

8) After year end, but before issuing the financial statements, the following events happened to Disaster Limited. Which of the following would be classified as a Type 1 subsequent event (i.e., would require that the financial statements be adjusted)?
a) One of the warehouses was flooded out and all the merchandise was ruined. The merchandise was insured.
b) Another warehouse burned down. The merchandise was not insured.
c) A customer that had been experiencing significant financial distress at year end had gone bankrupt. There were no funds available to pay suppliers. Disaster Limited still had a significant amount recorded as net accounts receivable for the customer in the year-end financial statements.
d) The market value of investments held declined significantly below market values at year end.

9) Tamagotchi Limited had the following cash flows for the year ended December 31, 2001:

Fixed asset purchase	$400,000
Cash from sale of long-term investments	$200,000
Share issue	$170,000
Payment of long-term debt	$15,000
Gain on sale of long-term investments	$50,000
Cash out to purchase company's stock	$65,000

What were the cash flows from investing activities that would be shown on the Statement of Cash Flows?
a) $200,000 outflow
b) $200,000 inflow
c) $265,000 outflow
d) $265,000 inflow

10) Assume the same information from 9. What would the cash flow from financing activities be?
a) $155,000 inflow
b) $155,000 outflow
c) $90,000 outflow
d) $90,000 inflow

11) Which of the following items would not be included in the calculation of cash flow from operating activities:
   a) cash from customer sales from last year collected this year
   b) cash spent to pay accrued vacation pay from last year
   c) repayment of current portion of long-term debt
   d) cash from sale of inventory

SOLUTIONS TO MULTIPLE CHOICE QUESTIONS

1) a) There are many limitations relating to the balance sheet, the main ones being the use of historical cost, the fact that accrual accounting requires the use of estimates such as for bad debts and the fact that due to inability to measure certain items such as contingencies, many items are left off the balance sheet.

2) d) By definition, items that are immaterial are not relevant to decision making and therefore, if all material information is disclosed, there is sufficient information for decision-making.

3) b) Any cash that is restricted for long-term use should not be included in current assets since it does not meet the definition which would require that the cash be available for use within the year. The other cash balances are available to meet expenditures within the current year.

4) c) Normally, the current portion of long-term debt must be included in current liabilities. However, if the debt is to be refinanced with new-long term debt then the company will not have to use any of its current assets to meet the obligation. There has to be evidence, however, that the debt will indeed be settled through other long-term debt such as a contract (*Handbook* Section 1510 par. .06). Unearned revenues would be included on the basis that the revenues would be earned within the year, which is usually the case.

5) a) When there is a range of estimates and no one number provides a better estimate than the next, the *CICA Handbook* states that the minimum amount in the range would be accrued (*Handbook* Section 3290 par. .14). This would tend to go against the conservatism principle; however, it at least provides at least a measure of consistency between companies.

6) d) Benny should accrue $0 since this is a contingent gain and contingent gains are not recognized due to the realization and conservatism principles.

7) d) Since the company will suffer no loss, there is no reason to disclose or accrue anything.

8) c) The customer had been in trouble before year end. Therefore, the condition of possible loss existed at year end and, the eventual bankruptcy confirms this loss. This loss should be adjusted for in the financial statements. The fact that there was no insurance on the merchandise would not in itself lead to a loss; this would be a type two event and the event would be recorded in the subsequent year, when the fire occurred.

9) a) $400,000 cash out for purchase less $200,000 cash in from sale. The gain is a non-cash item.

10) d) $170,000 inflow less $15,000 outflow less $65,000 outflow. The re-purchase of the company's shares are considered to be financing activities.

11) c) Repayment of long-term debt will always be a financing activity even if the debt is classified as a current liability.

PROBLEMS

1) Purpose: To illustrate the impact of certain atypical transactions on the financial statements.

Below are some events that took place at Nikki Limited (NL) after year end. These events have not yet been accounted for in the financial statements. The year end of the company is December 31, 2001. It is now February 28, 2002 and the financial statements are about to be issued.

(a) On January 5, 2002, a major customer of NL declared bankruptcy. NL stands little or no chance of recovering the accounts receivable from the customer. At year end, NL had a suspicion that this would happen, although the customer was denying the possibility. Up to December, the customer had been paying their bills.

(b) Litigation involving NL was settled February 1, 2002. NL lost the lawsuit, which related to injury to an employee in 1999. Nothing had been accrued in the accounts to date since it was not measurable. The incident was not covered by insurance.

(c) NL decided to sell off their warehousing operations (which were significant to the company) on January 1, 2002. A buyer was found and they estimated that there would be a gain on sale. Operations were shut down on January 31 and the sale took place shortly thereafter.

(d) On February 20, 2002, someone stole all the software for running NL's computers. The software was unique and although backup copies had been made, they did not reflect the most up-to-date version. Data masterfiles were also stolen. NL's systems were completely automated and highly computerized. The computer made many decisions (based on pre-programmed parameters) such as when to order raw materials, ship goods, and make payments. NL's staff relied heavily on the computers. NL had to temporarily stop taking orders and paying bills while the mess was sorted out.

Required

Explain if and how the financial statement should be adjusted for each event. Note which year, if any, should be adjusted.

2) Purpose: To illustrate how to calculate cash from operations.

Yaroslavsky Limited (YL) is in the process of preparing its financial statements for the year ended December 31, 2002. The following are some excerpts from the draft statements:

YAROSLAVSKY LIMITED
Draft Income Statement
For the Year Ended December 31, 2002

Sales	$545,000
Cost of sales	399,000
Expenses	122,000
Income taxes	12,000
Net income	12,000

Other information:

- Income taxes have not yet been paid.
- Sales consist of cash sales ($100,000) and credit sales ($445,000).
- $38,000 in cash was collected from 2001 accounts receivable (the full balance) and the closing balance in accounts receivable for 2002 was $56,000.
- Opening accounts payable was $0 and closing balance was $34,000, excluding taxes payable.

Required

Calculate cash provided from operations for disclosure in the statement of cash flows.

3) Purpose: To focus on the process of classifying information on the balance sheet.

Classifying assets, liabilities, and equity on the balance sheet is not always as straightforward as it might appear. While it is obvious how to classify accounts in certain cases (e.g., common shares and retained earnings are part of equity), it is not so obvious in other cases and professional judgement must be used. Below are some items that require professional judgement in classifying them on the balance sheet. Refer to the conceptual framework as well as common sense definitions of the items.

(a) A real estate company has a significant amount invested in buildings. The buildings are normally held for resale; however, due to a downturn in the economy, the company has not been able to sell them and is instead leasing the buildings out. Are the buildings inventory or capital assets?

(b) A company issued debentures that bear interest at 10% per annum. The debentures have no set maturity date and would not be repaid unless the company was wound up. In that case, the debentures would rank in preference to other distributions of capital since they are secured by the fixed assets of the company. Are the debentures debt or equity?

(c) Long-term debt is due in the upcoming year; however, it is expected to be refinanced with new long-term debt prior to the repayment date. Is the debt a current or long-term liability?

SOLUTIONS TO PROBLEMS

1)

(a) This is a subsequent event since it occurred subsequent to year end. The question is whether it is a type 1 or a type 2 subsequent event since this will determine how the financial statements will be adjusted, if at all.

We might argue that it is a type 1 event that gives additional information about an event that existed at the balance sheet date (i.e., the customer was in trouble). Therefore, the accounts receivable should be written off in 2001. Alternatively, we might argue that this is a 2002 event and should be recorded in 2002. There was little evidence of financial distress at year- end and the customer had been paying his bills. Therefore, at most, note disclosure would be given since the event would affect the 2002 net income. A more conservative application of GAAP would require type 1 treatment.

(b) This should be booked as a loss in the 2001 income statement, with note disclosure explaining the loss. This is a type 1 subsequent event.

(c) This would appear to be a type 2 subsequent event since the decision to discontinue the operations took place in 2002. The timing is somewhat suspect, however, since it happens one day after year end. Consideration might be given to showing pro forma statements since the operations are significant and note disclosure should be made of the details since this will affect future operations of the company.

(d) The issue here is whether the company can continue to operate given the significant loss. The company has stopped taking orders and paying bills. NL would have to prove that they are still a going concern, otherwise it would be misleading to continue to show the financial statements as though they were. If they could prove that they could continue to operate (i.e., with manual records or with the older software), this would be a type 2 subsequent event and note disclosure may not even be made.

If, however, they could not continue to operate, or if it was determined that the event would affect future operations, consideration would have to be given to additional disclosures or a different basis of presentation of the financial statements. Perhaps NL should delay issuing the statements until it has a better idea of the impact. The problem with this is that the decision-relevant information is being withheld from the users.

2) The cash from operations for YL would be calculated as follows:

Net income	$ 12,000
Add back/(deduct)	
Cash collected from 2001 sales	38,000
2002 non-cash sales	(56,000)
Non-cash expenses	
—year-end accounts payable	34,000
—year-end income tax payable	12,000
Cash from operations	$ 40,000

This topic is covered in more detail in Chapter 23.

3)

(a) Assets that are held for resale are normally treated as inventory, while assets that are used to produce income are treated as capital assets. In this case, the assets would have originally been treated as inventory but would now be treated as capital assets and be depreciated. On the balance sheet, real estate companies usually do not call assets inventory or capital assets, but rather assets held for resale and revenue-producing properties.

(b) The instrument has both the attributes of debt and equity. On the one hand, it is secured by the assets of the company, is interest bearing, and has the legal form of debt. But on the other, it would appear that it is part of the permanent financing of the company since there is no fixed maturity date. Therefore, it does not fit neatly into either category. The *CICA Handbook* dictates economic substance over legal form. *Handbook* Section 3860 on financial instruments would classify this as a financial liability due to the requirement to pay interest.

(c) Since the debt is due next year, it meets the definition of a current liability. However, since it will not use up any of the company's current assets or resources in settlement, it is questionable whether it belongs with other current liabilities that will. Classification between current and long-term debt will affect the presentation of the balance sheet and key financial ratios (e.g., working capital ratio), especially if the amount is significant.

Management of the company might want the amount to be classified as long-term if it makes the statements and the company look better. Therefore, before the amount is left as long-term, there must be concrete evidence that the refinancing will take place. This might take the form of a signed agreement.

CASES

1) BROOKFIELD PROPERTIES CORPORATION— www.brookfieldproperties.com

Normally, GAAP requires that the balance sheet be classified between current and non-current assets and liabilities. This helps users assess liquidity and the ability of the company to meet short-run obligations with current assets. For real estate companies, however, it is generally accepted within the industry that the balance sheet should not be classified and that no reference should be made to current assets or current liabilities.

Furthermore, it is generally accepted that the balance sheet for real estate investment and development activities be ordered in such a way such that longer term assets and liabilities are shown first with more liquid assets and liabilities following in order of significance.

A summary of excerpts from the balance sheets of Brookfield Properties Corporation follows to illustrate the above:

CONSOLIDATED BALANCE SHEET

December 31 (US Millions)	note	2000	1999
Assets			
Commercial properties	2	$ 6,326	$ 5,897
Development properties	3	637	447
Residential inventory		559	562
Receivables and other	4,5	893	945
Cash and cash equivalents		209	217
		$ 8,624	$ 8,068
Liabilities			
Commercial property debt – recourse to properties	6	$ 5,085	$ 4,460
Residential construction financing and advances	7	568	765
		5,653	5,225
Accounts payable		368	276
Capital base and other shareholders' interests			
Interests of others in properties	8	159	326
Preferred shares – subsidiaries and corporate	9	607	607
Common shares and convertible debentures	10,11	1,837	1,634
		2,603	2,567
		$ 8,624	$ 8,068

On behalf of the board,

GORDON E. ARNELL
Chairman

J. BRUCE FLATT
President and Chief Executive Officer

See accompanying notes to the consolidated financial statements.

REQUIRED

a) Describe the nature of the real estate development industry including the relationship between the assets and the financing. Use the above partial balance sheet to assist you. What is the difference between commercial and development properties?

b) Note the ordering of the assets in terms of liquidity and the unclassified nature of the balance sheet. Why do you think that the balance sheet presentation is different for real estate companies? Should the CICA mandate compliance with the *CICA Handbook* (i.e., classified balance sheets) to make it less confusing for users?

2) ROYAL BANK OF CANADA—www.royalbank.com

The Royal Bank (RBOC) is in the banking business. Operations are located primarily in Canada. And the company is jointly audited by Deloitte & Touche & Pricewaterhouse-Cooper out of their Toronto offices.

The financial statements are presented in accordance with both Canadian as well as U.S. GAAP, and include a note showing a reconciliation between Canadian as well as U.S. GAAP.

REQUIRED

Explain why RBOC produces two sets of financial statements under two sets of GAAP. Discuss within the context of the conceptual framework vis-à-vis providing useful information.

3) COMPARATIVE FINANCIAL STATEMENTS

In Canada, GAAP requires that comparative financial statements be shown "when it is meaningful" (*CICA Handbook* Section 1500). However, beginning January 1, 1990, the Ontario Securities Commission issued a document requiring that comparatives be shown and that the auditors' report extend to the comparative financial statements. That is, the auditors must report both on the current year and the preceding year and conclude whether both years' financial statements are presented fairly.

More recently, there has been a trend, originating in the United States, to show three years' worth of financial statements. Presumably, this is in line with the trend to provide more and better disclosures.

REQUIRED

Is more necessarily better? Does the trend to increase the amount of information on the face of the financial statements result in more useful statements? Do the costs outweigh the benefits?

SOLUTIONS TO CASES

1) BROOKFIELD PROPERTIES CORPORATION

(a) The real estate development industry is high-risk. The business operating cycle is lengthy since it often takes several years to develop and complete a property/project. This requires that the company predict several years in advance whether the market for buildings, houses or space will be strong or weak. Furthermore, the industry is highly leveraged; that is, most development is financed by loans. This means high interest payments and large exposures if the project is unsuccessful. Because of the large amounts of money involved in each project, failure of one or two can lead to financial problems and even bankruptcy. In a recession, often the real estate companies are the first to go under. In Canada, in the past decade, numerous large real estate companies have succumbed to the recession.

Commercial properties are revenue producing properties that are being rented or leased out by the company. Development properties are in the process of being developed and will become revenue producing in the future (hopefully).

(b) Part of the reason for the difference is that the operating cycle is usually much longer than a year and the one-year time frame for assessing liquidity is unrealistic and meaningless. A bank will often finance a construction project with a loan that becomes due when the project is finished. The loan covers all costs related to construction. More permanent financing is put in place depending on whether the asset is sold or leased.

The presentation generally accepted for real estate companies shows the most important assets and liabilities first along with the ones with the most risk. Since the properties are usually shown first, as is the related financing, this draws the users' attention to the relationship between the two (i.e., how much is financed and hence what the exposure is).

Given the different nature of the business, it would not make sense to mandate the same GAAP as for other industries. Besides, cross comparisons between the real estate and other industries are meaningless as the balance sheet structures and the businesses are so different.

2) ROYAL BANK OF CANADA

RBOC produces two sets of financial statements since the shares of the company trade on both the U.S. and Canadian stock exchanges. Under U.S. securities law, U.S. GAAP (as stated by FASB and the SEC) must be used to prepare the financial statements and the statements would be prepared in U.S. dollars. Under Canadian securities law, Canadian GAAP (as stated by the CICA) must be used to prepare the financial statements (Canadian dollars).

While the standard-setters in Canada and the U.S. argue that their respective GAAP is most relevant to decision-making in their country, users of the financial statements find this very confusing and the practice begs the question of which set of statements reflects economic reality.

Because of this, Canada and the U.S. are attempting to harmonize GAAP. Indeed, there is an international initiative to harmonize GAAP globally. As international capital markers become more accessible to investors, this issue will become more and more prominent.

3) COMPARATIVE FINANCIAL STATEMENTS

More is not always better since too much information in one document might tend to obscure the more critical elements. For instance, if three years' financial statements are shown, then three years' worth of notes and backup schedules must also be shown. This could result in many additional notes that may not even be relevant to the current situation.

Also, is it important that the three years all be in the same document? Presumably, the user could obtain an older set of financial statements for the earlier years. Putting it all together creates additional costs and these might not outweigh the benefits which may be nothing more than convenience.

On the other hand, the trend towards more disclosures is generally a good thing as long as it does not result in information overload and obscure the important data. More information adds value if it was not previously available and if it is useful.

SELECTED SOLUTIONS FROM THE TEXTBOOK

EXERCISE 5-2

1.	H.	11.	B.
2.	D.	12.	F.
3.	F.	13.	A.
4.	F.	14.	H.
5.	C.	15.	C.
6.	A.	16.	B.
7.	F.	17.	A.
8.	G.	18.	A.
9.	A.	19.	G.
10.	A.	20.	F.

EXERCISE 5-5

UHURA CORP.
Balance Sheet
December 31, 2002

Assets

Current assets

Cash			$230,000
Temporary investments—at fair value			120,000
Accounts receivable		$357,000	
Less allowance for doubtful accounts		17,000	340,000
Inventories, at lower of average cost or market			401,000
Prepaid expenses			12,000
Total current assets			1,103,000

Long-term investments

Land held for future use		175,000	
Cash surrender value of life insurance		90,000	265,000

Property, plant, and equipment

Building	$730,000		
Less accumulated amortization— building	160,000	570,000	
Office equipment	265,000		
Less accumulated amortization— office equipment	105,000	160,000	730,000

Intangible assets

Goodwill			80,000
Total assets			$2,178,000

Liabilities and Shareholders' Equity

Current liabilities

Accounts payable			$ 105,000
Bank overdraft			30,000
Notes payable (due next year)			125,000
Rent payable			49,000
Total current liabilities			309,000

Long-term liabilities

Bonds payable	$500,000		
Add premium on bonds payable	53,000	$553,000	
Pension obligation		82,000	635,000
Total liabilities			944,000

Shareholders' equity

Common shares, authorized 400,000 shares, issued 290,000 shares		290,000	
Contributed Surplus		160,000	
Retained earnings		784,000	

Total shareholders' equity		1,234,000
Total liabilities and shareholders' equity		$2,178,000

Exercise 5-11

CAVAMANLIS INC.
Statement of Cash Flows
For the Year Ended December 31, 2002

Cash flows from operating activities		
Net income		$44,000
Adjustments to reconcile net income to net cash provided by operating activities:		
Amortization expense	$ 6,000	
Increase in accounts receivable	(3,000)	
Increase in accounts payable	5,000	8,000
Net cash provided by operating activities		52,000
Cash flows from investing activities		
Purchase of equipment		(17,000)
Cash flows from financing activities		
Issuance of common shares	20,000	
Payment of cash dividends	(23,000)	
Net cash used by financing activities		(3,000)
Net increase in cash		32,000
Cash at beginning of year		13,000
Cash at end of year		$45,000

Exercise 5-14

KELLY CORPORATION
Balance Sheet
December 31, 2002

Assets			
Current assets			
Cash		$ 197,000	
Temporary investments, at market value		153,000	
Accounts receivable	$ 435,000		
Less allowance for doubtful accounts	(25,000)	410,000	
Inventories		597,000	
Total current assets			1,357,000
Long-term investments			
Investments in bonds		299,000	
Investments in shares		277,000	
Total long-term investments			576,000

Property, plant, and equipment

Land		260,000	
Building		1,040,000	
Less accumulated amortization		(152,000)	888,000
Equipment		600,000	
Less accumulated amortization		(60,000)	540,000
Total property, plant, and equipment			1,688,000

Intangible assets

Franchise	160,000	
Patent	195,000	
Total intangible assets		355,000
Total assets		$3,976,000

Liabilities and Shareholders' Equity

Current liabilities

Accounts payable	$ 455,000	
Short-term notes payable	90,000	
Dividends payable	136,000	
Accrued liabilities	96,000	
Total current liabilities		$ 777,000

Long-term debt

Long-term notes payable	900,000	
Bonds payable	1,000,000	
Total long-term liabilities		1,900,000
Total liabilities		2,677,000

Shareholders' equity
Paid-in on capital shares

Common shares	$809,000		
Contributed surplus	80,000	889,000	
Retained earnings**		410,000	
Total shareholders' equity			1,299,000
Total liabilities and shareholders' equity			$3,976,000

**Calculation of Retained Earnings:

Sales	$8,100,000
Investment revenue	63,000
Extraordinary gain	80,000
Cost of goods sold	(4,800,000)
Selling expenses	(2,000,000)
Administrative expenses	(900,000)
Interest expense	(211,000)
Net income	$ 332,000

Beginning retained earnings	$ 218,000
Net income	332,000
Correction of prior year's error	(140,000)
Ending retained earnings	$ 410,000

PROBLEM 5-7

(a)

MAS INC.
Income Statement
For the Five Months Ended May 31, 2002

Sales ($22,770 + $5,320 + $4,226)		$32,316
Cost of goods sold		
Purchases ($14,400 + $256 − $130)	$14,526	
Less inventory—May 31, 2002	(1,840)	12,686
Gross profit		19,630
Operating expenses		
Salaries and wages ($5,500 + $240)	5,740	
Utilities ($4,000 + $270)	4,270	
Rent ($1,800 × 5/6)	1,500	
Insurance ($1,920 × 5/12)	800	
Advertising	424	
Amortization ([$3,000 ÷ 5] × 5/12)	250	
Maintenance	110	13,094
Income from operations		6,536
Interest expense*		116
Income before income taxes		6,420
Income taxes (20%)		1,284
Net income		$ 5,136
Earnings per share ($5,136 ÷ 1,000)		$ 5.14

*Quarterly *principal* payments are calculated as follows:

Total principal	$2,880
Total quarters	÷ 12
Quarterly payments	$ 240

On April 1, 2002, *interest* was paid as follows:

2,880 × 10% × 3/12 = $72

First payment on April 1 is therefore:

Principal	$240
Interest	72
Total payment	$312

Interest for April and May then is as follows:

Interest [($2,880 − $240) × 10% × 2/12] $44

Interest expense through May 31 is therefore as follows:

Jan.–Mar.	$ 72
April–May	44
	$116

(b)

MAS INC.
Balance Sheet
May 31, 2002

Assets

Current assets		
Cash ($33,600 − $31,446)		$ 2,134
Accounts receivable		4,226
Inventory of baking materials-at cost		1,840
Prepaid insurance ($1,920 × 7/12)		1,120
Prepaid rent ($1,800 × 1/6)		300
Total current assets		9,620
Display cases and equipment	$3,000	
Less accumulated amortization	250	2,750
Total assets		$12,370

Liabilities and Shareholders' Equity		
Current liabilities		
Current portion of instalment loan ($240 × 4)		$ 960
Accounts payable ($256 + $270)		526
Wages payable		240
Income taxes payable		1,284
Interest payable		
[($2,880 − $240) × .10 × 2/12]		44
Total current liabilities		3,054
Instalment loan ($2,880 − $240)	$2,640	
Less current maturities	960	
Total long-term debt		1,680
Total liabilities		4,734
Shareholders' equity		
Common shares, 1,000 shares issued		
and outstanding	2,500	
Retained earnings	5,136	
Total shareholders' equity		7,636
Total liabilities and shareholders' equity		$12,370

REVENUE RECOGNITION

Current Environment

- Revenue recogntion criteria

Earnings Process

- Sale of goods
- Risks and rewards
- Disposition of assets other than inventory
- Consignment sales
- Continuing managerial involvement
- Completion of production
- Rendering of services and long-term contracts
- Percentage-of-completion method
- Completed contract method
- Long-term contract losses
  Disclosures

Measurement Uncertainty

- Sales with buy-back
- Sales when right of return exists
- Trade loading and channel stuffing

Uncertainty Associated with Collectibility

- Instalment sales
- Instalment method
- Cost recovery method

chapter 6

REVENUE RECOGNITION

PERSPECTIVE: THE EARNINGS PROCESS

This is not a complex area although the general principles established here are central to the analysis of many business transactions. The principles for revenue recognition, as laid down in the CICA Handbook Section 3400, leave much room for professional judgement. For this reason, this topic is one of the most intriguing areas of accounting.

This area is best dealt with by becoming familiar with the general principles and honing professional judgement in applying them.

INSIGHTS

- *The main issue here is **timing of recognition** of revenues. **Measurement** issues are often minor.*
- *Understanding the earnings process is central to dealing with revenue recognition issues.*
- *The material on the different **revenue recognition methods**, such as completed-contract, percentage-of-completion, instalment and cost recovery methods, is straightforward and therefore lends itself to self-study. You should do as many of these problems as possible to reinforce the concepts.*

STUDY STEPS

1. Understanding the Business Transaction—Business Content

STUDY STEPS

The earnings process and the time line

Revenue is defined as an **increase in the economic resources of the company from ordinary operations or business of the company**. It is therefore critical to understand how the entity earns its money. What does the company do to earn revenues and how do they go about doing it?
This is called the **earnings process**.

To help identify the relevant stages in the earnings process, it is useful to draw a diagram that shows the sequence of events. This is called a **time line**.

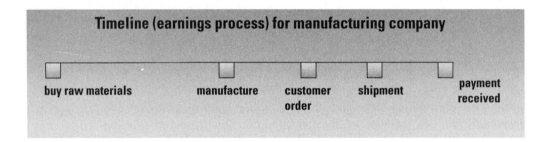

Sometimes there is one very important step or act in the earnings process that defines a sale. This is called the **critical event.** For sale of goods, this is often shipment. At this point, **possession** passes, as does **legal title** in many cases, and it is felt that there is minimal future uncertainty with respect to the sale not going through or the earnings process not being culminated. Prior to that point (i.e., when the customer places the order), there is a great deal of **uncertainty** as to whether the inventory will be in stock or whether the company will be able to deliver the inventory on time and in satisfactory condition, etc.

The critical event is often evidenced by an outside exchange. In this case, the exchange is the delivery of the inventory to someone outside the company for consideration.

When there is just one critical event, the earnings process is known as a **discrete earnings process.** Sometimes there is no single defining event, rather, there may be several significant events of equal importance. In this case, the earnings process is known as a **continuous earnings process.**

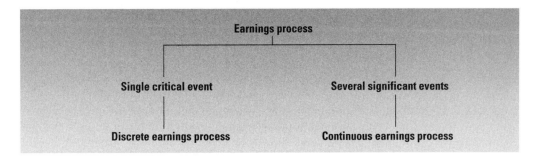

An example of a continuous earnings process is the long-term construction of a bridge. The earnings process might look as follows:

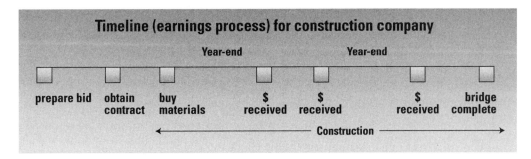

Here, the bridge is effectively sold before it is built. (In a normal manufacturing business, the product is made and then sold, with the outside exchange happening at the end.) Also, the **process takes longer**, often spanning more than one reporting period. Even though the bridge is pre-sold, the company must still **earn** the revenue by building it (i.e., **performance).**

One might argue that the **critical event** is the completion of the bridge. However, if this is true, then all of the revenue would be **recognized** in that period, implying that it was **earned** in that reporting period. Is this truly the case? Furthermore, the completion of the bridge would not signify a sale if there was no pre-signed contract. In this situation, especially since the bridge was sold up-front, the earnings process appears to be made up of several significant events and is, therefore, more like a **continuous process.** Revenue would be recognized as the significant events are completed or over time.

> When analysing accounting issues, sometimes it helps to determine the norm. When is revenue normally recognized (i.e., shipment)? Then look at whether earlier or later recognition makes sense in the specific case and explain why.
>
> **Tip!**

Sale of goods—the risks and rewards of ownership concept

For goods, a sale occurs when the **risks and rewards of ownership are transferred** from the seller to the purchaser and/or when all **significant acts in the earnings process are complete.** Therefore, it is important to focus on the definition of risks and rewards of ownership, as well as, on the earnings process. The earnings process has been discussed above and the risks and rewards will be discussed below.

Consider the house that you live in. What are the risks and rewards of owning the house?

Risks:

- loss in value
- loss from vandalism, fire or other unforeseen circumstances

Rewards:

- increases in value
- use—can live in it or rent it out to someone else for profit
- able to mortgage the property for raising funds

Note that there are many risks and rewards of ownership and that they differ from asset to asset. **Ownership is evidenced by having legal title to the asset, but may also be evidenced by possession** in certain circumstances. **Legal title** allows you to live in the house, pledge it to obtain financing, and entitles you to increases in its value. It also means that you are at risk for such things as loss and declines in value. **Possession** might also signal the existence of some or all of these rights/burdens. Therefore, these two facts are important in determining who has the risks and rewards of ownership and when they pass. Usually the party who is at risk for loss will acknowledge this through **insurance**.

Tip! When looking at any transaction where an asset is changing hands in terms of legal title or possession, an analysis must be done of who has the risks and rewards of ownership. Many complex transactions involve the transfer of risks and rewards of ownership.

Tip! Look at who has possession or legal title or who is paying for insurance. These often give hints as to who has the risks and rewards of ownership.

Tip! The concept of risks and rewards is also central to the definition of an asset i.e., the definition of an asset looks at existence and access to future benefits or rewards.

Dealing with uncertainty

Another major consideration to focus on is the **uncertainty** factor. Are the goods returnable? Are the funds collectible? Can the transaction be measured? These are a few factors that must also be considered. If there is too much uncertainty, then it is questionable as to whether a sale exists. This topic will be further discussed in Study Step 2 under measurement.

> **Where there is uncertainty, professional judgement must be applied. Extreme uncertainty might mean that the transaction should not be booked.**   *Tip!*

Franchise arrangements

A franchise arrangement is when one party—the franchiser—grants another party—the franchisee—the right to use the franchiser's name and sell a product or service. The value to the franchisee is the goodwill associated with the name, e.g., McDonald's, and the expertise and experience of the franchiser who usually assists in the setup of the new business and training of the franchisee.

For these rights, the franchisee pays what is known as an **up-front or initial fee**, which is often quite substantial and an ongoing fee. The **ongoing fee** is normally a percentage of sales and is paid to cover ongoing training and advertising.

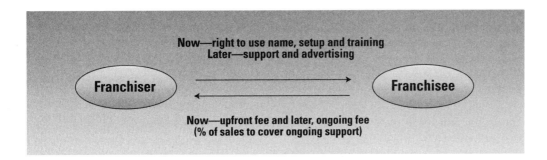

The accounting issues usually relate to the initial fee and when to recognize it. These will be discussed in Step 2.

> **Because initial fees are recognized as revenues up-front, there is a tendency or bias to maximize the amount of initial fee in the contract. Care should be taken to ensure that amounts identified as up-front or initial fees are indeed for services, etc. to be provided up-front by the franchiser.**   *Tip!*

Consignment sales

Consignment sales are a special type of arrangement whereby the vendor displays inventory on the premises of another party until a customer buys it. The middle party does not buy the goods up-front and then sell to the customer, rather, the middle party **allows the goods to be displayed.**

The accounting issue is one of recognition and will be discussed in Step 2 below.

> ## Tip!
> Legal title to the goods remains with the company until the customer buys the product even though it is displayed for sale in the showroom/store of the middle party.

Barter transactions

Barter transactions, also known as nonmonetary transactions, will also be discussed in Chapter 11; however, it is worth a brief mention here. A barter transaction is an **exchange of goods** where there is **no monetary consideration**. Because there is no monetary consideration, there is a **measurement issue** and, more importantly, there is an issue as to whether a real sale took place or whether the transaction was merely an exchange of similar assets. The accounting implications will be discussed in Step 2 below.

2. Understanding How the Transaction Fits into the Financial Reporting Model and the Conceptual Framework—Analysis and Critical Thinking

The big issue, as already mentioned, is one of **recognition,** i.e., when to recognize revenues. See Exhibit 6-1 on opposite page.

3. Becoming Proficient in Using Specific Revenue Recognition Methods

There are methods for recognizing revenues that have become generally accepted in certain industries (e.g., the instalment method in retail sales, franchise accounting in the fast food industry, percentage-of-completion and completed-contract methods in the construction industry, etc.). Furthermore, certain methods make more sense when dealing with sales and uncertaint,y e.g., instalment method/cost recovery method.

Not all are dealt with specifically in the *CICA Handbook*. The general principles covered in Section 3400 of the *Handbook* are often the only guidance provided. Franchise fee accounting is dealt with separately in the Accounting Guidelines section in the *Handbook*.

You should develop a proficiency in the **mechanics of instalment and cost recovery** methods, as well as, **franchise accounting** and **completed-contract and percentage-of-completion** methods. There are problems included for each of these methods in the Problems section that follows. Tips have been included there to assist in your studies. You may wish to do these prior to the multiple choice questions.

Exhibit 6-1

Business transaction: Sales are at the very core of what a business is all about. It is important to analyze the earnings process of a company in order to assess whether revenues have been earned or whether the earnings process is substantially complete.

	How it relates to revenues	Relevant criteria/definitions	Topic specific analysis- how it should be	What makes the analysis challenging–how it is
BASIC **Recoginition**	• when to recognize revenues and related profits	• **performance** achieved (**risks and rewards; earnings process/significant acts completed**) and **measurable** and **collectible**	• the idea is that revenues will be recognized when **earned** or when **significant acts in the earnings process are substantially complete** (including transferring R&R) • in order to recognize, must be **measurable** and **collectible** so that profit can be properly measured and reflected	• most companies would like to recognize revenues earlier rather than later and therefore a bias exists • often uncertainty with respect to returns or collection—if extreme— may not recognize • default to **installment method** or **cost recovery** method to defer profit recognition
Measurement	revenues, costs, and profits	• at **transactions cost** • **measurable?** • **matching** costs with revenues	• usually not a problem unless payments deferred over a # of years, in which case, consider **discounting** • must **accrue all costs** related to the sale in order to measure profits • collection and returns **uncertainty** (attempt to measure -look at history)	• see comments above re. uncertainty • attempt to measure returns or uncollectible amounts based on past history and current environment requires PJ
Presentation/ Disclosure	how to present in f/s and note disclosure required	• **full disclosure**	• due to differing methods for revenue recognition, **disclose** method in notes to statements	
LONG-TERM CONTRACTS and SERVICES Recognition	when to recognize revenues where earnings process is long (>1year)	• use **% of competion** method or **completed contract** method, whichever relates revenue to work accomplished	• if many significant acts (continuous earnings process) and can **measure % complete**—use % completion method	• may be difficult to estimate % complete
FRANCHISE— Initial Fee Recognition	when to recognize initial fee	• when **substantially all initial services performed**	• normally this would be when the franchise is ready for operation	• bias towards earlier recognition
Measurement	how much is the upfront fee and how much is the ongoing fee?	• **measurable?** • **economic substance over legal form**	• normally noted in the franchise agreement	• bias towards front end loading of revenues i.e., may call the fees upfront fees but may be for something else, like interest or future services
Presentation/ Disclosure	how to present in financial statements	• **full disclosure**	• normally show revenues from initial fees since non-recurring • segregate revenues and expense from other operations	
CONSIGNMENT TYPE TRANSACTIONS Recognition	whether to recognize a sale	• see under BASIC	• normally when **R & R** pass to outside party—for consignment sales this would not happen until the end customer purchases and takes legal title	• even though possession is with middle person, legal title still with vendor— watch also for unusually lenient return policy or unusually high returns that may signify no sale
BARTER TYPE TRANSACTIONS Measurment	• is this a sale @ FMV or an exchange of similar assets at NBV? • since non monetary, how to value?	• **culmination of the earnings process** • **economic substance over legal form**	• normally treat as sale of item with asset taken back considered to be consideration • look for whether asset taken back is **similar or dissimiar**— if similar, **economic substance** is that no sale, as left with similar asset with similar **R&R of ownership** • if sale (dissimilar) measure at FMV of asset given up unless FMV of asset taken back easier to value	

The following chart is designed to assist you in determining when a particular method might be appropriate.

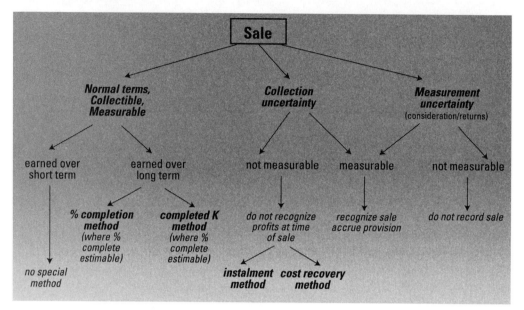

MULTIPLE CHOICE QUESTIONS

1) Under the revenue recognition principle, revenue is recognized when:
   a) Performance is complete and the money is collected.
   b) Performance is substantially complete and collection is reasonably assured.
   c) Performance is complete and collection is reasonably assured.
   d) Performance is substantially complete and the money is collected.

2) Which of the following earnings processes best illustrates the term discrete earnings process?
   a) A company makes paper and ships it to wholesalers.
   b) A company builds tunnels under the ocean connecting islands to the mainland.
   c) A construction company builds shopping centres.
   d) An engineering firm explores areas for oil and gas.

3) For consignment sales, the critical event is:
   a) Shipment of goods to the consignee i.e., when the goods leave the consignor's loading dock.
   b) Sale of goods to a third party other than the consignee.
   c) When the goods are received by the consignee.
   d) When the goods are received by the consignor.

4) ABC Co. uses the cost recovery method for accounting for revenues. During 1998, revenues were $15,000 and cash collections were $8,000. During 1999, revenues were $20,000 and collections for 1998 sales were $2,000 (the rest of the receivables related to 1998 were written off in 1998). ABC also collected $10,000 in cash relating to 1999 sales. ABC's profit margins for 1998 and 1999 are 40% and 45%, respectively. ABC should recognize gross profits in their 1998 and 1999 income statements as follows:

	1998	1999
a.	$3200	$ 800
b.	$3200	$(2200)
c.	$0	$1000
d.	$0	$0

5) According to Section 3400 of the *CICA Handbook*, the completed-contract method would be used when:

a) it best relates the revenue earned to the work accomplished.

b) the earnings process involves a single critical event.

c) the percentage-of-completion method would be appropriate and if the percentage complete is not determinable.

d) all of the above.

6) ABC Construction Limited contracted to construct an office building for XYZ Holdings Inc. for $2,000,000. Construction began in January 1994 and was completed in December 1995. Details of the activities related to this contract are summarized as follows:

| | (in $000s) | |
	1994	1995
Cost incurred to date	400	1,700
Estimated costs to complete	1,200	—
Progress billings to date	300	2,000
To date	250	2,000

How much gross profit can be recognized for this contract in 1994 under the percentage-of-completion method?

a) $0

b) $100,000

c) $133,333

d) $266,667

(CGA adapted-FA2 March 1996)

7) Based on the information in 6 above, how much gross profit can be recognized for this contract in 1995 under the cost recovery method?

a) 0

b) $50,000

c) $300,000

d) $450,000

(CGA adapted-FA2 March 1996)

8) Anchor Limited builds underground tunnels between buildings—usually for access and/or storage. In the most recent contract, they bid $5,000,000 and estimated costs would be $3,000,000. During the second year of the contract, the workers went on strike and delayed the work significantly. Due to this, costs soared to $5,300,000 (estimated to completion). Profits recognized to date, are $500,000. In the current year, using the percentage of completion method, what amount would be booked through the income statement?

a) $500,000 profit.

b) $300,000 loss.

c) $800,000 loss.

d) $800,000 profit.

9) Chang Corp. recently mounted a new campaign whereby their salespeople aggressively marketed the company's products. As part of the campaign, the company offered the products for sale at deep discounts and allowed unlimited returns. The transactions were recognized as revenues and as at year-end, there was a significant increase in sales.

a) The revenue recognition policy is acceptable since the legal title and possession to the goods has passed.
b) Revenue should not be recognized, as these goods will likely be returned.
c) Revenue may be recognized as long as a significantly increased allowance for returns is accrued at the same time.
d) Revenues may be recognized and no allowance is needed.

10) According to the cost recovery method of accounting, gross profit on an instalment sale is recognized in income.
a) on the date of sale.
b) on the date the final cash collection is received.
c) in proportion to the cash collection.
d) after cash collections equal to the cost of sales have been received.

11) Redmond Limited accounts for sales using the instalment method. Redmond's sales and collections for the year were $70,000 and $40,000, respectively. Uncollectible accounts receivable of $10,000 were written off during the year. Redmond's gross profit rate is 25%. What amount should Redmond recognize as profit from instalment sales on the income statement at year end?
a) $10,000
b) $0
c) $7,500
d) $17,500

12) Assuming that Redmond uses the cost recovery method to recognize net income, what would Redmond record as profit at year end?
a) $5,000
b) $0
c) $7,500
d) $17,500

SOLUTIONS TO MULTIPLE CHOICE QUESTIONS

1) b) Accrual accounting requires accountants to estimate transactions and events and record.

2) a) A discrete earnings process occurs when there is one main or critical event that signals performance or that the revenue has been earned. Up to the point of the critical event, too much uncertainty exists. The first example best fits this profile—the other earning processes being too lengthy and having many significant events.

3) b) Because the risks and rewards of ownership do not pass until a third party buys the goods, the earnings process is not complete until then. Prior to that, the consignor still has legal title and is exposed to the risks of ownership.

4) c) is the correct choice. In 1998, cash collections are less than the cost of the sale and therefore, no profits are recognized. In 1999 for the 1998 sales, collections of $2,000 mean that the full cost is recovered, plus $1,000 extra, which is recognized as profits. For the 1999 sales, the cost of sales is $11,000 amd cash collections are only $10,000. Again, they are less than cost of sales and therefore, no profits are recognized for 1999 sales.

5) d) Technically, the *CICA Handbook* states that the method should be the one that best relates the revenue to the work accomplished. However, pratically speaking, when the percentage-of-completion method might meet this criteria, a problem of estimating the percent may arise, in which case, the default would be to use the completed contract method. Where there is one single critical event, it may be appropriate to use this method since the work would all be done at one point after which the revenue would be recognized. This would cetainly be a situation where the completed-contract method best reflects the work accomplished.

6) b) $100,000 calculated as follows:
   Profit = $2,000,000 − 1,600,000 = $400,000
   % complete = $400,000/1,600,000 = 25%
   Gross profit = 25% × $400,000 = $100,000

7) c) $300,000. Since the contract is complete and the full amount has been collected, the full amount of the actual profit ($2,000,000—1,700,000) may be recognized. Note that none of the profit was recognized in 1994 since the full amount of the costs incurred had not yet been collected.

8) c) The company would have to reverse the profits from last year ($500,000) and accrue the estimated losses of $300,000 since they are likely and measurable.

9) c) Although this is aggressive, as long as an accrual is measurable and booked for the returns, recognition would be acceptable. Disclosure would be important.

10) d) Gross profit is deferred and recognized only after all costs have been recovered.

11) a)

Total Profit	$17,500
Less deferred 20,000 × .25	(5,000)
Less profit lost on uncollectible	(2,500)
Recognized	10,000

12) b) No profit would be recognized until the costs of $52,500 have been recovered.

PROBLEMS

1) Purpose: To illustrate the percentage-of-completion method.

Buildit Construction Limited (BCL) builds roads. In 2001, BCL obtained a contract to upgrade a private road that was being taken over by the municipality. Their contract required that the road be straightened, graded, and resurfaced. The road was 16 kilometres long and BCL had agreed to complete the job by mid-2002 for $100,000. The estimated profit on the job was $30,000. By the end of 2001, about 50% of the work had been completed. On signing, the municipality had advanced $10,000 and by the end of the year, they had paid a further $50,000. Supplies costing $40,000 had been purchased ($15,000 used) and $20,000 worth of labour cost had been incurred to date. At year-end, there was one outstanding billing of $8,000.

Required

Prepare the journal entries for BCL for the year ended December 31, 2001.

2) Purpose: To illustrate the completed-contract method.

Required

Using the completed-contract method, prepare the journal entries for BCL assuming the same data as in 1 for the year ended December 31, 2001.

3) Purpose: To illustrate the instalment method.

Bricker Limited (BL) sells appliances and offers an extended payment plan under which customers can pay on a monthly basis over three years. Most customers opt for the extended payment plan. The appliances are delivered to the customer's home upon sale; however, if the customer falls behind in payments, BL will repossess the appliance.

During 2002, BL sold $100,000 worth of appliances on instalment and received instalment payments of $40,000. The gross margin is 30%. BL also received payments from last year's instalment sales of $20,000. The profit margin last year was 25%.

Required

Prepare the journal entries for BL for the year ended December 31, 2002.

4) Purpose: To illustrate the use of the cost recovery method.

Action Limited (AL) had sales of $230,000 during the year (cost of sales $150,000). Customers remitted $100,000 of the amount by year-end. At the beginning of the following year, payments of $60,000 were made.

Required

Prepare the journal entries for AL including the journal entry for the most recent payment.

5) *Purpose:* To illustrate accounting for franchises.

Popcorn Unlimited Limited (PUL) was started up 10 years ago by Greg Gargantuan when he was in university. The company sold popcorn of many flavours and operated out of small portable booths in shopping malls. The concept was so successful that when Greg graduated from university, he decided to franchise the idea. This is the first year of operating as a franchise and Greg has managed to find 10 franchisees. Greg has standardized the contract which is as follows:

- $5,000 down payment.
- Three payments of $5,000 at the end of the next three years, beginning at the end of the first year.
- PUL promises to negotiate with various malls to obtain permission to set up each booth, provide a finished booth with all the necessary equipment, provide training, and provide ongoing support.
- The equipment has a two-year life expectancy and, therefore, since Greg anticipates that franchises will operate beyond that, he has included a second set of equipment (worth $4,000) in the initial fee (included in the $20,000 above). This equipment is held by PUL until required by the franchise.
- Franchisees must also pay 1% of monthly revenues Aside from these and the payments noted above, franchisees are not required to pay anything else.
- Interest rates are 10%.

The first contract was signed on January 1, 2002 and the down payment was made on the same date. PUL had the booth set up on June 1, 2002 and operations began that same day. Sales for this outlet were $40,000 for the first year. The franchisee appears to be financially stable.

Required

Prepare the journal entries relating to the first deal for the year ended December 31, 2002.

SOLUTIONS TO PROBLEMS

> **Tip!**
> The percentage-of-completion method is used for the rendering of services and long-term contracts where the method relates the revenues to the work accomplished. Generally, the percentage-of-completion method would work best where a good estimate of the work accomplished can be estimated.

1) To record the deposit:

Cash	10,000	
Billings on construction		10,000

To record purchase of supplies:

Inventory	40,000	
Cash		40,000

To record payroll costs:

Construction-in-progress	20,000	
Cash		20,000

To record materials usage:

Construction-in-progress	15,000	
Inventory		15,000

To record subsequent cash received:

Cash	50,000	
Billings on construction		50,000

To record the last billing:

Accounts receivable	8,000	
Billings on construction		8,000

To record revenues:

Construction-in-progress	15,000	
Construction expenses (I/S)	35,000	
Revenues		50,000

Revenues have been calculated based on the amount of costs incurred which happens to represent the status of the project (i.e., 50% complete).

Costs incurred/total costs expected = $35,000/$70,000 = 50%
50% x $100,000 or the total contract price = $50,000

The expenses incurred to earn this revenue (i.e., $15,000 materials and $20,000 labour) are booked on the income statement in order to match costs with revenues. These had previously been booked as assets in the construction-in-progress account. The difference represents the profit on the revenues to date.

> **Tip!** Profit is also booked to the construction-in-progress account with the end result that the CIP account accumulates not only all the costs incurred on the job, but also the profit element. In a sense, this asset account shows the worth of the project to date.

> **Tip!** The profit is a plug to balance the revenue journal entry but can also be calculated separately as 50% of the total expected profit on the job.

> **Tip!** On the balance sheet, the construction-in-progress account net of the billings account represents the value of the construction in excess of the amounts billed. In this case, the billings are greater than the value of the construction and, therefore, a net credit results. When revenues are recognized based on costs incurred to date, the construction-in-progress account is equal to the revenues recognized to date and the net amount would represent billings in excess of revenues recognized.

2) The journal entries would be exactly the same as under the percentage-of-completion method except for the last entry, which would not be booked. Revenues and related expenses would only be booked on the income statement in 2002, that is, when the project is complete and the title passes over to the buyer.

> **Tip!** The completed-contract method is usually only used where the % complete is not estimable.

> **Tip!** For the completed-contract method, the journal entries are the same except that no revenues are recognized until the end or completion of the contract.

3) To record the instalment sales:

Instalment AR	100,000	
Instalment sales		100,000

> **Tip!** The instalment method is used where there is uncertainty as to the realization of a sale. This is often inherent in instalment type sales since the terms of the sale are more lenient, allowing the customer to pay over a longer period yet take possession of the goods up-front.

To record cost of sales:

Cost of sales	70,000	
Inventory		70,000

To record payments received:

Cash	60,000	
Instalment AR 2002		40,000
Instalment AR 2001		20,000

To recognize profits from prior year:

Deferred profit 2001 (B/S)	5,000*	
Gross profit earned on instalment sales (I/S)		5,000
* $20,000 \times 25\%$		

The credit would be shown on a separate line item on the income statement after gross profit.

To defer unearned profit on this year's sales:

Deferred profit	18,000*	
Deferred profit (B/S)		18,000

* $60,000 \times 30\%$—The rest is earned since a payment of $40,000 has been received (i.e., $40,000 \times 30\% = \$12,000$ earned). ($18,000 + \$12,000 = \$30,000$ total profit on $100,000 sale @ 30% gross margin.)

The income statement would be shown as follows:

Instalment sales	$100,000
Cost of sales	70,000
Gross profit	30,000
Deferred gross profit	(18,000)
Gross profit earned on instalment sales from 2001	5,000
Net income	$ 17,000

Using the above journal entries, the instalment sales will be shown on the income statement in the year that they are earned. Alternatively, the sales and cost of sales can be reversed when the profit is deferred with the following entry for 2002:

Sales	100,000	
Cost of sales		70,000
Deferred profit 2002 (B/S)		18,000
Gross profit earned on instalment sales		12,000

This journal entry would be booked instead of the preceding entry and would result in nothing on the income statement for instalment sales except the one line for earned profits. Where instalment sales are significant, it makes more sense to use the former method so that instalment sales are shown as revenues in the year that they are made and that they are shown separately. Again, from a user's perspective, instalment sales are more risky in that they carry a higher collection risk.

> **Where instalment sales are significant, it makes sense to show them separately in the year that they are earned and defer only the profit recognition.**   *Tip!*

> **As the cash is collected from the customer, the uncertainty surrounding profit realization decreases and therefore, part of the profits may be recognized.**   *Tip!*

> **The cost recovery method is used where there is even more uncertainty than situations where the instalment method might be appropriate. Basically, the cost recovery method would be used where there is no reasonable basis for estimating collectibility, although, in this case, perhaps no sale should be recorded at all.**   *Tip!*

4) To record the sales:

AR	230,000	
Sales		230,000
Cost of sales	150,000	
Inventory		150,000

To record payment:

Cash	100,000	
AR		100,000

To defer profit:

Deferred profit (I/S)	80,000	
Deferred profit (B/S)		80,000

None of the profit will be recognized in the same year since the total costs of $150,000 have not yet been recovered (only $100,000 of the $150,000 has been received in cash). Under the instalment method, $34,783 would be recognized ($100,000/$230,000 × $80,000).

> **Tip!** With the cost recovery method, the amount of uncertainty increases and, therefore, the profits are not recognized until all costs are recovered.

To record payment:

Cash	60,000	
AR		60,000

To recognize profit:

Deferred profit (B/S)	10,000	
Realized gross profit (I/S)		10,000

Only $10,000 is realized since that is the amount of cash received to date for those sales less the costs incurred to make the sales (i.e., $100,000 + $60,000 − $150,000 = $10,000). Subsequent payments would result in profits equal to the payment being recognized. Under the instalment method, profits of $20,870 would be recognized ($60,000/$230,000 × $80,000).

5) January 1, 2002
To record the signing of the contract and the down payment:

Cash	5,000	
Deferred revenues		5,000

The revenue is deferred at this point since PUL has only signed the contract and has not yet otherwise fulfilled its obligations, including finding the location and setting it up. This might be arguable if the deposit was non-refundable.

June 1, 2002.
To record the revenues:

Deferred revenues	5,000 (1)	
Notes receivable	15,000 (2)	
Franchise revenues		12,434 (3)
Deferred revenues		4,000
Deferred interest rev.		3,566

(1) to reverse the downpayment that was originally deferred.
(2) $5,000 × 3
(3) Present value ordinary annuity of $5,000, 3 years at 10% less $4,000 for the equipment. Since the note is non-interest bearing (i.e., the question states that no other payments are required), then some of the initial fee relates to implicit interest on the notes. This represents the time value of the money. The interest revenue will be recognized over time. Since the delivery of the equipment does not happen until two years into the future, the $4,000 must be separated from the other revenues and recognized on delivery.

December 31, 2002.
To record the second payment:

Cash	5,000	
Notes receivable		5,000
Deferred interest	1,243	
Interest revenue		1,243

$12,434 \times 10\% = \$1,243$

To record the continuing fee:

Cash	4,000	
Fee income		4,000

$40,000 \times 10\%$

CASES

1) INVESTICO LIMITED

Investico Limited (IL) is a small real estate development company that was started up by two investors. Adam Adams, one of the investors, runs the company and makes the key decisions, whereas Brent Boudreau, the other investor, put up half of the initial capital required, and is basically a silent partner. The main objective of the company, initially agreed upon by the two men was to invest in low-risk real estate properties and sell them for profit once the real estate appreciated to a certain point.

The first project that IL invested in was some vacation property. Adam found the property, and made the decision to buy it without consulting Brent. Adam planned to subdivide and service the resulting lots and to sell them as vacation properties. Even though the purchase did not quite fit in with IL's objectives, Adam figured that he could sell the lots at a better than average profit before Brent could have a chance to object.

Adam subdivided the lots and was able to sell all of them on the following terms:
- $2,500 downpayment (5% of the sale price).
- IL would take back a note receivable from the purchaser under an agreement of sale. The note is interest-free and title to the land remains with IL until the note is fully repaid (five-year term).
- The purchaser would take immediate possession.
- IL would service the lot with electricity within a year of the purchase date.

Most of the lots were sold at the beginning of 2001; however, by the end of 2001, about 30% of the purchasers were behind in their loan payments. Adam was not anxious to repossess the properties and had worked out a deal with the owners that they would allow him to cut down the wood on the properties for resale. The owners felt that the resale value on the wood would more than cover the overdue payments.

Meanwhile, Brent found out about the property and that it had all been sold and was considering taking some of his investment out of the company. He wished to see the financial statements for the year ended December 31, 2001. Adam has hired you, a chartered accountant, to advise him as to how he should prepare the financial statements. He is considering selling the notes receivable connected with the sales of property in order to have some cash on hand, should Brent want his money back.

Required

Assume the role of the chartered accountant and prepare a memo to Adam analysing the accounting and reporting issues. Your memo should consider users and constraints and provide recommendations.

2) MicroStrategy—www.microstrategy.com

The following information was taken from a U.S. Securities and Exchange Commission (SEC) Document dated December 14, 2000, regarding proceedings instituted against MicroStrategy Inc. to determine whether the company violated the law. The restated consolidated financial statements of the company for the December 31, 1999 year end were also consulted. All amounts are stated in U.S. dollars.

According to the financial statements of the company, MicroStrategy provides intelligent e-business software and related services that enable the transaction of one-to-one electronic business through web, wireless, and voice communication channels. The company was incorporated in 1989 and went public in 1998. Since going public, the company had announced increasing revenues in each consecutive quarter. Share prices increased along with the revenues. After going public, the company began to enter into increasingly larger and more complex transactions as well as extensive software application development and customization consulting arrangements. The customized software was generally built on the MicroStrategy platform and customized for the particular customer. A licensing arrangement would be made to enable the customers to use the customized product which had at its base, the MicroStrategy software. In 1996, the majority of the revenues were from product licence sales although this emphasis began to shift.

On March 20, 2000, MicroStrategy announced that it would restate its financial statements for the years ended December 31, 1999 and 1998. The restatement caused 1999 revenues to drop from $205 million to $151 million and net income to move from a $13 million profit to a $34 million loss. The drop in revenues was primarily due to a decline in product sales revenues. 1998 revenues and net income dropped from $106 million and $6 million profit to $95 million and $2 million loss. The shares of the company had traded as high as $333 per share but by the end of the day, they were trading at $86. Subsequent to the restatement a class action suit was initiated on behalf of the investors against the company, its senior officers and directors and the company's auditors PricewaterhouseCoopers LLP.

The SEC in the document alleges that the company overstated revenues in several ways. One specific instance is noted below:

The company entered into an agreement with ShopKo Stores Inc. to provide software licences as well as consulting and development services as well as a stock warrant allowing ShopKo to purchase the company's common shares. The deal was measured at $4.5 million. The company agreed to provide services that would develop software applications for ShopKo that would work using the MicroStrategy software platform. The SEC alleges that the majority of the software licences purchased were to be used in conjunction with the yet to be developed applications. According to the SEC document, the entire amount was recognized as revenues in the fourth quarter in 1998.

U.S. GAAP is significantly more specific and rule-oriented than Canadian GAAP when it comes to revenue recognition. The SEC has also issued specific guidance regarding revenue recognition, the most recent release being issued during the financial reporting period in question.

REQUIRED

Critically analyse the financial reporting issues related to how the company recognized revenues in the two transactions noted. *NB:* It is not necessary to consider U.S. GAAP. Instead, apply Canadian GAAP.

SOLUTIONS TO CASES

1) INVESTICO

Overview

Brent is a key user and needs information to determine (1) whether to divest himself of the interest in the company, and (2) whether Adam is looking after the company (stewardship function); and (3) to assess risk since the objective of the company is to invest in low-risk properties. Therefore, he needs realistic financial statements that focus on the real value of the asset.

The potential purchasers of the notes receivable need conservative financial statements to determine whether to purchase the notes.

GAAP will be a constraint in providing reliable statements to the users. Even though the users may want financial statements that are conservative and realistic, Adam will want to portray the company and himself in the most favourable light to show Brent that he is looking after Brent's best interests and to induce someone to purchase the notes. Adam will want to downplay risk due to the intended nature of the company.

Analysis and Recommendations

The issues are as follows:

1. When to recognize revenues.
2. How to value the notes receivable given the collectibility problem.
3. Other—how to value the wood.

Revenue recognition:
The earnings process is as follows:

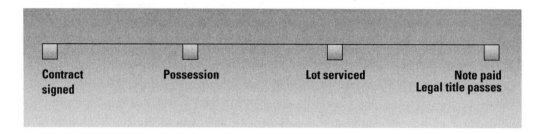

Revenue could be recognized when the contract is signed (customer found up-front) or when **possession** occurs, since it could be argued that the **risks and rewards** of ownership have passed (i.e., possession has passed and consideration has been received evidencing a reasonable amount of certainty that the deal will go through as planned). At this point, there has been an **exchange with an outside party**. Also, the sales price is **measurable**, since fixed by agreement.

However, **legal title** has not yet passed and it could be argued that the earnings process is not substantially complete as the lots have not yet been serviced (it may also be difficult to estimate costs). **Collectibility** is also a problem as evidenced by the tardy payments.

This position is aggressive and would support Adam's financial reporting objective, but there is uncertainty with respect to **measuring the profit** on the sale and **collectibility**.

Another alternative would be to wait until the end of the earnings process. At this point, **legal title** would have passed and there is no question as to **collectibility**. All revenues and costs are **measurable** at this point.

This position is very conservative, however, and does not meet Adam's needs.

Recommendation

Even though Adam wants aggressive financial statements, revenue should probably not be recognized until the lots are at least serviced. At this point, the uncertainty will be cleared up regarding costs and IL will have a better idea of collectibility. This might be considered aggressive since legal title has not yet passed; however, the intent is that the payments will be made and that the title will pass and, therefore, the substance is that a sale has been made.

Asset Valuation:
GAAP requires that a provision for bad debts be estimated if there are collections problems. However, in this case, payments are still being made albeit in kind.

One alternative is to set up a provision as required under GAAP. This would provide a more realistic value for the potential purchasers of the notes. As a chartered accountant, knowing that potential purchasers will rely on the value in the financial statements, you will want to ensure that they are properly valued in order to minimize lawsuits. Even though the payments are being made in kind at the present, there is uncertainty as to whether the note holders will be able to make future payments if they are in trouble now. Another alternative is to make no provision since payments in kind are just as good as monetary payments since they have value. Also, the payments are up to date. Adam does not want to let Brent see the riskiness of the venture given Brent's wariness.

Recommendation

Likely, a provision would be set up due to the high exposure to legal action if the potential purchasers rely on the value and subsequently suffer a loss. Perhaps there could be a compromise position of recognizing revenues earlier but providing a conservative estimate of bad debts.

Value of the Wood

This issue is tied in with the one above. How should the value of the wood be determined? It must be valued to assess whether the wood covers the overdue payments. The value must be net of any additional costs to sell the wood.

2) MICROSTRATEGY

Overview

At the time of the restatement, the company had been in business for over 10 years and was seen as being very successful. Company management took pride in announcing increasing revenues in each consecutive quarter and share prices rose to a high of over $300. The shares were seen as a great investment by many since they were in a high growth area and since many other similar companies were still in the development stage and had not yet managed to produce revenues yet alone profits. MicroStrategy had both. Analysts' expectations for the shares were high and the company was followed closely by many.

Management and directors benefited from this period of growth as they sold some of their shares at significant gains. Investors in the class action suit accused the company and its auditors of issuing false and misleading statements. Having shares that traded on a public stock exchange, the company was constrained by GAAP.

The company earned its money from three sources: (1) selling product licences; (2) providing services such as maintenance, technical support, and training; and (3) providing consulting and development services.

Analysis and Recommendations

The issue is one of revenue recognition—specifically when the revenue should be recognized. As the company's reputation and new products gained momentum, sales contracts grew in dollar value and technical complexity. The sales consisted of both products (licences) and services (development of customized platforms and applications, as well as training and ongoing support). In many cases, the software licences that were sold (products) enabled the customers to use the customized software that had been created for them using the MicroStrategy software application.

The earnings process could be seen as follows:

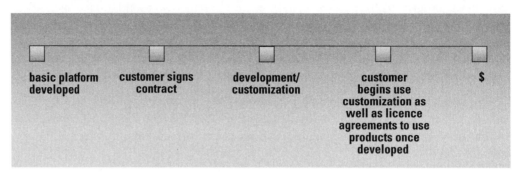

| basic platform developed | customer signs contract | development/ customization | customer begins use customization as well as licence agreements to use products once developed | $ |

This earnings process is not meant to represent all transactions entered into by the company but rather to illustrate one of the processes by which the company added value. Each contract would differ in terms of when the customer paid for the product, how long the development stage took, and even when the customer began to use the product. In reality, companies also paid for the rights to resell MicroStrategy products developed among other things.

Notwithstanding the foregoing, the question arises as to when the company might be able to recognize revenues and how it viewed its revenue stream, i.e., as **product, services** or **both**. In 1996, the emphasis was on **product sales** and therefore the **critical events** in the earnings process would be the **signing of the contract** and the **shipment** assuming in the earlier days, the products were less complex and needed less customization. At that point, **possession** would pass to the customer and the customer would be **legally entitled** to use the product. Could the product be downloaded? In the latter case, the critical event might be considered to be the contract signing.

With all software sales however, there is a **service** component—at a minimum a technical help hotline and other support. The question is whether this should be part of the product sale or deferred until the "service" was provided and/or the coverage period expired. The test would be **performance** and the issue would be whether performance consisted of a **discrete process** represented by a **critical event** (such as shipment as with products) or a **continuous earnings process** represented by **several significant events**— the development and testing of the application of customized software being these events. The issue would be one of **measurement**, i.e., how do you separate the support from the product and what value do you attach? If it is not measurable, does that mean all revenues should be recognized or all deferred? Which of the two is more significant?

Looking back to the transaction in the case, it was significant and involved the company developing customized applications. The SEC took exception to the fact that all of the revenues were allocated to product sales and none to the service component. The SEC questioned how revenues could be recognized for licensed product sales when the product was in the process of being developed.

SELECTED SOLUTIONS FROM THE TEXTBOOK

EXERCISE 6-4

(a)
Gross profit recognized in:

	2001	2002	2003
Contract Price:	$1,500,000	$1,500,000	$1,500,000
Costs:			
Opening balance of costs	0	400,000	935,000
Costs incurred during the year	400,000	535,000	135,000
Costs incurred to date	400,000	935,000	1,070,000
Estimated costs to complete	600,000	165,000	0
Total estimated costs	1,000,000	1,100,000	1,070,000
Total estimated profit	500,000	400,000	430,000
Percentage complete	40%*	85%**	100%
Total gross profit recognized	200,000	340,000	430,000
Gross profit recognized in			
previous years	0	(200,000)	(340,000)
Gross profit recognized current year	$200,000	$140,000	$90,000

*$400,000 ÷ $1,000,000
**$935,000 ÷ $1,100,000

(b)

Construction in Process	535,000	
($935,000 − $400,000)		
Materials, Cash, Payables, etc.		535,000
Accounts Receivable ($900,000 − $300,000)	600,000	
Billings and Construction in Process		600,000
Cash ($810,000 − $270,000)	540,000	
Accounts Receivable		540,000
Construction Expenses	535,000	
Construction in Process	140,000	
Revenue from Long-term Contracts		675,000*
*$1,500,000 × (85% − 40%)		

(c)
Gross profit recognized in:

	2001	2002	2003
Gross profit	$ -0-	$ -0-	$430,000

*$1,500,000 − $1,070,000

EXERCISE 6-15

(a) Realized gross profit recognized in 2002 under the instalment method of accounting
is $110,400

Sale Year	Gross Profit Percentage	2002 Collections	2002 Realized Profit
2001	25%	$ 240,000	$60,000
2002	28%	180,000	50,400
		Total	$110,400

(b) The balance of "Deferred Gross Profit" could be reported on the balance sheet for
2002:

   (1) As a current liability, as an unearned revenue on the theory that it is related to
        Instalment Accounts Receivables that are normally treated as current assets.

   (2) As a contra account to the related Instalment Accounts Receivable. This is
        because the deferred gross profit is a part of revenue from instalment sales not
        yet realized. The related receivable will be overstated unless the deferred gross
        profit is deducted.

(c) Realized gross profit of $20,000 is recognized on the 2002 income statement.

	2001 Sales	2002 Sales
Sales	$480,000	$620,000
Gross profit 25 %	120,000	
Gross profit 28 %		173,600
Costs	360,000	446,400
Collections to date:		
in 2001	(140,000)	
in 2002	(240,000)	(180,000)
Gross profit recognized	$20,000	
Costs remaining to be recovered		$266,400

PROBLEM 6-7

(a)

Calculation of Recognizable Profit/Loss
Percentage-of-Completion Method
($000 omitted)

	2001	2002	2003
Contract Price:	$1,950	$1,950	$1,950
Costs:			
Opening balance of costs	0	150	1,200
Costs incurred during the year	150	1,050	900
Costs incurred to date	150	1,200	2,100
Estimated costs to complete	1,350	800	0
Total estimated costs	1,500	2,000	2,100
Total estimated profit	450	(50)	(150)
Percentage complete	10%	60%	100%
Gross profit recognized	45	(50)	(150)
Gross profit recognized in previous years	0	(45)	50
Gross profit recognized current year	$45	($95)	($100)

(b)

Calculation of Recognizable Profit/Loss
Completed-Contract Method
($000 omitted)

	2001	2002	2003
Costs incurred to date	$ 150	$1,200	$2,100
Estimated costs to complete	1,350	800	0
Total estimated costs	1,500	2,000	2,100
Contract price	1,950	1,950	1,950
Loss to date on contract	0	(50)	(150)
Loss recognized previous year	0	0	50
Loss recognized current year	0	($50)	($100)

PROBLEM 6-9

	2001	2002	2003
Sales	$385,000	$426,000	$525,000
Cost of sales	270,000	277,000	341,000
Gross margin on sales	115,000	149,000	184,000
Gross margin realized on instalment sales (see calc. below)	36,300	72,600	119,050
Total gross profit	151,300	221,600	303,050
Selling expenses	77,000	87,000	92,000
Administrative expenses	50,000	51,000	52,000
Total selling and administrative expenses	127,000	138,000	144,000
Net income	$24,300	$83,600	$159,050

Calculation of gross margin realized on instalment sales:

	2001	2002	2003
Rate of gross profit	33%	39%**	41%***
Gross margin realized:			
33% of $110,000	$36,300		
33% of $90,000		$29,700	
39% of $110,000		42,900	
33% of $40,000			$13,200
39% of $140,000			$54,600
41% of $125,000			$51,250
	$36,300	$72,600	$119,050

$$*\frac{\$320,000 - \$214,400}{\$320,000} = 33\%$$

$$**\frac{\$275,000 - \$167,750}{\$275,000} = 39\,\%$$

$$***\frac{\$380,000 - \$224,200}{\$380,000} = 41\%$$

PROBLEM 6-17

(a)

Schedule to Calculate Gross Profit for 2001
($000 omitted)

	A	B	C*	D	E	Total
Contract Price:	$300	$350	$280	$200	$240	
Costs:						
Costs incurred to date	248	67.8	186	123	185	
Estimated costs to complete	67	271.2	0	87	15	
Total estimated costs	315	$339.0	186	210	200	
Total estimated profit (loss)	(15)	11	94	(10)	40	
Percentage complete	79%	20%	$100%	59%	92.5%	
Gross profit (loss) recognized	($15)	$2.2	$94	($10)	$ 37	$108.2
Revenue (contract price × % complete	$237	$70	$280	$118	$222	$ 927

* all of the losses are recognized when measurable

Schedule to Calculate Contract Costs
and Recognized Profit in Excess of Billings
($000 omitted)

	A	B	C*	D	E	Total
Construction In process	$248	$67.8		$123	$185	$623.8
Accrued loss to date on contract	(15)	2.2		(10)	37	14.2
Balance construction in process	233	70		113	222	$638.0
Billings on construction contract	200	110		35	205	
Contract costs and gross profit in excess of billings	$ 33			$ 78	$ 17	
Billings in excess of contract costs and gross profit		($40)				

*Contract is complete, construction costs have been closed

(b)

Partial Income Statement

Revenue from long-term contracts	$927,000
Costs of construction	818,800
Gross profit	$108,200

Refer to totals of costs and construction in process plus gross profit or less losses in second schedule part (a)

Partial Balance Sheet

Current assets:		
Accounts receivable		$65,000
($830,000 − $765,000)		
Inventories (below)		
Construction in process	$568,000	
Less: Billings	440,000	
Unbilled contract costs		
and recognized profit		
in excess of billings		128,000
Current liabilities:		
Billings ($110,000) in excess of		
costs and recognized profit		
($70,000)—Project B	$40,000	

($000 omitted)

	A	D	E	Total
Construction In process	$248	$123	$185	$556
Accrued loss to date on contract	(15)	(10)	37	12
Balance construction in process	233	113	222	568
Billings on construction contract	200	35	205	440
Contract costs in excess of billings	$ 33	$ 78	$ 17	$128

(c)

Schedule to Calculate Gross Profit for 2001
($000 omitted)

	A	B	C	D	E
Contract Price:	$300	$ 350	$ 280	$200	$240
Costs:					
Costs incurred to date	248	67.8	186	123	185
Estimated costs to complete	67	$271.2	0	87	15
Total estimated costs	315	339.0	186	210	200
Total estimated profit (loss)	(15)	11	94	(10)	40
Percentage complete	79%	20%	100%	59%	92.5%
Gross profit (loss) recognized	($15)		$94	($10)	

Schedule to Calculate Contract Costs in Excess
of Billings and Billings in Excess of Costs
($000 omitted)

	A	B	C*	D	E
Construction in process	$248	$67.8		$123	$185
Accrued loss to date on contract	(15)	0.0		(10)	0
Balance construction in process	233	67.8		113	185
Billings on construction contract	200	110		35	205
Contract costs in excess of billings	$33			$78	
Billings in excess of contract costs and accrued losses		($42.2)			($20)

*Contract is complete, construction costs have been closed

(d) The principal advantage of the completed-contract method is that it reports revenue based on the final results and not on estimates made throughout the construction period. However, the disadvantage of using this method is that for contracts, which extend more than one accounting period, income recognition is distorted. For example, in this exercise Shen Corp. would recognize $39,200 less gross profit using the completed-contract method than if it was using the percentage-of-completion method ($108,200-$69,000). This difference exists because the only project completed at the end of 2001 was project C and so that is the only project from which Shen may recognize revenue and gross profit. Therefore, even though a portion of the work was completed on projects B and E, no revenues or gross profit can be recognized until those projects are completed.

On the other hand, the percentage-of-completion method does recognize revenue and gross profit before the completion of a project. If Shen can determine reliable estimates of its progress and meets the other conditions for this method, Shen can recognize revenues as the work progresses. The use of this method provides financial statement users with a more current picture of the results of the company's operations; however, problems may occur if the estimates are poor. If revised estimates, or even rising costs, show that a project will result in a loss, the company must reverse gross profit previously recognized for that project. Thus, it is possible that the financial statements may present a good picture one year and the next year present a picture that is not as good because of the change in estimate treatment.

The end results will be the same under either method and so the difference is simply one of timing. Therefore, if a company can determine reliable estimates of its progress towards completion and meets the required conditions, the percentage-of-completion method is preferred. Otherwise the completed-contract method is more appropriate.

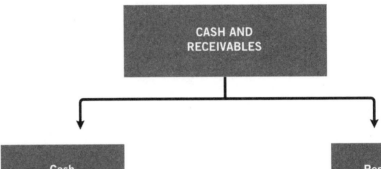

chapter 7

CASH AND RECEIVABLES

PERSPECTIVE

This chapter deals with some fundamental areas that may have been covered in previous account-ing courses. It is nonetheless a key area since cash management for a company is critical. Companies need to know that there is sufficient cash available to cover expenses and current lia-bilities in the near term. A company that cannot cover its operating costs in the short term, has a liquidity problem and may not be able to continue to operate in the longer term. Therefore, it is crucial that liquid assets are properly classified in the financial statements and any restrictions on how the cash may be spent are properly disclosed.

There is a new Accounting Guideline that discusses Transfers of Receivables.

INSIGHTS

- *The more fundamental skills, such as completing bank reconciliations, should be mastered as every accountant should be proficient in them.*
- *Also of importance here is the ability to estimate bad debt expense.*

STUDY STEPS

1. Understanding the Importance of Cash and Liquid Assets in Any Business

STUDY STEPS

As mentioned above, cash and liquid assets are crucial to any business since a company needs to keep a certain amount of liquid assets in order to pay off operating expenses and short-term payables. Users of financial statements, therefore, often focus on liquid assets and short-term liabilities to assess the **liquidity** of a company.

Use of receivables to generate cash

Sometimes a company will experience a cash shortage because it has a significant amount of working capital tied up in accounts receivable; therefore, some companies will use receivables to generate cash. One way of doing this is to **pledge** or **assign** the receivables to a lender. Another method of using receivables to generate cash is to sell or dispose of them. This is sometimes called **factoring, discounting** or **securitization**. It is important to understand this business transaction prior to understanding the accounting issues. Generally, the company will give up rights to the future stream of cash receipts that will be collected from the receivables for immediate receipt of cash.

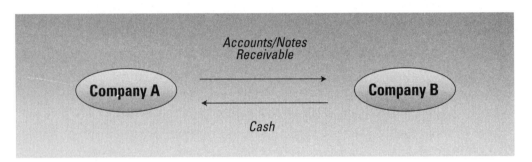

Company B has **possession** of and **legal title** to the receivables after the transaction. The arrangement may be such that Company B in the above situation has no **recourse** to Company A if the receivables prove to be uncollectible in future periods. Conversely, the arrangement may allow Company B to seek compensation from Company A if they cannot collect the full amount of the receivables from the customers. In the latter case, Company B has **recourse** to Company A.

Generally, the amount of cash received by Company A would be less than the Net Book Value (NBV) of the receivables. This discount is to compensate Company B for their collection efforts and for any potential losses from uncollected amounts. Company B would probably rather have recourse to Company A for uncollectible amounts, although, it may be willing to give this right up for a lower cash payment.

> **Tip!** Pledging or assigning receivables is a method of generating cash from receivables up front usually in the form of a loan. The legal right to the cash from collecting the receivables remains with the company unless the company defaults on the loan.

> **Tip!** Factoring or discounting is another method of generating cash from receivables up-front. In this case, however, the legal right to collect the receivables is transferred to the other party.

The sale of receivables may be with or without recourse.

Recourse signals that the risks and rewards of ownership may still rest, at least partially, with the company.

---

2. Understanding How the Transactions Related to this Area Fit into the Financial Reporting Model and the Conceptual Framework—Analysis and Critical Thinking

STUDY STEPS

Overall

For all liquid assets, there is an issue of **disclosure** in certain situations. Users of financial statements assume that the assets on a balance sheet are **unencumbered** or **available for paying off obligations**; therefore, if this is not the case, it is important to make this information available in order for users to assess liquidity.

For all receivables, there exists a collection risk and this must be **re-measured** at each reporting date.

Transfer of receivables

For transactions involving the transfer of receivables (and related transactions where the receivables are used to raise funds), the issue is a **recognition** issue as analysed below:

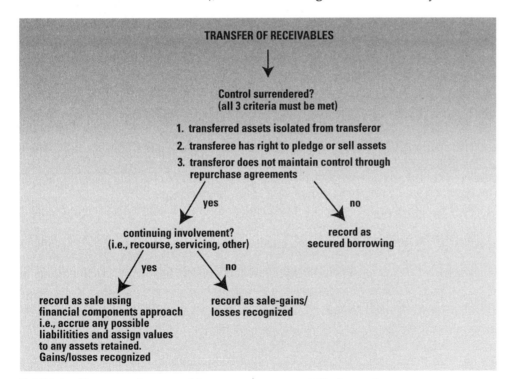

TRANSFER OF RECEIVABLES

↓

Control surrendered?
(all 3 criteria must be met)

1. transferred assets isolated from transferor
2. transferee has right to pledge or sell assets
3. transferor does not maintain control through repurchase agreements

yes / no

no → **record as secured borrowing**

yes → **continuing involvement?**
(i.e., recourse, servicing, other)

yes → **record as sale using financial components approach i.e., accrue any possible liabilities and assign values to any assets retained. Gains/losses recognized**

no → **record as sale-gains/losses recognized**

Exhibit 7-1 illustrates the recognition, measurement and disclosure issues.

Exhibit 7-1: Relevant criteria, definitions and issues

Business perspective: The amount of cash and receivables signal liquidity and flexibility signalling users whether or not the company is able to meet its short-term commitments

	How it relates to cash and receivables	Relevant criteria/definitions	Topic specific analysis—how it should be	What makes the analysis challenging—how it is
BASIC Recognition/ Measurement	• some receivables may not be collected	• **lower of cost and NRV** • **estimated realized amount** (HB 3025.14)	• write down when **known to be uncollectible** (HB 3020.10) • write down when **no reasonable assurance** as to collection (HB 3025.03) • **disclose method** and also HB 1508 recommends **nature and extent of uncertainty**	• very judgemental—many different ways to calculate— **% of sales or % of receivables** • for impaired loans value depends on intent **see Chapter 15**
Disclosure	note disclosure of valuation method	• **full disclosure**		
TRANSFER OF RECEIVABLES Recognition/ Derecognition	whether to recognize a sale/ profit/loss on transfer of receivables	• **risks and rewards** of ownership transferred • **economic substance** • **3 criteria** Accounting Guideline 12 1. assets isolated from transferor 2. transferee has right to pledge or exchange asset 3. transferor gives up effective control • **continuing involvement?**	• in principle, if **R&R** of receivables transferred to another party should be treated as a disposition and gain or loss recognized	• complicated by specific details of the transaction. May be either a disposition or a financing type transaction. Where the receivables are merely pledged or assigned, it is a financing and the receivables stay on the books. Where it is a transfer, it may be like a financing or a disposition/sale. If recourse, may be more like a financing. If not, may be like a sale. See EIC #54 and Accounting Guideline 12.
Measurement	can the risks retained be measured and accrued	• **reasonable assurance** as to measurement • **financial components** approach	• must measure and recognize any assets and liabilities retained	• measurement of the consideration and potential losses under recourse provisions are a matter of professional judgement and not necessarily easy to predict
Presentation/ Disclosure	how to present in the f/s and note disclosure required	• **full disclosure**	• due to differing ways of treating and complexity of some of these transactions— **full disclosure**	

Prepared by Irene Wiecek
©2002 John Wiley & Sons Canada, Ltd

STUDY STEPS

---

3. Becoming proficient in the Related Calculations

The key calculations required in this area are as follows:

- Bank reconciliations
- Estimation of bad debts

An example of a bank reconciliation is covered in problem 2 along with some tips to assist in preparation of the reconciliation. Estimation of bad debts is covered in the multiple choice questions as well as in problem 1.

MULTIPLE CHOICE QUESTIONS

1) Which of the following items on a bank reconciliation will require an adjustment to the general ledger balance for cash?
   a) outstanding cheques
   b) bank error
   c) proceeds of note collected by bank
   d) deposit in transit
(CGA FA2 March 1994)

2) Which of the following items would require an adjustment to the bank balance in the bank reconciliation?
   a) bank service charges
   b) bank error
   c) bank debit memo
   d) book error

3) Ninja Limited has accounts receivable of $500,000 at year-end. The allowance for doubtful accounts is $30,000 before adjusting for the following:

   • $10,000 cash was received for accounts receivable previously written off

   • Ninja uses the percentage-of-receivable approach for estimating bad debts and has found in past that the allowance should represent 5% of the accounts receivable.

   By how much should the allowance account be debited/credited to adjust the balance to the required amount?
   a) $5,000 debit
   b) $15,000 debit
   c) $5,000 credit
   d) $4,500 debit

4) A method of estimating uncollectible accounts that emphasizes income measurement rather than asset valuation is the allowance method based on:
   a) ageing the receivables
   b) direct write-off
   c) credit sales
   d) gross sales less sales returns
(CGA FA2 March 1994)

5) Which of the following items should be included in the cash and cash equivalents balance in the current asset section of the balance sheet?
   a) IOUs in the petty cash fund
   b) Cash in a foreign bank account which has been frozen by the foreign government
   c) Cash being accumulated in a savings account which will be used exclusively to pay down the mortgage when it matures in two years
   d) None of the above
(CGA adapted FA2 June 1995)

6) Before adjusting entries are made, River Corp.'s accounts receivable balance is $220,000 and the allowance for doubtful accounts has a debit balance of $700. An ageing of accounts receivable results in a $15,750 estimate of uncollectible accounts at year-end. Bad debt expense for the year is:
   a) $16,450
   b) $15,750
   c) $15,050
   d) $14,350

(CGA adapted FA1 June 1996)

7) The year-end trial balance of Kodiak Limited shows accounts receivable of $164,000; allowance for doubtful accounts of $200 credit; sales of $600,000. Uncollectibles are estimated to be 1.5% of sales. Bad debt expense for the year is:
   a) $8,800
   b) $9,000
   c) $9,200
   d) $9,400

(CGA adapted FA1 June 1996)

8) The term cash and cash equivalents is used as a grouping on the balance sheet and statement of cash flows to indicate available cash. Which items would not be included in cash and cash equivalents?
   a) short-term borrowings
   b) post-dated cheques
   c) term deposits
   d) petty cash

9) The main difference between factoring and asset securitization is that:
   a) the receivables are sold to an external party with recourse, with factoring.
   b) the receivables are sold to an external party without recourse, with factoring.
   c) the receivables are of a higher quality with securitization.
   d) there is a fee involved with factoring.

10) Bohui Limited transferred receivables to a separate entity. In order to determine whether the transaction is accounted for as a sale or borrowing, which of the following criteria must be met.
   a) no continuing involvement
   b) assets isolated, transferee has right to pledge/sell assets and no recourse
   c) assets isolated, transferee has right to pledge/sell assets and no control retained through repurchase agreements
   d) assets transferred must not be serviced by transferee

SOLUTIONS TO MULTIPLE CHOICE QUESTIONS

1) c) Since the company would not yet have been notified of the deposit, and since it would already have been received, this would need to be adjusted for. The bank error is not adjusted for since it is an error; the bank should adjust the bank account to correct it. The deposit in transit would be known and recorded by the company, as would outstanding cheques that had not yet cleared the bank.

2) b) A bank error is something that has been incorrectly recorded by the bank. It would not have been recorded on the books, nor should it be. Therefore, the bank balance would be adjusted to correct the error.

3) b) The allowance account would be increased for the $10,000 subsequently collected and then reduced to the required amount ($500,000 × 5% = $25,000). Therefore, it would need to be debited $15,000 to bring it down to $25,000 ($30,000 + 10,000 − 15,000).

4) c) This method looks at sales that occurred during the year, as opposed to the balance sheet amount in the accounts receivable account.

5) d) None of these items should be included as they do not represent cash that is readily available to settle current obligations of the company. The definition of an asset includes the criteria that the company must have control over and/or access to the asset. Therefore, even though (b) represents cash, the company cannot access it.

6) a) The bad debt expense is whatever it takes to ensure that the ending balance in the allowance account is equal to the required allowance. The latter has been calculated as $15,750 based on the ageing. Therefore, the allowance balance must first be brought to $0 ($700 + $15,750 = $16,450).

7) b) The expense would be calculated as a % of sales: $600,000 × 1.5% = $9,000.

8) b) The post-dated cheques are classified as receivables.

9) c) With securitization, there are many investors involved, who have invested in the pool of assets for a return, who would otherwise not have invested in the pool. The seller often remains involved with the collection of the assets after the securitization deal. Otherwise, in both cases, there is a fee or discount, and the sale may be with or without recourse.

10) b) All three criteria must be met. The transferor may agree to a recourse provision and may even service the transferred assets. The financial components method ensures that any assets or liabilities incurred/retained are recognized.

SHORT PROBLEMS

1) *Purpose:* To prepare an aged trial balance and estimate a provision for doubtful accounts.

Credit Sale Incorporated (CSI) has the following customer accounts listed in its accounts receivable at year-end, which is December 31:

		(in $000)
A Co.	Jan. 1	$ 100
	Nov. 1	100
	Dec. 3	200
	Dec. 31	300
B Co.	Dec. 22	455
	Dec. 31	300
C Co.	Nov. 30	240
	Dec. 29	566
D Co.	July 13	900
	July 30	677
E Co.	Nov. 12	122
	Dec. 12	156
total accounts receivable per subledger		$4,116

The bad debt expense is estimated annually by providing fully for amounts over 90 days and 50% of amounts between 61 and 90 days. The balance in the accounts receivable control account in the general ledger is $5 million versus $3 million at the end of last year. Sales have remained constant. The economy has worsened steadily over the past year.

Required

(a) Prepare an aged trial balance for the current year.

(b) Calculate the bad debt expense for the year using the percentage-of-receivables approach.

(c) Discuss any other factors that might affect the calculation and note how they would be dealt with.

2) *Purpose:* To illustrate preparation of bank reconciliations and related journal entries.

Cash Corp. (CC) is in the process of preparing the monthly bank reconciliation for November. The following details have been assembled:

Cash balance per general ledger	$3,999,909
Cash balance per bank account statement	3,939,410
Cash booked in November, deposited in December	200,000
Cheques that have not yet cleared the bank	145,000

Bank service charges not yet recorded in books	499	
Bank debit memo incorrectly charged to account	5,000	

Required

(a) Prepare a bank reconciliation using both the two-column method and the one-column method (i.e., going from bank to book).

(b) Prepare any journal entries to adjust the books. Note any other action to be taken.

3) Purpose: To illustrate transfer of notes receivable with and without recourse.

Cashshort Corp. (CC) decided to transfer some notes receivable in order to raise some extra cash. The book value of the receivables transferred was $4,563,787. The transferee has charged a commission of 1.25% of the book value and has decided to hold back a further 5% for sales discounts, etc. The transferred assets are held in a special purpose entity which is outside the control of CC. There are no repurchase agreements.

Required

(a) Prepare the journal entry to record the transfer.

(b) Assume that the risks and rewards of ownership still lie with CC (i.e., control is not surrendered). Prepare the required journal entries to book the transaction.

SOLUTIONS TO SHORT PROBLEMS

1) (a) and (b)

(in $000)

			0-30 days	31-60 days	61-90 days	>90
A Co.	Jan. 1	$100				$100
	Nov. 1	100			$100	
	Dec. 3	200	$200			
	Dec. 31	300	300			
B Co.	Dec. 22	455	455			
	Dec. 31	300	300			
C Co.	Nov. 30	240		$240		
	Dec. 29	566	566			
D Co.	July 13	900				900
	July 30	677				677
E Co.	Nov.12	122		122		
	Dec. 12	156	156			

total accounts receivable
per subledger

	$4,116	$1,977	$362	$100	$1,677
provision	$1,727	—	—	$50	$1,677

> **Tip!** Invoices should be classified according to their age.

(c) Other considerations:

- The aged trial balance does not agree with the general ledger account. These two should be reconciled before preparing the ageing so that the ageing includes all amounts.

- Accounts receivable have increased over last year, yet sales have remained constant. Therefore, it may make sense to increase the provision (although the increase is partially due to the abnormally large sale of $900 that was not collected but has been fully provided for).

- Since the economy has worsened, it may make sense to increase the provision.

> **Tip!** Consideration should always be given to the current economic environment as well as past collection rates.

2) (a)

	Per bank	Per books
Balance	$3,939,410	$3,999,909
Deposits	200,000	
Cheques	(145,000)	
Error	5,000	
Service charge		(499)
Correct balance	$3,999,410	$3,999,410
Balance per bank	$3,939,410	
Add deposits	200,000	
Deduct cheques	(145,000)	
Add back error	5,000	
Add back service charges	499	
Balance per books	$3,999,909	

> **Tip!** The more commonly used method is the two-column method or the method that goes from book and bank to the correct cash balance.

(b)   Bank charges   499
         Cash   499

The bank should be notified of the $5,000 error and asked to adjust it.

3)(a)   Cash   4,278,551   (See 3 below)

             Loss on sale   57,047   (See 1 below)

             Receivable   228,189   (See 2 below)

                   Notes receivable   4,563,787

(1) $4,563,787 \times 1.25\%$

(2) $4,563,787 \times 5\%$—Recording this as a receivable implies that the transferee will remit the amounts to CC if collected. The specific arrangement would have to be reviewed. Perhaps the amount would otherwise be part of the loss. This would be an area of professional judgement.

(3) To balance ($4,563,787 less 6.25% of $4,563,787)

(b)   Cash   4,278,551

           Deferred discount   57,047

               Loan payable   4,335,598

The notes receivable would remain on the books and a loan payable would be set up. The discount would be deferred and amortized over the period of the notes as an interest adjustment (judgemental). When the notes were finally fully collected, the loans payable would be debited, the notes receivable credited for the full amount, and the receivable collected in cash, assuming no bad debts or discounts, etc.

If sales discounts or returns, etc. arise, the amount receivable from the transferee would be reduced (cr. receivable, dr. loss or sales returns and allowances or discounts).

CASE

Dixie Dundee, the V.P. of Finance of Dundee Developments (DD) stared at the draft financial statements for the November month-end. The financial statements looked as though the company was facing a liquidity crisis. There were current liabilities that had to be paid, as well as a large repayment of principal on one of the loans. Unless there were some drastic changes, the year-end financial statements would look even more grim.

Dixie was not worried about getting the funds. They were already negotiating to renew the loan in question, although the bank was nowhere near finalizing the deal and would not be before the year-end statements were issued. However, unless something very disastrous happened, the loan would go through and DD would get the funds.

Dixie's prime concern was how the market would react to the perceived liquidity problem as presented in the financial statements and whether the reaction would cause the stock prices to tumble. DD was also in the process of making a new share offering in order to finance an expansion of the company into the United States. The deal was not worth doing unless a certain share price could be obtained.

In this regard, DD was considering entering a deal to transfer certain notes receivable to EE Ltd. (EE). The notes were long-term and had always provided DD with a much needed steady stream of cash from the interest. The terms were as follows:

- DD would transfer the notes to EE on a non-recourse basis for the fair value of the notes less a small discount since the notes were considered fully collectible.

- DD guaranteed a rate of return of 12% on the notes to EE. That is, if market rates went down, DD would pay to EE the difference between the variable interest rate paid to EE under the note and 12%. Conversely, if market rates went up, EE would pay the difference to DD.

- DD also retained the right to repurchase the notes at the book value plus a small premium.

- The debtor owing the money will make payments directly to EE.

The deal was consummated within a few days, resulting in DD obtaining a significant inflow of cash. At year-end, market interest rates had declined significantly.

REQUIRED:

Discuss the accounting and reporting issues and advise Dixie as to how they affect the year-end financial statements.

SOLUTION TO CASE

DUNDEE DEVELOPMENTS

Overview

The V.P. of Finance is concerned that the financial statements portray the company in a negative light. This is troubling since this could cause stock prices to fall at a time when the company needs higher stock prices to maximize proceeds from an impending stock issue. Stakeholders of the statements would include the bank, especially due to the loan renewal, and potential investors. Both would want information that is realistic and perhaps even conservative. GAAP is a constraint since the shares are publicly traded.

Assuming that you work for DD, the financial reporting objective would be to down play the apparent liquidity problem as it appears in the financial statements. If your role is that of the auditors, the needs of the users would play a more important role. Since the company plans to use the statements for refinancing, the engagement would be high risk and you would advise Dixie along more conservative lines. That is, if there are liquidity problems, this is information that would affect the users and, therefore, it should be apparent in the financial statements, regardless of what Dixie wants. Full disclosure of complex transactions would also be important.

Analysis and Recommendations

The issues are as follows:

- How to account for the transfer of the notes.
- How to present the loan that is currently due.

Notes Receivable

- Should the transfer of the notes be treated as a disposition or merely a financing?
- The resolution would appear to revolve around whether the **risks and rewards** of owning the notes have passed to EE, as well as whether control has been surrendered.
- Firstly, the financial reporting implications will be reviewed. If it is seen as a bona fide transfer, the long-term receivables will be removed from the financial statements at a small loss, and replaced with cash. This would greatly enhance the perceived liquidity position.

> Cash
> Loss
>   Notes receivable

If it is perceived as a financing, the transaction would increase liabilities (questionable whether this would be current or long-term) and cash. The discount would be deferred and amortized. If it was booked as long-term liabilities, this would also improve the appearance of the statements; although if booked as current liabilities, it would be of no help.

> Cash
> Deferred discount
>> Current or non-current liability

In order to determine whether this is a sale or borrowing Accounting Guideline 12 (*CICA Handbook*) looks at three criteria:

1. Are the assets isolated from the transferor?
   In this case EE is a separate legal entity and is also an arm's length party. Therefore the criterion is met.

2. Does EE have the right to pledge or sell the receivables?
   Yes since legal title to the receivables has passed.

3. Does DD maintain control through any repurchase agreements?
   In this case, there is a repurchase agreement in place i.e., DD has the right to repurchase. On the one hand, the agreement does not obligate the transferor to reaquire the assets and therefore it may be concluded that DD has transferred the risks of ownership. However, the right to reacquire means that they have retained some of the rewards of ownership.

DD notes that it values the "steady stream of income."

This might be an inducement for DD to exercise this right. Also, DD does not really need the cash if the loan and equity financing go through, as they likely will. It should be acknowledged that the transaction appears to have been entered into for its short-term window-dressing value only.

DD has guaranteed a certain rate of return to EE and, therefore, is at **risk** for fluctuations in interest rates.

It might be acceptable to argue that the arrangement is a financing arrangement but that the **intent** is not to re-purchase the notes until after the upcoming year. This would result in a long-term liability and would still enhance the financial statement picture. However, declining interest rates will be an inducement to re-purchase in the shorter run.

Given the intent, treat the transaction as financing, especially since it is not clearly evident that the risk and rewards have passed. Treat as long-term liability since this is justifiable and will achieve the financial reporting objective (assuming the role of an employee of DD). Full disclosure of the arrangement will be required due to the significance of the transaction and due to the interest guarantee which will affect cash flows.

Loan Refinancing

The loan will have to be classified as current even though there is **intent** to refinance, since the refinancing is not in place by the financial statement issue date. Consider disclosing the intent to refinance in the notes to the financial statements since the negotiations are in progress, and since this will affect future cash flows.

SELECTED SOLUTIONS FROM THE TEXTBOOK

EXERCISE 7-1 (10–15 MINUTES)

(a)   Cash includes the following:

1.	Commercial savings account First National Bank	$ 600,000
2.	Commercial chequing account First National Bank	900,000
3.	Money market fund Volonte	5,000,000
4.	Petty cash	1,000
5.	Currency and coin on hand	7,700
	Cash reported on December 31, 2002, balance sheet	$6,508,700

(b)   Other items classified as follows:

1.   Travel advances (reimbursed by employee)* should be reported as receivable employee in the amount of $180,000.
2.   Cash restricted in the amount of $1,500,000 for the retirement of long-term debt should be reported as a noncurrent asset identified as Cash restricted for retirement of long-term debt.
3.   An IOU from Marianne Koch should be reported as a receivable from officer in the amount of $190,000.
4.   The bank overdraft of $110,000 should be reported as a current liability.**
5.   Certificates of deposits of $500,000 each should be classified as temporary investments.
6.   Postdated cheque of $125,000 should be reported as an accounts receivable.
7.   The compensating balance requirement does not affect the balance in cash. A note disclosure indicating the arrangement and the amounts involved should be described in the notes.
8.   Commercial paper should be reported as temporary investments.

* If not reimbursed, charge to prepaid expense.
** If cash is present in another account in the same bank on which the overdraft occurred, offsetting is required.

Exercise 7-9 (8–10 minutes)

Balance 1/1 ($700 − $155)	$ 545	Over one year
4/12 (#2412) ($1,710 − $1,000 − $300)	410	Eight months and 18 days
11/18 (#5681) ($2,000 − $1,250)	750	One month and 12 days
	$1,705	

Inasmuch as later invoices have been paid in full, all three of these amounts should be investigated in order to determine why Gerald Manley, Inc. has not paid them. The amounts in the beginning balance and #2412 should be of particular concern.

Exercise 7-23 (15–20 minutes)

(a)

BRUNO CORP.
Bank Reconciliation, August 31, 2002
National Bank of Ottawa

Balance per bank statement, Aug. 31, 2002		$ 8,089
Add: Cash on hand	$ 310	
Deposits in transit	3,800	4,110
		12,199
Deduct: Outstanding cheques		1,050
Correct cash balance		$11,149
Balance per books, August 31, 2001		
($10,050 + $35,000 − $34,903)		$10,147
Add: Note ($1,000) and interest ($40) collected		1,040
		11,187
Deduct: Bank service charges	$ 20	
Understated cheque for supplies	18	38
Correct cash balance		$11,149

(b) Cash	1,040	
Notes Receivable		1,000
Interest Revenue		40
(To record collection of note and interest)		
Office Expense Bank Service Charges	20	
Cash		20
(To record August bank charges)		
Supplies Expense	18	
Cash		18
(To record error in recording cheque for supplies)		

(c) The corrected cash balance of $11,149 would be reported in the August 31, 2002, balance sheet.

Problem 7-12

Part I

(a)

	Cash	200,000	
	Accounts Receivable	200,000	
	Sales		400,000
	Note Receivable	50,000	
	Sales		50,000
	Cash	160,000	
	Accounts Receivable		160,000
12/31	Interest Receivable	2,750	
	Interest Revenue		2,750

(b)

$$\text{Current Ratio Dec. 31, 2002} = \frac{\text{Current Assets}}{\text{Current Liabilities}}$$

$$= \frac{(\$15,000 + \$80,000 + \$2,750 + \$50,000 + \$80,000)}{\$70,000 + \$16,000}$$

$$= 2.648$$

$$\text{Current Ratio Dec. 31, 2001} = \frac{\$20,000 + \$40,000 + \$85,000}{\$65,000 + \$15,000}$$

$$= 1.813$$

$$\text{Accounts Receivable Turnover} = \frac{\text{Sales}}{\text{Average Receivables}}$$

$$= \frac{\$450,000}{(\$80,000 + \$40,000)/2}$$

$$= 7.5 \text{ times (or about 49 days)}$$

Current Ratio of 2.648 is much higher than last year 1.813. Accounts Receivable turnover of 7.5 times is much lower than last years 10.37. Thus, while the current ratio is higher, Horn is not collecting receivables as quickly as in the prior year.

Part II

(c)

	Cash	52,000	
	Loss on Sale of Note Receivable	750	
	Note Receivable		50,000
	Interest Receivable		2,750

(d)

	Cash	36,000	
	Due from Factor	2,400	
	Loss on Sale of Accounts Receivable	5,600	
	Accounts Receivable		40,000
	Recourse Liability		4,000

(e)   Current Ratio $= \dfrac{\text{Current Assets}}{\text{Current Liabilities}}$

$= \dfrac{\$15{,}000 + \$52{,}000 + \$36{,}000 + \$40{,}000 + \$80{,}000 + \$2{,}400}{\$70{,}000 + \$16{,}000 + \$4{,}000}$

$= \dfrac{\$225{,}400}{\$90{,}000}$

$= 2.5$

Accounts
Receivable $= \dfrac{\text{Sales}}{\text{Average Receivables}}$
Turnover

$= \dfrac{\$450{,}000}{(\$40{,}000 + \$40{,}000)/2}$

$= 11.25$ times (or about 32 days)

Horn has been able to speed up collection of receivables by transferring the note to the bank and selling accounts receivable to First Factors.

(f)   With a secured borrowing, the receivables would stay on Horn's books and Horn records a Note Payable. This would reduce the current ratio and leave the receivable turnover ratio at approximately the same level as in Part 1.

VALUATION OF INVENTORIES: A COST BASIS APPROACH

Inventory Classification and Control

- Classification
- Management and control
- Basic valuation Issues

Physical Goods Included in Inventory

- Goods in transit
- Consigned goods
- Special sales agreements
- Inventory errors

Costs Included in Inventory

- Purchase discounts
- Product costs
- Period costs
- Manufacturing costs
- Variable versus absorption
- Standard Costs

Cost Flow Assumptions

- Framework for analysis
- Specific identification
- Average cost
- FIFO
- LIFO

Evaluation and Choice

- Advantages of LIFO
- Disadvantages of LIFO
- Summary analysis
- Which method to select?
- Consistency

chapter 8

VALUATION OF INVENTORIES: A COST BASIS APPROACH

PERSPECTIVE

The emphasis in Chapter 8 is on inventory costing, which goods and costs to include, and cost flow assumptions. Costs that cannot be inventoried are expensed, and, therefore, you should focus on the relationship between inventory and cost of goods sold/net income.

INSIGHTS

- *Key calculations in this chapter include the **cost flow methods,** i.e., LIFO and FIFO, specific identification, and weighted average. Learn these as well as the impact of using these methods on net income.*

- *Often the method and accounting policies chosen are constrained by the industry and different businesses,*

STUDY STEPS

1. Understanding the Importance of Inventory in Business and Inventory Related Transactions

Inventory defined

Inventory is defined as goods held for resale or goods that will be used in the production of goods for sale. It is comprised of either **goods held for resale** or materials that will be used to produce goods for sale, i.e., **raw materials**. It also includes partially completed goods that will eventually be sold, i.e., **work in process**. The business objective is that the finished product will be sold, hopefully at a profit. Inventory differs from fixed assets in that fixed assets are **used** to produce profits whereas inventory is **sold** to produce profits.

Tip! Inventory includes items that will eventually be sold for profits and/or to recover costs.

Inventory is one of the **essential assets** in many businesses since the manufacture and sale of inventory is often the primary source of income. Inventory has a dual use. Not only will it be sold to generate profits, it may also be used as collateral to secure bank loans.

Tip! Because inventory affects the calculation of the current ratio, and because it is often used to secure loans, the amount of inventory included and the value are very important.

Ownership

Shipping terms

As previously mentioned, inventory in a manufacturing company consists of raw materials, work in process, and finished goods. Sometimes the raw materials may not have actually made it into the warehouse (i.e., they may be sitting on the loading dock, in a railway car, or even in a truck **in transit**). Are these goods part of the company's inventory? Analysis of this issue revolves around whether the **risks and rewards** of ownership have passed to the company buying the inventory. Sometimes this may be determined by looking at the **shipping terms**. The same applies to finished goods being shipped by the company.

If the goods are sent **f.o.b. shipping point** (free on board), the company selling the goods takes responsibility and retains the ownership only until the goods are shipped. After that, the purchaser obtains ownership. Likewise, if the terms are **f.o.b. destination**, the company selling the goods retains ownership until the goods reach the destination. For this reason, the goods should be insured by the company selling them up until they reach their destination.

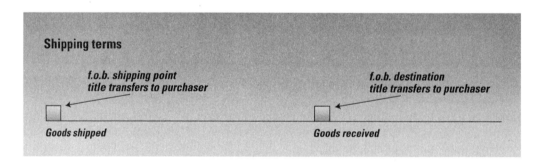

Shipping terms

f.o.b. shipping point
title transfers to purchaser

f.o.b. destination
title transfers to purchaser

Goods shipped

Goods received

Tip! Shipping terms are very important in identifying whether an asset should be recorded on the balance sheet since risks and rewards stay with seller up to the point designated in the shipping terms.

Inventory on consignment

See discussion of business arrangement under consignment sales in Chapter 6 of the Study Guide.

Parking transactions/product financing arrangements

These arrangements are usually characterized by a sale of inventory plus an agreement to buy the inventory back over a future period of time. This may be seen as two separate transactions, i.e., a sale and then a future purchase, or as one transaction, i.e., a financing transaction.

> **Professional judgement should be used to determine whether a real sale has occurred and whether the inventory still, in substance, belongs to the company.** *Tip!*

Sales involving uncertainty

See also the comments under revenue recognition in Chapter 6 of the Study Guide.

> **Inventory remains on the books of the company when there is major uncertainty as to collection or measurement.** *Tip!*

2. Understanding How Inventory Issues Fit into the Financial Reporting Model and Conceptual Framework—Analysis and Critical Thinking

The key issues in this area are as follows:

- **which items** to include in inventory (e.g., goods in transit, consignment items)—**recognition**
- **which costs** to include (e.g., freight, factory overhead, labour)—**measurement/classification costing**

Exhibit 8-1: Valuation of inventories: Cost Flow methods
Relevant criteria, definitions and issues

Business perspective: Inventory is an essential asset and since it is included in current assets, it is essential that it is properly reported and valued.

	How it relates to inventory	Relevant criteria/definitions	Topic specific analysis—how it should be	What makes the analysis challenging—how it is
Recognition	when to recognize or de-recognize inventory	• overall, when **R&R** have passed • consider shipping terms **fob shipping point vs fob destination** • for complex transactions **economic substance**	• normally when received/shipped **(possession)** and **legal title** • is it a real sale/purchase?, or a financing type of transaction?	• complicated by complex selling terms where company may have either legal title or possession but not both

Measurement	what to include as inventory cost (partly classification issue)	• **laid down cost** plus **direct costs** and **applicable share of overhead** (HB 3030.05 and .06)	• include any cost incurred to get the inventory to the company and any further costs to get it ready for sale	• complex transactions, such as parking transactions where company sells but agrees to buy back—difficult to determine who has R&R of inventory • **standard costs** may be used if not significantly different from actual cost • PJ needed in deciding how much overhead to allocate • costs from abnormal situations generally not included
	what cost flow method to use	• **FIFO, LIFO, weighted average, specific ID** • fairest **matching of costs with revenues** (HB3030.09)	• the key is to match costs with revenues (actual inventory flow need not be the detemining factor) • consider practicality and nature of inventory	• the method chosen may have a significant impact on net income and therefore, potential exists for a bias to exist
Presentation/ Disclosure	note disclosure	• **full disclosure**	• disclose basis of valuation and cost flow method since choice	

Prepared by Irene Wiecek
©2002 John Wiley & Sons Canada, Ltd

3. Becoming Proficient in Using Inventory Costing and Valuation Methods

Determining the **cost of inventory** would be easy if there were only a few high-priced items. However, inventory often consists of a multitude of different products of varying values which were purchased at different times and at different prices. Even identical products that were purchased at different times may have different prices.

If all the items were purchased at different prices but are identical and only half were sold, which items are left? Is it the ones that were purchased first, or the most recent purchases? An assumption must be made about the inventory flow (i.e., which items were sold first). The two most common assumptions are **LIFO (last in, first out)** and **FIFO (first in, first out)**. FIFO probably reflects reality, since most people would want to sell the oldest inventory first.

Examples and tips are given under multiple choice questions and problems 3 and 4. Brief explanations of the methods follow.

FIFO

With FIFO, the most recent prices are used to value the inventory.

Tip! This provides a better valuation of inventory and is easier to apply since more recent prices are easier to obtain.

LIFO

With LIFO, the original cost of the inventory the first time that the company purchased inventory is maintained as the value. Subsequently, sales come from the more recently purchased goods with the new prices being booked as costs of sales. The old inventory theoretically stays there at the same old price.

This provides a better measure of cost of sales and net income, especially in times of rising prices.

Specific identification method

If the inventory happens to be specifically identifiable (e.g., jewellery), there is no need to make assumptions as to which was sold first since it is easy to identify the remaining pieces and their individual costs.

Weighted average method

The weighted-average method calculates the weighted-average cost of all purchases during the year and uses this per-unit cost to value the remaining inventory.

Standard costing

With standard costing, standardized costs are determined periodically for each product. Management predetermines what the costs should be, including material, labour, and overhead costs. These costs are usually determined based on reasonable estimates of what costs should be incurred. **Care should be taken to ensure that if standard costs are used to value inventory that they do not differ significantly from actual costs at year-end.** Standard costs are used primarily for management costs control purposes.

Keeping track of quantities—periodic versus perpetual inventory methods:

The **perpetual method** of inventory involves keeping track of each inventory item and noting individual purchases and sales when they are made. Perpetual inventory records are like a subledger that gives details about the balance of inventory in the general ledger (like the accounts receivable subledger). It requires extra bookkeeping but allows the company to see the exact number of items on hand for each inventory item at any point in time. Also, like the accounts receivable subledger, it allows the company to verify the control account for inventory in the general ledger.

Under the **periodic method,** no such subledger is kept. The inventory account in the general ledger is verified only when an inventory count is performed (usually annually).

Under both methods, physical inventory must be taken. With a perpetual system, specific types of inventory can be spot checked and compared to the individual perpetual inventory amounts. Whereas with a periodic inventory, a full count must be performed. The perpetual system offers more control over inventory; however, it may be time consuming and costly. With more businesses using computers, this factor is becoming less and less an issue.

The inventory equation:

Cost of goods sold is often determined by the following equation:

Cost of goods sold = opening inventory + purchases − closing inventory

Cost of goods sold is a residual figure since opening inventory and purchases are known, and since closing inventory is usually determined by a physical count. It is important to acknowledge the relationship between these components and that an error in one will affect another of the components.

MULTIPLE CHOICE QUESTIONS

1) NG Limited's opening inventory for 2002 was $16,000. During 2002, NG made purchases of $12,300 and returned $200 of merchandise. The purchase discounts amounted to $600. If NG's closing inventory was $14,000 on December 31, 2002, what was the cost of goods sold?
   a) $13,500
   b) $13,700
   c) $14,100
   d) $14,300

(CGA adapted FA1 March 1996)

2) If Ko's income statement showed cost of goods sold at $39,000, purchases of $40,000, transportation in at $100, purchase returns of $300 and end of period inventory at $6,000, its beginning of the period inventory must have been:
   a) $5,100
   b) $5,200
   c) $5,800
   d) $6,000

(CGA adapted FA1 March 1996)

3) Based on the following information, what amount should Caume Corp. report as its inventory balance on December 31, 2002? Goods costing $5,000 marked f.o.b. shipping point on December 30, 2002 billed and shipped to Curtis Corp. were not included in the physical count of Caume's merchandise inventory. Goods costing $9,000 shipped f.o.b. shipping point on December 30, 2002 from Curtis Corp. to Caume were received on January 3, 2003. A physical count of merchandise inventory revealed an amount totalling $70,000.
   a) $70,000
   b) $65,000
   c) $84,000
   d) $79,000

(CGA adapted FA1 December 1994)

4) Which of the following items would not likely be classified as inventory on a balance sheet?
   a) cleaning supplies held by a janitorial firm
   b) lots of land held by a land developer
   c) laying hens held by a farmer
   d) work-in-process held by an equipment manufacturer

(CGA adapted FA2 December 1993)

5) ABC Incorporated was formed on August 2, 2002, to sell a single product. Its unit cost of inventory purchases has decreased steadily over the past two years. Physical quantities held in inventory are always equal to approximately three months' sales. Assuming the periodic inventory system, the inventory cost method which reports the highest amount for each of the following is:

	Inventory—December 31, 2002	Cost of sales—2002
a)	LIFO	FIFO
b)	LIFO	LIFO
c)	FIFO	FIFO
d)	FIFO	LIFO

(CGA adapted FA2 June 1994)

6) Limax Limited has inventory at the beginning of the year of $100,000. At year-end, it came to the accountant's attention that the previous year-end balance had been over-stated by $20,000 and that the current year-end balance ($100,000) was understated by $18,000. What was the impact of the two errors on the current and previous years' net income?

	Current year's NI	Previous year's NI
a)	$38,000 understated	$20,000 overstated
b)	$38,000 understated	$20,000 understated
c)	$38,000 overstated	$20,000 overstated
d)	$38,000 overstated	$20,000 understated

7) Assume the same information as for 6. What would be the impact on the following ratios of the errors for the current year?

	Current ratio	Asset turnover
a)	overstated	overstated
b)	understated	understated
c)	overstated	understated
d)	understated	overstated

8) Weldco. omitted recording inventory (cost $20,000) that was in transit f.o.b. shipping point to their warehouse at year-end. Current assets were $200,000 and current liabilities were $100,000—both unadjusted. The impact on the following ratios is:

	Current ratio	Rate of return on total assets
a)	overstated	overstated
b)	understated	understated
c)	overstated	understated
d)	understated	overstated

9) Most accountants, if asked to determine the cost of Canadian Tire's inventory by FIFO would probably reach similar conclusions. This is an application of the :
   a) cost-benefit constraint
   b) matching principle
   c) continuity assumption
   d) reliability characteristic

(CGA FA2 June 1996)

10) Jason Limited received goods and counted them in inventory on December 31, 2002—year-end. The related accounts payable was not recorded in the financial statements. Which of the following is true of the financial statements the following year when the accounts payable gets recorded?

	Inventory	Accounts payable
a)	overstated	understated
b)	overstated	okay
c)	understated	understated
d)	understated	overstated

SOLUTIONS TO MULTIPLE CHOICE QUESTIONS

1) a) $13,500, calculated as follows: op inventory $16,000 + purchases $12,300 − returns $200 − discounts $600 − ending inventory $14,000 = $13,500.

2) b) $5,200, calculated as follows: CGS $39,000 + closing inventory $6,000 − purchases $40,000 − transportation in $100 + returns $300 = $5,200

3) d) $79,000. The goods shipped by Caume should not be included, and have, therefore, been correctly handled. The goods shipped to Caume should be included since the terms are f.o.b. shipping point and they were shipped December 30.

4) c) The laying hens would not be considered to be inventory since they are not held for resale at a profit; rather, they are held to produce inventory and are therefore more like fixed assets.

5) a) In times of declining prices, the LIFO method which leaves the oldest costs in inventory would cause inventory to be the highest. Likewise, FIFO would cause COS to be the highest since the older costs would go to the income statement first.

6) a) Last year's inventory was too high and therefore the CGS was too low and net income too high—therefore overstated. This year's opening inventory was too high which would mean CGS was too high for the same amount and then closing inventory was too low—again result was that CGS was too high by the year-end amount. Therefore, the current net income would be understated by $20,000 and $18,000 = $38,000.

7) b) The current ratio would be understated (CA/CL) since inventory is understated at year-end. The asset turnover (sales/average total assets) would be understated since average total assets is greater $(100 + 100)/2 = 100$. Note that it should be less, $[($100 − 20) + (100 + 18)]/2 = 99$, and therefore the ratio should be higher if the numbers were correct.

8) a) Current ratio would be overstated. CA/CL = $200,000/100,000 = 2:1 versus $220,000/120,000 = 1.8 to 1. Rate of return on assets would be overstated since total assets, the denominator, would be understated. The numerator (NI) would not be affected by the error.

9) d) Reliability includes verifiability and, therefore, if most accountants would come up with the same number, it must by definition be verifiable.

10) b) the inventory would have already been included when the count was done at year-end. When the payable gets recorded, the balance will be okay; however, the inventory account will be debited again and will, therefore, be too high.

SHORT PROBLEMS

1) *Purpose:* To demonstrate how to calculate cost of sales and preparation of related year-end journal entries.

The following items are taken from a year-end trial balance:

Opening inventory	$388,000
Purchases	698,000

The perpetual inventory records indicate that there is $395,000 on hand at year-end (when valued) and the year-end inventory count has been valued and shows $345,000. Even though the company maintains separate perpetual records in a subledger, they only book cost of sales in the general ledger on reporting dates. The perpetual records are used for inventory control purposes and asset management.

Required

(a) Show the cost of sales and year-end inventory numbers that should be booked on the income statement and balance sheet respectively. Explain why the inventory count value might be different from the perpetual record.

(b) Prepare related journal entries required to adjust the inventory accounts.

2) *Purpose:* To illustrate how to deal with off-site inventory at year-end.

Assume that it is year-end and that the inventory is being counted. In order to establish an accurate count, the company has established a cut-off point of noon after which items will not be received or shipped until the count has finished. Assume the following:

(a) There is inventory sitting in a railway car behind the warehouse (railway car owned by company).

(b) There are goods in transit to the company shipped f.o.b. shipping point.

(c) There are goods in transit to the company shipped f.o.b. destination.

(d) Just before noon, a truck arrived with a shipment f.o.b. destination. The receiver decided not to unpack the goods and therefore not to include them in inventory although they were signed for and unloaded onto the receiving dock.

(e) There are goods that were shipped prior to the cut-off point to Sell It Limited, an outside company. The terms are that for every item sold by Sell It Limited, Sell It Limited will receive a commission of 3%. Any goods that do not sell are shipped back.

Required

For each item above, note whether it should be included in inventory for the year-end count or not. Explain your answer.

3) Purpose: To illustrate the application of different cost flow assumptions using the periodic method.

Assume the following:

Opening inventory	1,000 units @ $1.00 each
January 15 purchased	4,000 @ $1.10
February 29 sold	2,000
March 1 purchased	2,000 @ $1.20
June 30 sold	3,000
July 14 sold	500
September 5 purchased	4,000 @ $1.40
December 30 sold	3,000

Required

Calculate the value of closing inventory using the following cost flow assumptions. Assume that the company does not use perpetual inventory systems.

     (a)   FIFO.

     (b)   LIFO.

     (c)   Weighted-average cost.

4) Purpose: To illustrate the application of different cost flow assumptions using the perpetual method.

Assume the same information in Problem 3, except that the company uses perpetual inventory information systems.

Required

Calculate the value of closing inventory using the following cost flow assumptions:

     (a)   FIFO.

     (b)   LIFO.

     (c)   Moving-average market.

Tip! You should also review the questions from the text that deal with the impact of errors on financial statements. Use the Cost of Goods sold equation.

SOLUTIONS TO SHORT PROBLEMS

1)

(a) Calculation of cost of sales:

Opening inventory	$388,000	
Plus purchases	698,000	
Equals inventory available for sale	$1,086,000	
Less closing inventory	345,000	equals balance sheet amount
Equals cost of sales	$ 741,000	

The value from the valued inventory count is the relevant number for the calculations. This number should also be shown on the balance sheet. The perpetual records show the quantity of each product that is on hand at one point, taking into account individual purchase and sales of that particular product to date. Sometimes, the perpetual records also show the values.

Although fairly accurate, the perpetual records do not always allow for shrinkage due to theft, error, etc. The only way to establish this is to actually count the remaining inventory and compare it to the perpetual records. Assuming that the count is accurate, the perpetual records should be adjusted and reconciled to closing inventory per the financial statements.

(b)

Cost of sales	741,000	
Inventory-sales (B/S)		741,000

The shrinkage is included with cost of sales.

2)

(a) Since the car is owned by the company, the goods should be included. It is very important to include all goods owned by the company at the count date.

(b) Include these goods since the terms are f.o.b. shipping point. This means that the company has legal title.

(c) Exclude these goods since the goods have not yet arrived and the terms are f.o.b. destination. The risks and rewards of ownership would still rest with the vendor.

(d) Since the goods have effectively been officially received by the company before the cut-off date, they must be included in the count.

(e) It would appear that the goods are still owned by the company and that the arrangement is similar to a consignment sale. The inventory should be included in the inventory account until Sell It Limited sells the goods to a third party.

3)

(a) FIFO. Using this method, the easiest way is to look at the most recent purchases and move backwards until all inventory is costed. In this case, there are 2,500 units in closing inventory. The most recent purchase was 4,000 units @ $1.40. Therefore, the remaining units in inventory will be costed at this most recent cost: $2,500 \times \$1.40 = \$3,500$.

(b) LIFO. Using this method, the most recent purchases are deemed to have been sold first and the remaining inventory will be costed as follows:

1,000	@	$1.00	=	$1,000
1,500	@	$1.10	=	1,650
				$2,650

(c) Using this method, the weighted-average cost of all purchases, including opening inventory, is calculated and becomes the cost of the remaining inventory as follows:

1,000	@	$1.00	=	$1,000
4,000	@	1.10	=	4,400
2,000	@	1.20	=	2,400
4,000	@	1.40	=	5,600
11,000				$13,400

$$\$13,400 \ / \ 11,000 = \$1.22$$

Therefore, the closing inventory is $2,500 \times \$1.22 = \$3,050$

FIFO yields the highest value since the cost is influenced by the most recent, higher cost. LIFO, on the other hand, yields the lowest value since the cost is influenced by the opening inventory costs and the early, lower-cost purchases.

4)

(a) FIFO

Opening	1,000	@	$1.00	=	$1,000
Buy	4,000	@	1.10	=	4,400
Sell	(1,000)	@	1.00	=	(1,000)
	(1,000)	@	1.10	=	(1,100)
Buy	2,000	@	1.20	=	2,400
Sell	(3,000)	@	1.10	=	(3,300)
Sell	(500)	@	1.20	=	(600)
Buy	4,000	@	1.40	=	5,600
Sell	(1,500)	@	1.20	=	(1,800)
	(1,500)	@	1.40	=	(2,100)
	2,500				$3,500

This is the same as if the periodic inventory system was used.

(b) LIFO

Opening	1,000	@	$1.00	=	$1,000	
Buy	4,000	@	1.10	=	4,400	
Sell	(2,000)	@	1.10	=	(2,200)	
Buy	2,000	@	1.20	=	2,400	
Sell	(2,000)	@	1.20	=	(2,400)	
Sell	(1,000)	@	1.10	=	(1,100)	
Sell	(500)	@	1.10	=	(550)	
Buy	4,000	@	1.40	=	5,600	
Sell	(3,000)	@	1.40	=	(4,200)	
	2,500				$2,950	

(c) Moving-average market

Average cost

Opening	1,000	@	$1.00	=	$1,000		$1.00
Buy	4,000	@	1.10	=	4,400	5,400/5,000	= 1.08
Sell	(2,000)	@	1.08	=	(2,160)		
Buy	2,000	@	1.20	=	2,400	(5,400 − 2,160 + 2,400)/5,000	
							= 1.13

Sell	(3,000)	@	1.13	=	(3,390)	
Sell	(500)	@	1.13	=	(565)	
Buy	4,000	@	1.40	=	5,600	(5,400 − 2,160 + 2,400 − 3,390 −
						565 + 5,600)/5,500 = 1.32

Sell	(3,000)	@	1.32	=	(3,960)	
	2,500				$3,325	$1.33

CASES

1) ACME LIMITED

Acme Limited (AL) is a manufacturing company that produces various synthetic construction materials. The shares trade on the local stock exchange. In 2002, the company was able to negotiate an extremely low price on raw materials. As part of the deal, AL had to buy more material than was needed. However, since they had the excess cash, and since the production manager, Owen, was able to assure the purchasing manager, Enid, that the material would all be used up within the year, the deal was consummated.

Unfortunately, the following year, Acme found demand for its products had fallen dramatically because new housing starts were down significantly. As a result, cash was short and AL was considering going to the bank for financing.

After preliminary discussions with the bank, Warren, the V.P. of Finance, found out that AL was considered to be a high-risk company. The bank was reluctant to lend AL the funds and would do so only at a significant premium. Warren felt that the interest rate was excessive and was looking for alternative means of financing. He called a meeting with his managers to discuss the problem.

Warren:
We're short of cash and we need some operating capital. Our customers are taking longer to pay than usual due to the state of the housing markets and demand is down. Any suggestions?

Hiroko (controller):
I guess we've tried the usual sources, like the bank?

Warren:
Of course! The bank, however, is not willing to loan us funds unless we pay them some exorbitant interest rate. Owen, what are we doing with all this raw material? Can't we sell it off? That would generate the money that we need. Or do we need the inventory for production?

Owen:
Well, we don't really need it in the short run since demand has fallen off. However, I'm not sure that we can find a buyer. Besides, I don't really want to let too much of it go since I feel that demand will pick up again within the next few months. Prices have already started to rise.

Warren:
Well it seems to me that we have too much capital tied up in that darn inventory. Whose decision was it to buy that much?

Enid:
It was mine. At the time, we felt that the price was too good to pass up, but we had to buy a large quantity to get the price. I think that I might have a solution to our problem, however. Recently, I had lunch with the controller of Warehouses Unlimited. He was dismayed over the fact that they had excess warehouse space that couldn't "give away." I know that they have excess cash as well. Perhaps something can be worked out.

Warren:
I have another meeting to run to now. Enid, will you please follow up on your idea and report back to me as soon as possible?

Enid contacted Warehouses Unlimited (WU) and was able to strike the following deal:

WU agreed to:

- Buy the excess raw material from AL for $700,000 cash. AL's cost was $600,000.
- Store the inventory and insure it.
- Sell it back to AL over the next year as AL needed it with the proviso that it all had to be re-purchased within the year.

AL agreed to:

- Buy back the inventory over the year at a total cost of $800,000, sufficient to cover the inventory costs (including the carrying costs on the inventory) and provide a reasonable return on WU's money.

Enid called Warren immediately to tell him of the deal.

Enid:
Warren, I think that I've solved our problem. I've negotiated a deal that will get us $700,000 cash, ensure a steady supply of raw materials at not much more than market rates, and boost our net income before tax by $100,000!

REQUIRED:

Assume the role of an independent advisor to the company and comment on how the proposed transaction should be accounted for.

CANFOR CORPORATION—WWW.CANFOR.COM

Canfor Corporation (Canfor) is based in British Columbia and is a leading integrated forest products producer. The company is committed to the environment and practises sustainable forest management. It's shares trade on the TSE.

Aproximately 95% of all timberlands in British Columbia are owned by the province. The government manages these forests, allowing companies such as Canfor to manage the forested areas including cutting down trees. Two ways of accomplishing this are through the use of Tree Farm Licences (TFL) and Forest and Timber Licences. A tree farm licence may be granted by the government under which the licensee undertakes to manage the area and is allowed to cut down trees. These licences last 25 years and Canfor has recently renewed several of its tree farm licences (in 2000). A Forest Licence generally lasts for a term of 15 years and may be renewed by the government subject to satisfactory levels of performance by the licensee. Canfor holds 12 of these types of licences most of which were replaced/renewed in 1998/9. Timber licenses are non-renewable and once the timber is cut, the land is surrendered back to the government.

Under TFL and Forest Licences, an allowable annual cut is determined. The Provincial Chief Forester monitors this on behalf of the Province. Canfor is in substantial compliance with the harvesting terms of these agreements.

Maintaining the forests involves many activities, including fertilizing, building and maintaining road access, thinning, and other costs associated with the care and upkeep of the land and trees. Licences would not usually be revoked unless there is a change in ownership, illegal cutting, poor management, or other problems.

SOLUTION TO CASES

1) ACME LIMITED

Overview

Since AL is a public company, GAAP is a constraint. Stakeholders of the information will be WU, which may want the statements to determine the solvency of AL, and shareholders, who will want to determine stewardship and the value of their investment.

Management of AL (i.e., Enid and Owen) will want the financial statements to show that they are making good business decisions (stewardship). Since the first inventory transaction has turned out to be less than ideal, they will want to ensure that the second transaction shows good management.

As an independent advisor, however, you will have to ensure that the financial statements are not misleading and that the needs of the users are met.

Analysis and Recommendations

The issue is how to account for the deal that Enid has set up with a transaction:

1. Either the transaction may be treated like a sale, in which case, the inventory would be removed from the balance sheet and perhaps a profit recognized since the price is greater than the book value; or

2. The arrangement may be treated like a financing arrangement with the inventory being put up as collateral for a loan (i.e., the $700,000).

Sale of the Inventory:

The journal entry to record this as a sale would be as follows:

Cash	700,000	
Sales		700,000
Cost of sales	600,000	
Inventory		600,000

This would result in a profit being recorded of $100,000 and would result in AL not having to record any liability on the balance sheet. If they had borrowed the money from the bank, they would have had to record a liability. Possession of the inventory is with WU, as is legal title. This would seem to imply that the inventory should be removed from the books of AL.

Financing Arrangement:

The **underlying substance** of the transaction must be reviewed. In essence, this could be viewed as **off-balance-sheet financing.** Has a sale really taken place? In reality, it could be argued that the **risks and rewards** of ownership still rest with AL. The inventory is still theirs since they will end up buying it all back. They are also effectively covering the costs, albeit indirectly (they are paying more for the inventory when they buy it back, thus covering storage, insurance costs, and interest costs on the money). The return to WU is $800,000/$700,000 = 14.3%. Accounting Guideline 12 and EIC #121 support this treatment since control over the inventory is retained through the buy-back agreement.

Since the substance of the transaction is that the risks and rewards of ownership have not really passed to WU, the transaction should probably be treated as a financing arrangement with the inventory staying on the books and the $700,000 being recorded as a loan. Adequate note disclosure should also be made of the transaction since legal title to the inventory temporarily rests with WU.

2) CANFOR CORPORATION

Overview

Canfor's shares are publicly traded and therefore GAAP is a constraint. Since its future success depends on access to trees, which are situated on crown land, the company must maintain sound foresting practices. The government would be a user of the financial statements, which they would use in conjunction with other information, to determine whether they should renew the licences. Pulp and paper prices fluctuate with demand (which is cyclical) and therefore, it is very important to have a good idea of the costs of products in order to make key decisions about production levels and selling prices. Existing shareholders and potential investors will use the financial statements in investment decisions, focusing on profits in order to gauge the company's ability to compete in an increasingly global marketplace where sustainable foresting practices are becoming the norm.

REQUIRED:

Adopt the role of the company controller and discuss how the costs associated with maintaining and harvesting the trees should be accounted for. Focus on reforestation costs and maintenance costs such as fertilization, pest control, thinning and other "farming" type costs.

Analysis and Recommendations

Maintenance and other costs related to farming the trees

These costs could be seen as normal **period expenses** that are required to be incurred in order to operate. These costs are normal operating costs required to maintain the assets and are similar to insurance and other administration costs. The value of the property to the company would decrease if the property were not maintained and therefore, this is not really a **betterment** as it does not **extend the life of the property** (HB Section 3060.29). On the contrary, it could be argued that these costs are **product costs** that are similar to manufacturing costs in a manufacturing company. These costs are required to get the trees ready for harvest. The trees are analogous to work in process and HB Section 3030.02 states that the **laid down costs** for **direct materials** and **direct labour** and an applicable share of overhead may be included. Presumably, it could be argued that any costs for pesticides and fertilizers are **material costs** that are required for the growth of the trees and any labour to prune, etc. is akin to **direct labour,** to "manufacture" the trees. Costs such as the roads required to service the trees and any other infrastructure could be seen as **overhead.** The *Handbook* encourages **absorption costing** and allows all **variable overhead** and a portion of **fixed overhead** to be allocated as a product cost. If viewed as product costs, when sold, this will impact the gross profit ratio.

The above views the trees as inventory. The trees are grown, harvested and then sold for profit. This meets the definition of inventory, i.e., sold for profit. The property may also be viewed as fixed assets, where the asset is the land. In the real estate development industry, properties take a long time to produce and, generally, **all costs required to get the property ready for use** or sale are also capitalized.

As a general argument, it can be said that the maintenance costs provide **future benefit** to the company and, therefore, meet the definition of an asset. Furthermore, it makes sense to defer these costs to match them with the future revenues on sale of the trees.

In conclusion, a strong case could be made for cost deferral and this would result in higher asset values and net income. It would also give management better information about the true cost required to raise these trees for pricing purposes.

SELECTED SOLUTIONS FROM THE TEXTBOOK

EXERCISE 8-10 (15–20 MINUTES)

(a) Jan.   4 Accounts Receivable   640
               Sales (80 × $8)   640

    Jan. 11 Purchases ($150 × $6)   900
               Accounts Payable   900

    Jan. 13 Accounts Receivable   1,050
               Sales (120 × $8.75)   1,050

    Jan. 20 Purchases (160 × $7)   1,120
               Accounts Payable   1,120

    Jan. 27 Accounts Receivable   900
               Sales (100 × $9)   900

    Jan. 31 Inventory ($7 × 110)   770
               Cost of Goods Sold   1,750
                  Purchases ($900 + $1,120)   2,020
                  Inventory (100 × $5)   500

(b) Sales ($640 + $1,050 + $900) $2,590
     Cost of goods sold   1,750
     Gross profit $ 840

(c) Jan.   4 Accounts Receivable   640
               Sales (80 × $8)   640

               Cost of Goods Sold   400
                  Inventory (80 × $5)   400

    Jan. 11 Inventory   900
               Accounts Payable (150 × $6)   900

    Jan. 13 Accounts Receivable   1,050
               Sales (120 × $8.75)   1,050

               Cost of Goods Sold   700
                  Inventory ([(20 × $5) + (100 × $6)]   700

    Jan. 20 Inventory   1,120
               Accounts Payable (160 × $7)   1,120

Jan.   27   Accounts Receivable   900
                   Sales (100 × $9)   900

               Cost of Goods Sold   650
                   Inventory [(50 × $6) + (50 × $7)]   650

(d)   Sales $2,590
      Cost of goods sold ($400 + $700 + $650)   1,750
      Gross profit $ 840

Exercise 8-15 (15–20 minutes)

(a)   Cost of Goods Sold   Ending Inventory

      1. LIFO   500 @ $12 = $ 6,000   300 @ $10 = $3,000
                 500 @ $13 =   6,500   300 @ $12 =   3,600
                               $12,500 $6,600

      2. FIFO   300 @ $10 = $ 3,000   500 @ $13 = $6,500
                 700 @ $12 =   8,400   100 @ $12 =   1,200
                               $11,400 $7,700

(b)   LIFO   100 @ $10 = $ 1,000
                  300 @ $12 =   3,600
                  200 @ $13 =   2,600
                               $ 7,200

(c)   Sales $25,400   = ($24 × 200) + ($25 × 500) + ($27 × 300)
      Cost of Goods Sold   11,400
      Gross Profit (FIFO) $14,000

Note: FIFO periodic and FIFO perpetual provide the same gross profit and inventory value.

(d)   LIFO matches more current costs with revenue. When prices are rising (as is generally the case), this results in a higher amount for cost of goods sold and a lower gross profit. As indicated in this exercise, prices were rising and cost of goods sold under LIFO was higher.

EXERCISE 8-17 (15–20 MINUTES)

(a)

Mackain Limited
CALCULATION OF INVENTORY FOR PRODUCT
BAP UNDER FIFO INVENTORY METHOD
March 31, 2002

	Units	Unit Cost	Total Cost
March 26, 2002	600	$12.00	$ 7,200
February 16, 2002	800	11.00	8,800
January 25, 2002 (portion)	200	10.00	2,000
March 31, 2002, inventory	1,600		$18,000

(b)

Mackain Limited
CALCULATION OF INVENTORY FOR PRODUCT
BAP UNDER LIFO INVENTORY METHOD
March 31, 2002

	Units	Unit Cost	Total Cost
Beginning inventory	600	$8.00	$ 4,800
January 5, 2002 (portion)	1,000	9.00	9,000
March 31, 2002 (inventory)	1,600		$13,800

(c)

Mackain Limited
CALCULATION OF INVENTORY FOR PRODUCT
BAP UNDER WEIGHTED AVERAGE INVENTORY METHOD
March 31, 2002

	Units	Unit Cost	Total Cost
Beginning inventory	600	$ 8.00	$ 4,800
January 5, 2002	1,200	9.00	10,800
January 25, 2002	1,300	10.00	13,000
February 16, 2002	800	11.00	8,800
March 26, 2002	600	12.00	7,200
	4,500		$44,600

Weighted average cost ($44,600 ÷ 4,500)		$ 9.91*	
March 31, 2002, inventory	1,600	$ 9.91	$15,856

*Rounded off.

EXERCISE 8-18 (15–20 MINUTES)

(a) 1. 2,100 units available for sale − 1,400 units sold = 700 units in the ending inventory.

500 @ $4.58 =	$2,290	
200 @ 4.60 =	920	
700	$2,930	Ending inventory at FIFO cost.

2. 100 @ $4.10 = $ 410
   600 @ 4.20 =   2,520
   700              $2,930   Ending inventory at LIFO cost.

3. $9,240 cost of goods available for sale ÷ 2,100 units available for sale = $4.40 weighed-average unit cost. 700 units × $4.40 = $3,080. Ending inventory at weighted-average cost.

(b) 1. LIFO will yield the lowest gross profit figure because this method will yield the highest cost of goods sold figure in the situation presented. The company has experienced rising purchase prices for its inventory acquisitions. In a period of rising prices, LIFO will yield the highest cost of goods sold figure because the most recent purchase prices (which are the higher prices in this case) are used to price cost of goods sold while the older (and lower) purchase prices are used to cost the ending inventory.

2. LIFO will yield the lowest ending inventory figure because LIFO uses the oldest costs to price the ending inventory units. The company has experienced rising purchase prices. The oldest costs in this case are the lower costs.

EXERCISE 8-22 (10–15 MINUTES)

(a)   FIFO Ending Inventory 12/31/02
      76 @ $10.89* = $ 827.64
      24 @ $11.88** =   285.12
                          $1,112.76

      * ($11.00 × .99)
      ** ($12.00 × .99)

(b)   LIFO Cost of Goods Sold 2002
      76 @ $10.89   = $ 827.64
      84 @ $11.88   =   997.92
      90 @ $14.85* =   1,336.50
      15 @ $15.84** =   237.60
                          $3,399.66

      * ($15.00 × .99)
      ** ($16.00 × .99)

(c)

Weighted average cost per unit $\dfrac{\$5,191.66^*}{365}$ = $14.22

Ending inventory 100 x $14.22 =   = $14,220

      *   50 @ $20.00 = $1,000.00
          65 @ $15.84 =   1,029.60
          90 @ $14.85 =   1,336.50
          84 @ $11.88 =   997.92
          76 @ $10.89 =   827.64
      Total goods available $5,191.66

(d)   FIFO matches older costs with revenue. When prices are declining, as in this case, this results in a higher amount for cost of goods sold. Therefore, it is recommended that FIFO be used by Long Limited to minimize taxable income.

INVENTORIES: ADDITIONAL VALUATION ISSUES

Lower of Cost and Market

- What is "market"?
- How LCM works
- Application of LCM
- Recording market
- Evaluation of rule

Other Valuation Issues

- Net realizable value
- Relative sales value
- Purchase commitments

Estimation: Gross Profit Method

- Gross profit percentage
- Evaluation of method

Estimation: Retail Inventory Method

- Terminology
- Conventional method
- Special items
- Evaluation of method

Presentation and Analysis

- Presentation of inventories
- Analysis of inventories

chapter 9

INVENTORIES: ADDITIONAL VALUATION PROBLEMS

PERSPECTIVE: ADDITIONAL INVENTORY VALUATION PROBLEMS

Inventory accounting was introduced in Chapter 8. This chapter concludes the discussion with a review of the lower of cost and market (LCM) rule and other methods for inventory valuation that are specific to certain industries.

INSIGHTS

*The key methods to be learned here are the **retail method** and the **gross profit method**. Keep in mind that both are **estimation methods** that should only be used where there is no better information. Many computers and point of sale terminals keep detailed information such that these methods may not be necessary.*
***Lower of cost and market** is a key concept used to value inventory. There are several ways to determine market.*

STUDY STEPS

1. Understanding the Business Side

This has already been covered in Chapter 8 of the Study Guide.

2. Understanding How Inventory Issues Fit into the Financial Reporting Model and Conceptual Framework—Analysis and Critical Thinking

The main issue here is one of **measurement** or valuation. Inventory may get old or obsolete, and therefore, this should be reflected in the financial statements. Exhibit 9-1 discusses relevant measurement and presentation/disclosure issue.

Exhibit 9-1: Relevant criteria, definitions and issues

Business perspective: Inventory is an essential asset and since it is included in current assets, it is important that it is reported and properly valued.

	How it relates to inventory	Relevant criteria/definitions	Topic specific analysis— how it should be	What makes the analysis challenging—how it is
Measurement	• in most companies inventory gets old/obsolete and the cost may not be recovered through sale. This represents a loss that must be reflected. • in the retail industry, it is very costly to measure COS and inventory for interim reporting	• lower of cost and market (LCM)	• since inventory is a current asset, it is important to give users info about cash flows that it will generate when sold. If the cost will not be recovered, must write down to market. • market may be one of many alternatives including **replacement cost, net realizable value (NRV) or NRV less a profit margin.**	• since the definition of market includes several alternatives, it is open to PJ • in certain very specialized industries, NRV is used e.g., meat packing industry. This is unusual. • use of retail and gross profit methods subject to PJ
Presentation/ Disclosure	note disclosure	• full disclosure	• due to different definitions of market, CICA HB discourages the use of the term market and suggest a more descriptive term such as replacement cost, etc. • see also HB 1508—disclose nature and extent of **measurement uncertainty**	

Prepared by Irene Wiecek
©2002 John Wiley & Sons Canada, Ltd

STUDY STEPS

3. Becoming Proficient in Applying the Retail Method and Gross Profit Methods

Gross profit method

The **gross profit method** of determining ending inventory is used to **estimate** inventory where perpetual records are not kept and where a count is not practical. Inventory must be counted at least annually. However, if inventory values are needed more frequently, as they usually are (e.g., for interim reporting), the gross profit method may be used to estimate the number. Ending inventory would be calculated as follows under the gross profit method.

> *Ending Inventory = beginning inventory + purchases – cost of sales*
>
> *(= sales X gross profit %)*

The **gross profit percentage** must be determined. This is done by looking at gross profit divided by sales from **prior periods** or from budgets. Many companies use this to estimate cost of sales and ending inventory for interim reporting.

Tip!   The gross profit method is used to estimate CGS and ending inventory where no inventory count is taken.

> **It often uses a normalized historic gross profit % to estimate CGS and ending inventory and, therefore, it tends to smooth seasonal and quarterly fluctuations and to emphasize past trends rather than existing and future trends.** *Tip!*

Retail sales method

The **retail inventory method** is often used by retailers to value inventory where there is high volume/low unit cost. The method uses the same calculation as the gross profit method; however, it uses retail value (i.e., sales price) instead of cost to track and value inventory. Where the gross profit method is used to get an estimate of CGS and inventory when no inventory count is performed, the retail method is used for this and to estimate year-end inventory **$ values** even when a count is performed.

The inventory count is valued using retail value, not cost, as is usually the norm. Retail value or sales price is easier to obtain. The ending inventory is then **converted back to cost** by applying a percentage that represents cost of sales divided by sales. Normally the following method is used:

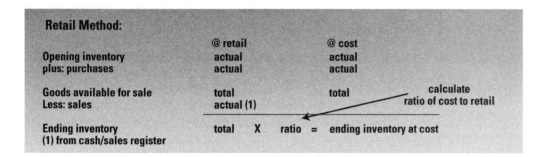

Retail Method:	@ retail	@ cost	
Opening inventory	actual	actual	
plus: purchases	actual	actual	
Goods available for sale	total	total	calculate
Less: sales	actual (1)		ratio of cost to retail
Ending inventory	total X ratio	=	ending inventory at cost
(1) from cash/sales register			

> **The retail method is a way of tracking costs using retail or sales prices. Where a company has a more sophisticated computerized system, the need for the retail method diminishes.** *Tip!*

> **Both the gross method and the retail method are estimation techniques that are used in the absence of better information. (i.e., Cost /Benefit)** *Tip!*

Examples of the retail method and the gross profit method are worked through in problems 2 and 3 and the multiple choice questions.

MULTIPLE CHOICE QUESTIONS

1) The gross profit method is often used to calculate inventory and cost of goods sold. Under which of the following scenarios would it not be acceptable:
   a) where ending inventory numbers are not available due to fire
   b) for interim reporting purposes
   c) for year-end reporting purposes
   d) for projection purposes

2) Ingo Limited has several product lines with very different gross profit margins. These products are each sold in markets that have different peak periods throughout the year. For first quarter reporting, Ingo has decided to use least year's annual gross profit % to calculate total gross profit for the company. They have put forth the following arguments to the company auditors to support this. Which argument is not acceptable?
   a) The year-end consolidated gross profit % has not been materially different for the past three years.
   b) For interim reporting, the gross profit method is acceptable.
   c) It is too time-consuming to do an inventory count, and in the absence of more accurate information, the gross profit method will serve as a good estimation.
   d) The first quarter gross profit %, even if incorrect, will even out by year-end.

3) The retail method and the gross profit method are both methods that are used to estimate cost of goods sold and ending inventory. In this regard, they are similar. From the list below, identify the main difference.
   a) Both methods use a % based on gross margins to calculate inventory cost and cost of goods sold.
   b) Both methods are often used for interim financial reporting.
   c) Both methods may not be used for year-end financial reporting.
   d) Both methods provide management with information for internal decision making.

4) In financial statements, it is useful to disclose how inventories have been valued. Specifically, it is useful to note the rule where inventories have been written down. Therefore, the *CICA Handbook* requires that the basis of valuation be disclosed. Which of the following phrases to describe the basis of valuation is not optimal from the CICA's perspective:
   a) lower of cost and replacement cost
   b) lower of cost and net realizable value
   c) lower of cost and net realizable value less normal profit margin
   d) lower of cost and market

5) Standard costs are another option for costing inventory. Standard costing is allowable for year-end financial statement purposes under GAAP under the following circumstances:
   a) where it does not differ materially from actual cost
   b) where actual cost is not available
   c) where management uses it for internal decision making
   d) where the company is a manufacturing company and needs the information in order to track variances

6) In certain cases, inventories are valued at net realizable value even when the cost is lower than the NRV. Which of the following does not justify the use of net realizable value as a valuation base when NRV is greater than cost?
   a) where there is a controlled market with a fixed price
   b) where cost figures are too difficult to obtain, i.e., in the meat packing industry
   c) where there is no specific customer identified for the inventory
   d) where costs of disposal are not estimable

7) Which of the following methods of estimating market (while using the lower of cost and market rule) is the most common in Canada?
   a) net realizable value
   b) replacement cost
   c) net realizable value less normal profit margins
   d) net realizable value less reserves for future declines in value

8) When using the retail method, the following is not included in the calculation of the cost ratio or cost to retail ratio :
   a) markups
   b) markup cancellations
   c) markdowns
   d) net markups

9) Dino Corporation agreed with a supplier to buy 10 tons of raw materials at a fixed price over the next year. The amount is material and the contract non-cancellable. Which of the following statements is true?
   a) The transaction should be recorded on the balance sheet as it represents a liability to the company.
   b) The transaction should be recorded since it is material.
   c) The transaction should not be recorded on the balance sheet since it represents an executory contract.
   d) The transaction should be recorded since it is non-cancellable.

10) Although both the retail method and the gross profit method have been used for interim reporting for many years, the advent of the computer and point of sales systems that track inventory at very detailed levels will likely signal the demise of these methods. Which of the following was the basic concept that supported these methods in past?
   a) relevance
   b) reliability
   c) understandability
   d) cost versus benefit

SOLUTIONS TO MULTIPLE CHOICE QUESTIONS

1) c) The gross profit method is an estimation technique only, and should not be used for the official, audited financial statements at year-end. Having said this, the method may be used where the numbers are otherwise not available, (theft, fire etc.), or where an estimate is acceptable (for internal decision making or interim financial reporting).

2) d) is the least supportable. True, the gross profit method is an acceptable estimation technique; and true, historical information would support using the prior year's number. However, the reason for quarterly reporting is to give timely, reasonably accurate information. Each quarter's transactions should be booked in the quarter. The company has several different products with several different profit margins and, therefore, depending on demand, the gross profit margin in any given quarter could vary significantly from year-end.

3) c) While the gross profit method is generally not acceptable for year-end reporting, the retail method is commonly used for costing inventory at year-end. The retail method is allowable where an inventory count has been taken and valued at retail. The method converts the inventory to cost for the balance sheet and income statement purposes.

4) d) Any of the options except d) are preferred. d) is not considered to be the best phrase due to the ambiguity of the term "market." Market value is often based on intent, i.e., what the management of the company plans to do with the inventory. If they plan to replace it, replacement cost might be more relevant. If they plan to get rid of it at any cost, and not replace it, net realizable value might be the most relevant.

5) a) It is only acceptable where the variance from actual cost is not material. Standard costing systems are put in place by management to control operations and to monitor costs. While this function is critical to a manufacturing company, the most relevant information for users of the financial statements is actual cost, and therefore, both must be tracked.

6) d) In order to write the inventory up to the higher market and to recognize profits, the costs to actually deliver and sell the inventory must be known and accrued. This would result in a matching of the costs with the inventory. C) does not preclude the revaluation upwards as a specific customer need not be known as long as a controlled market exists and it is certain that the product will be sold, i.e., gold. Interestingly, b) allows the revaluation since in the meat packing industry, it is impossible to allocate the cost of a cow to its individual butchered parts. Therefore, it is not even a question of the cost to obtain the allocation being too high. In this case it is impossible to obtain the information. Therefore, valuation at market less distribution costs is the only information available.

7) a) Net realizable value is the most common as it is usually the most readily available.

8) c) Markdowns are not used in the calculation of the ratio.

9) c) The contract would generally not be recorded as it represents a promise by both parties to do something in the future. Under present GAAP, these future commitments are not yet recorded. They may, however, have to be disclosed. If the value of the raw material declines, a loss would likely be accrued under contingency accounting.

10) d) In the past it was too costly to keep track of the inventory at a detailed level and, therefore, these estimation methods were used since the cost would have far outweighed the benefit.

SHORT PROBLEMS

1) *Purpose:* To illustrate the use of LCM and emphasize the difference between the choices available for valuation.

Wholesale Company Limited (WCL) imports products in bulk and resells them at a profit. Below is information relating to the inventory. Because of "free trade," tariffs and import duties have been removed from most of the products that WCL imports, resulting in lower replacement costs. However, management has decided not to pass these savings on to the customer since they feel that most customers will not realize how quickly the duties and tariffs have been removed.

	Cost	NRV	NRV-profit	Replacement cost
Product A	$10,000	$15,000	$10,000	$7,000
Product B	20,000	19,000	15,000	-0-
Product C	5,000	10,000	8,000	3,000
	$35,000	$44,000	$33,000	$10,000

A replacement cost for B is not available since the product is no longer popular and the manufacturer has gone out of business. WCL failed to assess the market correctly and may now be stuck with the product, although at present the market is still holding.

Required

(a) Prepare the journal entry to revalue the inventory, if required, using the following market definitions. Calculate the value at which inventory should be reported on the balance sheet using the totals.

• NRV.

• NRV less normal profit margin.

• Replacement cost.

(b) Comment on which definition you think should be used and why.

(c) How would your answer to (a) differ if NRV was used and the comparison was done on a category-by-category basis?

(d) Assume that you are the auditor for the company and that the cost and market information was given to you by management. Would your answer to (a) be any different?

2) *Purpose:* To illustrate the use of the gross profit method.

ABC Limited (AL) uses the periodic inventory method to value inventory and to calculate cost of goods sold. Inventory is counted once a year on December 31 and the inventory and cost of goods sold accounts are adjusted accordingly. It is now June 30 and AL needs to know the value of the inventory for the bank, as the inventory will be used as collateral for a loan. The following additional information is available:

Beginning inventory	$ 398,888
Purchases	1,989,079
Gross profit:	
—Cumulative historical	34%
—Year-to-date est.	30%
—Budgeted-YTD	31%
Sales	3,150,000

Gross profit has been declining in past years.

Required

Estimate the value of inventory using the gross profit method.

3) Purpose: To illustrate the use of the retail sales method.

Department Stores Incorporated (DSI) counts its inventory only once a year. The job is a mammoth one and usually takes every available employee. The store must be closed in order to do an accurate count and subsequent valuation takes another two weeks. The valuation is facilitated by a computer which has all retail prices programmed by product code.

During the year, inventory levels must also be monitored since a significant amount of capital is tied up in inventory. Since the inventory count takes so much time and effort, it is impractical to perform it on a monthly basis and inventory must be estimated. DSI, therefore, uses the retail sales method in the interim. The following information has been taken from the computer:

	@ Retail	@ Cost
Opening inventory	$4,567,090	$2,968,609
Purchases	9,888,787	7,199,927
Sales	12,080,333	

Required

Calculate ending inventory.

SOLUTIONS TO SHORT PROBLEMS

1)(a) NRV:
   No adjustment required since NRV > cost.

   NRV less normal profit:

Cost of sales-loss on inventory write-down	2,000	
Inventory allowance		2,000

Replacement cost:

Cost of sales	25,000	
Inventory allowance		25,000

This entry does not make any sense since the bulk of the write-down occurs because no replacement cost is available. WCL should attempt to obtain the replacement cost for a similar product if there is one (perhaps from a different supplier).

(b)   According to the *CICA Handbook*, any of the methods is acceptable. In this case, however, due to the lack of information about replacement costs, it may not be appropriate to use this method. As noted above, WCL should attempt to find the replacement cost of a similar product if they want to use this definition of market. To value product B at $0 is unrealistic if it can be sold for substantially more.

Use of NRV results in no write-down and the most favourable net income, although this should not be the basis for making the decision. (Accounting should be neutral.) Note that the higher market values for A and C offset the lower values for B.

Use of the NRV less profit makes sense since sales prices, which are exit values, are not comparable to cost, which represents an input value. However, recognizing a loss this period just so a normal profit may be recognized in the following year is really an allocation issue (i.e., allocation of the profits between periods).

The most commonly used definition is NRV. *Tip!*

(c)
NRV: Product B would be written down.

Cost of sales	1,000	
Inventory allowance		1,000

NRV less profits: Again, product B would be written down.

Cost of sales	5,000	
Inventory		5,000

RC: All products would be written down but the journal entry would be the same since the replacement costs are all below cost anyway.

(d)
Be sceptical about the NRV assigned to product B. It sounds as though there might not be a market for this product and that WCL might be stuck with it, in which case, it would be prudent to write down some or all of the product B inventory.

2) The question is which gross profit percentage to use. Since the gross profit has been declining, it does not make much sense to use the cumulative historical rate. Whether the estimated YTD figure is used, or the budgeted figure, is purely a matter of judgement. Both are estimates in reality. Therefore, use the estimated YTD figure (arbitrary).

Opening inventory	$ 398,888
Purchases	1,989,079
Less: estimated cost of sales	
$3,150,000 × (1-30%)	(2,205,000)
Estimated ending inventory	$ 182,967

Use of the budgeted profit would result in a higher ending inventory. Since the choice is arbitrary, management might use the budgeted percentage to calculate the inventory for the bank since it results in a higher value ($214,467).

3)

	@ Retail	@ Cost
Opening inventory	$ 4,567,090	$ 2,968,609
Purchases	9,888,787	7,199,927
Goods available for sale	14,455,877	10,168,536 70%
Sales	12,080,333	
Ending inventory	2,375,544 × 70% =	1,662,881

The ending inventory is $1,662,881 which is calculated by multiplying the estimated ending inventory (at retail) by the ratio of cost to retail.

$$\frac{\text{Goods available for sale at cost}}{\text{Goods available for sale at retail}} = \frac{10,168,536}{14,455,877}$$

$$= 70\%$$

The ending number is really only a rough estimate since it does not account for shrinkage. One way to deal with this would be to estimate shrinkage based on past years and to adjust the estimated inventory. Even so, it does not account for errors. This is why a physical count should be taken at least annually.

CASES

1) SHEUNG STEEL LIMITED

Sheung Steel Limited (SSL) manufactures steel. The market for its raw materials is fairly volatile and the prices are a function of supply and demand. In the past, SSL has often purchased more than necessary in order to get a good price. Chuck Chung, the general manager, was in the process of reviewing current raw material prices and inventory levels in order to determine how much he should buy. Samantha Tse, a recently hired employee, stopped by his office.

Samantha:
Free for lunch today Chuck?

Chuck:
Maybe a bit later, Samantha. I have to make a decision today on how much raw materials to purchase. The price is at an all-time low and I'm not sure that it will get any better. The problem is that we don't really need all this inventory now, not to mention the fact that the boss is worried about cash flows.

Samantha:
You know that there are other costs involved besides the purchase price. Have you considered the storage costs and the cost of tying up cash in assets that are not in use?

Chuck:
I guess not. I always make my decision based on the purchase price alone. I guess that I should factor in those other costs as well. But the purchase price is so low that it's probably still a good deal.

Samantha:
Why don't you see if you can lock into the price now but not take delivery of the product until we need it. That way, we wouldn't incur storage costs and we wouldn't have to pay until we take delivery. You might have to lock in at a higher price but considering the other benefits, it might be worth it.

Chuck:
Sounds good. I'll call the supplier right away. We've got a pretty good working relationship. Maybe he'll join us for lunch. I have to get this finalized today so that I can work on the year-end financial statements. It's already mid-December and before you know it, year-end and the auditors will descend on us. I'll have to think about how this would be accounted for.

It is now January 15, 2002 and Chuck has negotiated a deal with the supplier to purchase the raw materials at a very good price. SSL must take delivery of a fixed amount within the next six months and pay a fixed total price even if they do not take delivery of the full amount. The deal was signed December 15, 2001 and SSL has not yet taken delivery of the first shipment.

On December 31, 2001, the price of the raw material dropped even further. Chuck was annoyed since he could have saved $200,000 had he waited. Prices have since begun to creep upwards, however.

REQUIRED:

Assume the role of Chuck and consider how the raw material deal should be presented in the financial statements.

2) EATONS—www.eatons.ca

In note 2 to the consolidated financial statements under "Significant Accounting Policies", the method used for valuing/costing inventory is the retail method.

REQUIRED:

Discuss the appropriateness of the retail method for inventory costing in the case of Eatons (i.e., a major retail department store).

SOLUTION TO CASES

1) SHEUNG STEEL LIMITED

Overview

Favourable presentation of the deal will be important to Chuck. He might not be very keen on showing the fact that, had he delayed the signing of the deal, he could have saved the company $200,000. GAAP is a constraint since it is mentioned that the auditors will be coming in soon. Stakeholders of the statements will include shareholders who will want information in order to assess their investment in the company.

Analysis and Recommendations

The issue is how the raw material purchase commitment should be accounted for. The arrangement for the undelivered material is called an executory contract since both parties have agreed to do something but neither have fulfilled their part of the deal. SSL has agreed to take delivery of the material and to pay the supplier for the goods and the supplier has agreed to sell the goods to SSL at an agreed upon price. There is, as yet, no liability for the goods, that is, until they are delivered.

The commitment should be disclosed in the notes to the financial statements since it will help users predict cash flows of the company. Furthermore, there is the question of whether Chuck should accrue the difference between the contract price and the market price of the raw material at year-end.

Accrue the Loss:

Since the market price is below the committed purchase price at the financial statement date, the loss should be accrued. Otherwise when the inventory is delivered and recorded on the books it will be overvalued. And since it must be carried at the lower of cost and market, it will be written down to market. Since the decline in value occurred in the current year, it would make sense for the loss to be booked in 2001.

However, accrual would reduce net income and highlight the fact that the company could have saved money had they waited.

Should the loss be presented as part of cost of goods sold? Since it relates to inventory this would make sense. If booked to cost of goods sold, gross profit and gross profit ratio would decline.

Do Not Accrue the Loss:

Contingency accounting would require that the loss be accrued when it is estimable (which it is) and when it is likely that a future event will confirm the fact that the inventory value has been impaired. The latter is arguable. The fact that the market price is below market at the balance sheet date is surely relevant. However, if the market price increases after year-end and before the financial statements are issued, it is hard to argue that it is likely that a loss will be incurred. In fact, if the price keeps rising prior to the delivery dates, there will be no loss. In this case, the price is rising.

It might also be argued that since the price is volatile, it is not easy to estimate the potential loss, if any, and, therefore, the first criterion is not met either.

Recommendation

Since the price is volatile and since it is rising, no loss should be accrued in the financial statements. The notes to the statements should describe the deal but not necessarily that market is below cost. It is not likely that a loss will occur.

2) EATONS

The retail method is often used in the retail sales business, hence its name. The method was developed for retailers, in order to overcome the problem of accurately costing inventory where there is a large inventory population that is non-homogeneous and spread out over numerous locations. The cost of revaluing this type of inventory is very prohibitive and often does not justify the benefit of having accurate numbers. The retail method requires the use of retail costs to track and eventually value the inventory. Most retailers are very conscious of profit margins and it is critical to the success of the company to maintain these profit margins. Because of this, there is quite a bit of information available on retail prices and profit margins that may be used for operational decisions.

Retail prices are available for all items through the point of sales systems. At year-end, or at various times during the year, a count is made and the inventory valued at retail. The amount is then converted to cost using a calculated cost to sales ratio (inverse of the profit margin). In the case of retailers, much time and effort is saved doing it this way and, since the ratio incorporates markups and not markdowns, ending inventory is conservatively valued.

SELECTED SOLUTIONS FROM THE TEXTBOOK

EXERCISE 9-3 (20–25 MINUTES)

1) LCM—Canadian

Item No.	Estimated selling price	Estimated selling expense	Market = NRV	Cost	LCM	Quantity	Final Inventory
1320	$4.50	$.35	$4.15	$3.20	$3.20	1,200	$ 3,840
1333	3.50	.50	3.00	2.70	2.70	900	2,430
1426	5.00	.40	4.60	4.50	4.50	800	3,600
1437	3.20	.25	2.95	3.60	2.95	1,000	2,950
1510	3.25	.80	2.45	2.25	2.25	700	1,575
1522	3.80	.40	3.40	3.00	3.00	500	1,500
1573	2.50	.75	1.75	1.80	1.75	3,000	5,250
1626	6.00	.50	5.50	4.70	4.70	1,000	4,700
							$25,845

2) LCM—U.S.

Item No.	Cost per Unit	Replacement Cost	Net Realizable Value	Net Real. Value Less Normal Profit	Designated Market Value	Quantity	Final Inventory Value
1320	$3.20	$3.00	$4.15	$2.90*	$3.00	1,200	$ 3,600
1333	2.70	2.30	3.00	2.50	2.50	900	2,250
1426	4.50	3.70	4.60	3.60	3.70	800	2,960
1437	3.60	3.10	2.95	2.05	2.95	1,000	2,950
1510	2.25	2.00	2.45	1.85	2.00	700	1,400
1522	3.00	2.70	3.40	2.90	2.90	500	1,450
1573	1.80	1.60	1.75	1.25	1.60	3,000	4,800
1626	4.70	5.20	5.50	4.50	5.20	1,000	4,700**
							$24,110

* 4.15 − $1.25 = $2.90
** Cost is used because it is lower than designated market value

Exercise 9-5 (20–25 minutes)

(a)

	February	March	April
Sales	$29,000	$35,000	$40,000
Cost of goods sold			
Inventory, beginning	15,000	15,100	17,000
Purchases	20,000	24,000	26,500
Cost of goods available	35,000	39,100	43,500
Inventory, ending	15,100	17,000	13,000
Cost of goods sold	19,900	22,100	30,500
Gross profit	9,100	12,900	9,500
Gain (loss) due to market			
fluctuations of inventory*	(2,000)	1,100	700
	$ 7,100	$14,000	$10,200

*	Jan. 31	Feb. 28	Mar. 31	Apr. 31
Inventory at cost	$15,000	$15,100	$17,000	$13,000
Inventory at the lower of cost				
or market	14,500	12,600	15,600	12,300
Allowance amount needed to				
reduce inventory to market	$ 500	$ 2,500	$ 1,400	$ 700
Gain (loss) due to market				
fluctuations of inventory**		$ (2,000)	$ 1,100	$ 700

**$500 − $2,500 = $(2,000)
$2,500 − $1,400 = $1,100
$1,400 − $700 = $700

(b)

Jan. 31	Loss Due to Market Decline of Inventory	500	
	Allowance to Reduce Inventory to Market		500
Feb. 28	Loss Due to Market Decline of Inventory	2,000	
	Allowance to Reduce Inventory to Market		2,000
Mar. 31	Allowance to Reduce Inventory to Market	1,100	
	Recovery of Loss Due to Market		
	Decline of Inventory		1,100
Apr. 31	Allowance to Reduce Inventory to Market	700	
	Recovery of Loss Due to Market		
	Decline of Inventory		700

EXERCISE 9-12 (10–15 MINUTES)

(a)

Inventory, May 1 (at cost)		$160,000
Purchases (gross) (at cost)		640,000
Purchase discounts		(12,000)
Freight-in		30,000
Goods available (at cost)		818,000
Sales (at selling price)	$1,000,000	
Sales returns (at selling price)	(70,000)	
Net sales (at selling price)	930,000	
Less gross profit (30% of $930,000)	279,000	
Estimated cost of goods sold		651,000
Estimated inventory, May 31 (at cost)		$167,000

(b)

Gross profit as a percent of sales must be calculated:

$$\frac{30\%}{100\% + 30\%} = 23.08\% \text{ of sales.}$$

Inventory, May 1 (at cost)		$160,000
Purchases (gross) (at cost)		640,000
Purchase discounts		(12,000)
Freight-in		30,000
Goods available (at cost)		818,000
Sales (at selling price)	$1,000,000	
Sales returns (at selling price)	(70,000)	
Net sales (at selling price)	930,000	
Less gross profit (23.08% of $930,000)	214,644	
Estimated cost of goods sold		715,356
Estimated inventory, May 31 (at cost)		$102,644

EXERCISE 9-20 (20–25 MINUTES)

	Cost		Retail
Beginning inventory	$30,000		$ 46,500
Purchases	48,000		88,000
Purchase returns	(2,000)		(3,000)
Freight on purchases	2,400		
Totals	78,400		131,500
Add net markups			
Markups		$10,000	
Markup cancellations		(1,500)	8,500
Net markups	$78,400		140,000
Deduct net markdowns			
Markdowns		9,300	
Markdowns cancellations		(2,800)	
Net markdowns			6,500
			133,500
Deduct net sales ($99,000 − $2,000)			97,000
Ending inventory, at retail			$ 36,500

$$\text{Cost-to-retail ratio} = \frac{\$78,400}{\$140,000} = 56\%$$

Ending inventory at cost = 56% × $36,500 = $20,440

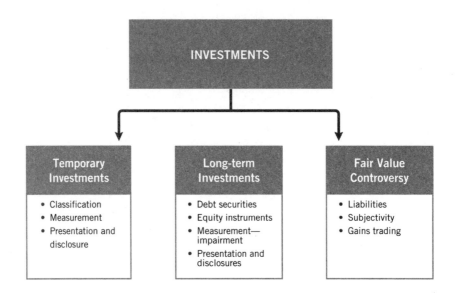

chapter 10

INVESTMENTS

PERSPECTIVE

This chapter deals with investments made by companies in other companies. These investments may take the form of bonds, common shares or preferred shares and may be short-term or long-term. Since the above represent very different types of investments, with very different business impacts, the accounting is quite different in each case. It is important to identify what type of investment has been made before attempting to account for it.

Aside from some basic principles, two methods of accounting for long-term investments in common shares are included here. Bond accounting is also covered. The latter topic is usually dealt with in reasonable detail at the introductory accounting level, and will only be reviewed briefly here.

INSIGHTS

- *The basics of **bond accounting** are fundamental and should be reviewed. The study of bond accounting is very mechanical in nature once a few basic concepts have been mastered.*
- *For **long-term common share investments**, both the **cost** and **equity methods** of accounting are important to learn.*
- *The significance of **management intent** is of interest in determining whether an investment is classified as temporary or long-term.*
- ***Long-term common share investments** are accounted for differently depending on the percent ownership since common shares carry voting rights and therefore, the more shares held, the more influence exists over the company.*

STUDY STEPS

1. Understanding the Fundamental Differences in Different Types of Investments

STUDY STEPS

The main groups of investments are shown below.

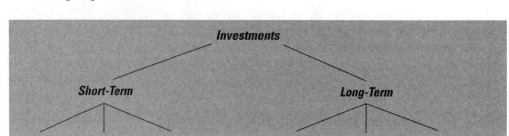

Traditionally speaking, investments are made in either **debt** or **equity instruments**. Debt instruments (e.g., **bonds**) will normally give a **fixed stream of income through interest**. Equity instruments may take the form of **preferred shares** or **common shares**. Preferred shares usually offer a fixed return on the investment over the longer term through **fixed rate dividends**. The dividend **payout ranks in preference** to the dividends paid out on other shares. If the company winds up, the preferred shareholders theoretically would get their investment back before other shareholders—hence the name "preferred."

> **Tip!** Preferred shareholders rank in preference to common shareholders in terms of dividend payout and return of capital.

Common shares are quite different from debt or preferred shares as they are **residual**. There is no fixed return on the shares rather the shares allow the holder to share in residual income (after deducting operating expenses and preferred dividends). On wind up of a company, the common shareholders would get whatever is left after the creditors and preferred shareholders have received their funds—hence the term "residual." Common shares generally carry **voting rights** and this, along with the potential for no return/opportunity for high returns, gives the holders the **risks and rewards of ownership**. Accounting for long-term investments in common shares is, therefore, quite different.

> **Tip!** Common shares carry voting rights and opportunity to receive excess returns—therefore, depending on % of shares held, this gives the holder the risks and rewards of ownership.

Often these investments are made for the purpose of vertically or horizontally integrating operations. For instance, a company that makes bread might buy shares in a flour company to enable it to have some control over the quality and cost of raw materials. Or it might buy shares in a distribution company in order to have access to distribution channels. Remember that equity or common shares carry voting rights, and therefore, depending on the number of shares purchased, enable the holder to exercise some control over the decisions made by the investee (the company invested in).

For all investments, management might decide to hold onto the investments for a short period, whereas for others the **intent** might be to take a longer term position for various reasons. This intent is reflected in whether the investments are shown as long-term or current assets.

2. Understanding How Investment Related Issues fit into the Financial Reporting Model and Conceptual Framework—Analysis and Critical Thinking

STUDY STEPS

Exhibit 10-1: Relevant criteria, definitions and issues

Business perspective: Companies invest in other companies for various reasons. Sometimes, the company is interested in investing excess cash for a short or long-term return; however, sometimes the investment is made to achieve operating synergies or for other business reasons. The accounting should reflect the underlying intent of management.

	How it relates to investment	Relevant criteria/definitions	Topic specific analysis— how it should be	What makes the analysis challenging—how it is
TEMPORARY INVESTMENTS: Measurement	• how to value the investment initially and whether to reflect changes in market value • how to value management intent changes	• **historical cost** • **LCM** • **concept of relevance versus reliability** • **management intent** • **conservatism**	• generally, assets are measured at **historical cost** subject to the LCM rule. For temporary investments, **market** is defined as the market price as at reporting date. • since **intent** is to hold for short-term, recent market is **relevant.** • generally not written up if market is greater due to potential **bias** and **conservatism**	• LCM is often seen as one-sided and it is felt that pure market provides better info • many specialized industries use pure market for valuation • for many temporary investments, market values available and **objective**, so no bias
Presentation/ Disclosure	• how to present in balance sheet and note disclosures	• **full disclosure**	• basis of valuation • if marketable securities, disclose market and carrying value • classify as current assets only if **capable of prompt liquidation and intent to liquidate**	
LONG-TERM INVESTMENTS IN VOTING SHARES Measurements	• how to measure changes in value of long-term investments	• **historical cost** • **LCM** • **concept of relevance versus reliability** • **management intent** • **conservatism** • **cost vs. equity method** • **significant influence** • **loss in value that is other than temporary**	• if no significant influence, (<20%), then **cost method** – dividends = income, write down if **longer term impairment** only since LT investment • if significant influence, then **equity method** and accrue share of profits/losses as earned/incurred by investee	• can't just go by % owned—must look to whether significant influence—PJ—consider i) representation on BOD ii) partcipation in policy making; iii) I/C transactions; iv) interchange of personnel or info • PJ as to whether loss in value other than temporary—consider i) **mkt < cost for prolonged period;** ii) **severe losses;** iii) **continued losses;** iv) **suspension in trading;** v) **going concern problems;** vi) **appraisal less then cost** • watch for **"liquidating dividends"** with portfolio investments
Presentation/ Disclosure	• how to classify and note disclosures required	• **full disclosure** • **management intent**	• disclose basis of valuation • if equity method, disclose any purchase price discrepancy • if cost method, disclose market and carrying value	

Prepared by Irene Wiecek
©2002 John Wiley & Sons Canada, Ltd

3. Becoming Proficient in the Cost and Equity Methods of Accounting for Common Shares Investments and Bond Accounting

Investments in Common Shares

Long-term investments are accounted for differently depending on the nature of the investment and the relationship between the investee and investor. This is often a function of **percentage ownership** and the amount of **influence** or **control asserted** by the investor over the financing, investing, and operating decisions of the investee. This is illustrated in the chart below.

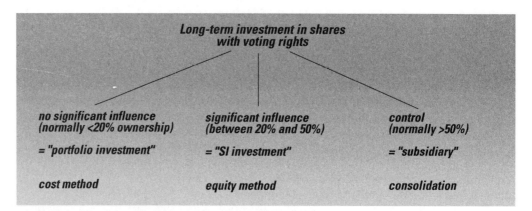

> **Tip!** In determining which type of investment has been made, the % ownership is merely a guideline and the real issue is whether "control" or "significant influence" exists. Criteria for significant influence are examined in exhibit 1. "Control" is relevant for subsidiaries and is studied in advanced accounting courses.

The **cost method** recognizes that the investor has no power to influence decisions, including the distribution of profits to the shareholders. Therefore, the **critical event** in the **earnings process** and the point when revenues are recognized by the investor, is when dividends have been declared by the investee or are receivable (dr. cash/AR and cr. dividend income). Dividends do not affect the investment account on the balance sheet.

> **Tip!** Under the cost method, the critical event in the earnings process for recognition of investment income is the declaration or receipt of dividends from the investee.

Under the **cost method,** the investment is booked at cost and is not adjusted afterwards, except under two circumstances:

1. The first is if there is a **loss in value that is other than temporary**. Conditions that evidence this situation are outlined in *Handbook* Section 3050 and in Exhibit 1. Generally, if the market value or earnings have been depressed for three to four years, this would signify a non-temporary decline (booked as dr. loss on investment and cr. investment [B/S]).

2. The other situation occurs when there are **liquidating dividends**. These are dividends paid by the investee out of pre-acquisition earnings (i.e., dividends paid after the

acquisition date that exceed cumulative profits earned by the investee in the period since the shares were acquired). The excess of the dividends paid to the investor over the investor's share of post-acquisition profits is known as a liquidating dividend and is credited to the investment account (B/S), instead of to dividend income. These are technically not real liquidating dividends in a legal sense—i.e., a return of capital but the concepts are the same.

> Cash
>> Dividend income
>> Investment account (B/S)

The **equity method** recognizes that the investor has **influence over the dividend decision** and, therefore, the critical event in the earnings process (i.e., for the investor to recognize earnings from the investee) is the point when the investee earns the income. The declaration of the dividend is secondary. Theoretically, revenue could be recognized by the investor as each dollar is earned by the investee; however, practically speaking, it is only booked monthly or even annually (dr. investment and cr. equity pickup or investment income). If the investor owns 25% of the shares of the investee, then it would record 25% of the profits of the investee, or 25% of the losses.

When the dividends are actually received, income is not recognized, but rather the journal entry appears as follows: dr. cash and cr. investment (B/S). This is because the income has already been accrued when the investee earns the income.

Under the equity method, pro-rata income is accrued by the investor and dividends are treated as a decrease in the investment account on the balance sheet.   *Tip!*

The investment is booked at cost originally, and is increased as earnings are accrued and decreased as dividends are received. This makes intuitive sense since as the investee earns profits, the value of the investment/company increases and as the investee pays out cash, the value of the investment/company decreases.

In addition, an assessment of whether there has been a **decline in value that is other than temporary** should be made at every reporting date. The criteria used to assess this are the same as for cost investments.

The income recognized by the investee under the equity method must be adjusted for amortization of the **purchase price discrepancy** (PPD). The PPD is the difference between what the investor paid for the shares and the value of the company.

The purchase price discrepancy must be calculated when an investor invests in common shares of a company and obtains significant influence or control of that company through the purchase.   *Tip!*

For instance, Beakman Limited (BL), might pay $4 million for 25% of World Limited (WL) as follows:

- Paid $4 million for 25%.
- Net Book Value (NBV) = $12 million.
- Fair Market Value (FMV) of underlying net assets $15 million.

The purchase price equation (PPE) shows what the investor paid and what they received. For BL, the PPE is as follows:

Amount paid for 25% interest	$4,000,000
NBV of 25% interest	
($12,000,000 × 25%)	3,000,000
Difference	1,000,000

Why would BL pay more for the shares than the recorded NBV? There are two reasons: one being that the recorded values of assets seldom reflect the FMV of the underlying assets due to **the historical cost principle.** The other reason is that there are often unrecorded assets such as **goodwill.** Goodwill is the extra value attributable to a going concern company and results from the reputation of the company, the company having established suppliers, steady customers, etc. Goodwill is not recorded on the balance sheet of a company unless it is purchased. Therefore, in this case, BL could have paid more for the shares because the assets have FMV > NBV, or because of goodwill, or both.

Tip! PPD arise due to perceived excess value inherent in a company purchased. PPD arises either because the underlying tangible assets are seen to have a greater worth than the NBV or that there are unrecorded assets such as goodwill.

Tip! In most cases, there is at least some amount of PPD that is attributable to the perceived excess value of tangible assets since the historical cost principle dictates that assets cannot be written up in the financial statements to reflect increases in value.

The "difference" calculated above must be allocated between these two things as follows:

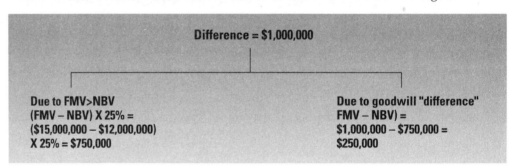

Finally, we must adjust the **equity pickup** or **investment income** booked by BL for amortization of these differences. The FMV>NBV is amortized over the life of the underlying assets (e.g., if the asset is a building with a 20-year life with 15 years remaining, then the amortization would be as follows: $750,000/15 = $50,000). This amount would be booked each year by BL as a reduction of the investment income. Goodwill is not amortized.

The amortization only gets booked by the investor and only affects the amount of income recognized by the investor for the investee.

A summary of both methods follows:

	Cost (no significant influence)	Equity (significant influence)
1. investment purchase	– booked at cost	– booked at cost
2. income recognition	– when dividend is receivable	– accrued when investee earns income
3. subsequent adjustment of investment account	– liquidating dividend – non-temporary decline in value	– increase for earnings – decrease for dividends – non-temporary decline in value
4. adjustment to earnings	NA	– adjust for amortization of purchase price discrepancy

The **consolidation method** is taught in Advanced Accounting courses and therefore will not be discussed here.

Investment in bonds

Bonds often trade on the stock exchange at values that differ from their face values (e.g., a $100 bond might sell for $95). A primary reason is that the market interest rates might differ from the stated rates. In this case, the market interest rates would be higher than the interest rate on the bonds, making them a less desirable investment and therefore cheaper. Theoretically, bonds are priced by discounting the stream of interest and principal repayments using a discount rate that reflects market rates.

> **A bond is issued at a discount when the interest rate on the bond is less than the market interest rate.** **Tip!**

> **A bond is issued at a premium when the interest rate on the bond is greater than the market interest rate.** **Tip!**

Bonds are recorded at cost, which includes any acquisition fees. The difference between the cost and the face value is known as the discount or premium. The discount or premium is amortized over the life of the bond.

For instance, if a bond with $100 face value was purchased for $98 including acquisition costs, the discount would be $2 and the journal entry would be as follows:

Investment in bond	100	
Deferred discount		2
Cash		98

Often the investment and the discount are shown net on the balance sheet.

In this case, if the bond had a two-year life, the discount would be booked to income over two years:

Deferred discount	1	
Interest income		1

The discount or premium amortization gets booked through interest income. This results in the **effective interest** being closer to **market interest** rates. In this case, market rates must have been higher than the bond rates since the bond was purchased for less than face value. The credit to interest income resulting from the bond amortization serves to increase the interest income, thus bringing it closer to market interest.

> **Tip!** The market interest rate is the currently prevailing market rate for bonds of similar risk. The effective interest rate on a bond is the yield on the bond when taking into account the cost of the investment and the return.

There are two ways to amortize the discount: the **straight-line amortization** (e.g., $2/2 years = $1 per year) or the **effective interest method** of amortization. The latter sets up an amortization table and calculates amortization on the declining or increasing balance of the bond book value. The straight-line method results in equal amounts of amortization annually, while the effective yield method results in greater amortization initially, and less later.

> **Tip!** The effective interest method is most often used to amortize net income and uses a standard amortization table.

MULTIPLE CHOICE QUESTIONS

1) Which items should not be classified as temporary investments?
    a) Marketable securities where original management intent is to hold as short-term investments.
    b) Marketable securities (representing 100% of total outstanding shares) purchased with a clearly demonstrated intention of disposing of the shares in the foreseeable future.
    c) Investment in shares of a private company held with the intent to dispose in the near future. There is no market for trading these shares at the present time.
    d) Investment certificates purchased with short-term excess cash.

2) Which of the following investments would appropriately be accounted for under the equity method?
    a) a 30% investment in preferred shares of a company
    b) a 20% investment in common shares of a company where there is no significant influence
    c) a 25% investment in subordinated non-voting shares of a company
    d) a 15% investment in the common shares of a company where significant influence exists

3) Which of the following statements is incorrect?
    a) Under the cost method, investment income never reduces the investment account on the balance sheet.
    b) Under the equity method, investment income increases the investment account on the balance sheet.
    c) Under the cost method, dividends are recorded as investment income.
    d) Under the equity method, dividends reduce the investment account on the balance sheet.

4) On January 1, A Company Limited   purchased 30% of the common shares of B
   Company Limited for $3 million. B's shares trade on a public stock exchange. The
   book value of B at the time was $9 million. The excess paid was due to intangible
   assets, which will be amortized over 20 years. During the year, B Company Limited
   had profits of $400,000 and dividends of $300,000 were paid out. Market value of the
   shares at year-end was $2.7 million. Assume significant influence. What is the
   amount that should be recorded as investment income for the year?
   a) $120,000
   b) $127,500
   c) $105,000
   d) $0

5) Assuming the same information as 4 above, what would the investment income be,
   assuming no significant influence?
   a) no change
   b) $90,000
   c) $82,500
   d) $0

6) Assume the same information as 4, including significant influence, however, assume
   that, at the date of purchase, the intent of company management was to resell the
   shares in January of the following year. What is the incremental impact on net
   income of this investment for the year?
   a) $105,000 increase
   b) $90,000 increase
   c) $210,000 decrease
   d) $187,500 decrease

7) B Company Limited issued five hundred $1,000 10-year bonds at a discount at the
   beginning of year one. The bonds have a 10% interest rate and market rates are 12%.
   Interest is paid annually at the end of December. The carrying value of the bonds at the
   end of the second year is:
   a) $450,322
   b) $443,496
   c) $500,000
   d) $484,685

8) On September 30, A Company Limited issued 3-year bonds with $1 million face
   value for $1.025 million. The bonds were dated June 30 and 10% interest due semi-
   annually on June 30 and December 31. Which of the following statements about the
   bonds is true?
   a) The bonds were issued at a discount because the market interest rate was >10%.
   b) The bonds were issued at a premium because the market interest rate was <10%.
   c) The bonds were issued at a premium due to accrued interest.
   d) The bonds were issued at a discount due to accrued interest.

9) A Company Limited pools its excess cash and invests in marketable securities for
    short-term returns. Last year, the company had to recognize a loss on the portfolio
    since total market cost of shares in the portfolio was less than total cost of the shares
    in the portfolio by $300. This amount is still in the valuation account at year-end. At
    year-end, the portfolio consisted of the following:

	Cost	Market
ABC company shares	$1,050	1,150
DEF company shares	1,000	1,500
GHI company shares	1,000	400

Calculate the gain or loss that should be recognized on valuation of the portfolio at year-end.

a) $600 loss
b) $300 loss
c) $300 gain
d) Under $0

10) B Company Limited has shares that are classified as temporary investments on the December 31 balance sheet. The shares were purchased last year at $400,000 and are currently valued by the market at $100,000 (on December 31). B has decided to keep the shares for a long-term investment and, therefore, plans to classify them as long-term investments. It is felt that the shares will recover in value to at least $250,000 in that period. Just before the financial statements are issued, the share value plummets to $50,000. What should the shares be valued at in the December 31 balance sheet?

a) $100,000
b) $50,000
c) $400,000
d) $250,000

SOLUTIONS TO MULTIPLE CHOICE QUESTIONS

1) c) Investments must be capable of reasonably prompt liquidation. In this case, this is not necessarily true. If there is no market, then it may be difficult to find a buyer. B) would be classified as short-term, even though it is a subsidiary since management intent right from the beginning was to dispose of the asset as soon as possible (HB1590.12).

2) d) the existence of significance influence is the key factor here, regardless of the percent ownership. Note also that the shares must be voting.

3) a) Although in most cases, dividend income is recorded as income and, therefore, does not change the investment account on the balance sheet, care should be taken to isolate dividends received in excess of the investor's pro-rata share of post-acquisition earnings. These are recorded as a reduction of the amount of the investment (HB 3050.02(c)) and are sometimes referred to loosely as "liquidating dividends" as they are seen as a return of the capital invested.

4) c) • Paid   = $3,000,000
       30% × 9,000,000   =   2,700,000
                                    300,000
                                 ÷ 20 years
                                     15,000
                           amortization

- Income   =   400,000
-                             $\times$ 30%
-                             120,000
- 120,000 − 15,000   =   105,000

5) b) The investment income would be based on the dividends as follows: $300,000 $\times$ 30% = $90,000. The purchase price discrepancy is ignored as is the earnings of B.

6) c) Since the asset would be accounted for as a temporary investment, investment income would be 30% of the dividends = $90,000. In this case, however, as a temporary investment, the investment would be written down under the LCM rule.

       3,000,000 − 2,700,000

     =   300,000

          90,000   (dividends)

        210,000   net decrease

7) a) $500,000 $\times$ .32197 + $50,000 $\times$ 5.65022   = $443,496

     $443,496 $\times$ 12% = $53,220; $53,220 − 50,000 =   3,220

                                                   $446,716

     $446,716 $\times$ 12% = $53,606 − 50,000   =   3,606

                                                $450,322   at the end of
                                                           second year

8) c) The extra $25,000 represents accrued interest ($1,000,000 $\times$ 10% $\times$ 3/12) since the bonds were dated June 30 but issued September 30.

9) c) The LCM rule is applied on the whole portfolio as evidenced by the way it was calculated last year—GAAP gives a choice however; the same method must be applied from year to year. Based on this, there is no gain or loss for the current year as they offset each other; however, since there is still an allowance of $300 from last year that is not needed, this may be taken into income.

10) a) $100,000 is the value since the shares must be valued at LCM prior to reclassification. This becomes the new cost base. The decline in value after a year end is a Type II subsequent event, which management may wish to disclose in the notes.

SHORT PROBLEMS

1) Purpose: To illustrate the journal entries under the cost method.

Werner Limited (WL) purchased 20% of the voting common shares of Wonder Incorporated (WI) for $3.4 million. WI is a major distributor for the products produced by WL. The net book value of WI at the time was $15 million and the fair market value of the net assets was $17 million (the excess being attributable to equipment with a remaining useful life of five years). For the current year, WI earned $1 million in profits, $700,000 since the date of acquisition. WI also paid out $500,000 in dividends. The market value of the shares at year-end is $3 million.

Required

Prepare the journal entries for WL relating to the investment for the year. Assume the cost method is appropriate.

2) Purpose: To illustrate the accounting for a liquidating dividend.

Assume the same information as in 1 except that the dividend was $900,000.

Required

Prepare the journal entry for WL to record the dividend received from WI.

3) Purpose: To illustrate accounting for the investment under the equity method.

Assume the same information as in 1; however, assume further that WL was able to appoint two people to the five-member Board of Directors of WI and that it was agreed that a senior manager from WL be transferred to WI for a two-year work term.

Required

Prepare the journal entries for WL for the year.

4) Purpose: To illustrate the calculation of interest revenue on bonds using straight-line amortization.

Bondex Limited (BL) acquired 10-year bonds on January 1, 2002 for $196,000 plus accrued interest (face value $200,000). The bonds bear interest at 10% and market interest is 10.2%. Interest is payable semi-annually on June 1 and December 1. The bonds will mature in 10 years.

Required

Prepare the journal entries to account for the bonds for the year-ended December 31, 2002. Assume straight-line amortization.

5) Purpose: To illustrate accounting for a bond on sale.

Assume that the bond mentioned in 4 is sold on January 31, 2003 for $198,000 including interest. The transaction costs were $500.

Required

Calculate the gain or loss on sale and prepare the journal entry to record the sale.

SOLUTIONS TO SHORT PROBLEMS

1) To record the investment:

Long-term investments	$3,400,000	
Cash		3,400,000

Based on the information given, we will assume that this is a long-term investment since WI is a distributor of WL products. It is therefore likely that WL management consciously made this investment for the purposes of having some influence over the decisions made by WI.

To record the dividend received during the year:

Cash	$100,000	
Investment income		100,000

This is not a liquidating dividend since post-acquisition earnings of $700,000 exceed the dividends of $500,000. The dividend is recorded as dividend income since the cost method is being used.

Since this is a long-term investment, there is no need to write down the investment at year-end, even though the fair market value is less than the book value by $400,000. What we are looking for in long-term investments are declines in value that are other than temporary. In this case, a decline in value during the year is seen as temporary since the value of long-term investments is usually assessed in terms of a three to four-year time frame (i.e., if the market has been below cost for three to four years, this might be considered a decline in value that is other than temporary).

If this had been a temporary investment, it would have been revalued since GAAP requires temporary investments to be booked at the LCM. The journal entry would have been:

Loss on investment	$400,000	
Investment allowance (B/S)		400,000

2) To record dividends:

Cash	$180,000 (See 1 below)	
Dividend income		140,000
Long-term investment		40,000 (See 2 below)

(1) $900,000 × 20%
(2) dividend received $900,000 × 20% = $180,000
    less % of post-acquisition earnings
    $700,000 × 20%   140,000
    = Liquidating dividend $ 40,000

3) To record the investment:

| Long-term investment | $3,400,000 | |
| Cash | | 3,400,000 |

Again, this is recorded as a long-term investment for the same reasons as 1. That WL has been able to appoint two members to the Board of Directors and also has placed a senior manager in WI further support this classification.

To accrue earnings:

| Long-term investment | $140,000 (See 1 below) | |
| Equity pickup or investment income | | 140,000 |

(1) $700,000 × 20%

Only WL's share of earnings since the date of acquisition is accrued.

To record dividends:

| Cash | $100,000 | |
| Long-term investment | | 100,000 |

The dividend reduces the investment account. It is not booked as income again since it has already been booked as income when earnings were accrued.

To record amortization of the difference paid for the shares over the net book value of the company:

| Equity pickup or investment income | $80,000 | |
| Long-term investment | | 80,000 |

First, a purchase price equation must be prepared:

Amount paid	$3,400,000	
Net book value $15,000,000 × 20%	3,000,000	
	$ 400,000	
Attributable to		
FMV>NBV		
($17-$15) × 20%	400,000	/ 5 years = $80,000*
Goodwill	-0-	

* Since the assets have a remaining life of five years, the difference will be amortized to income of WL over the five-year period. The journal entry to book this has been recorded separately above; however, it is often combined with the entry to accrue the earnings (booked earlier).

4) To record the bond purchase:
January 1, 2002

Long-term investment in bonds	$200,000	
Accrued interest receivable	1,667 (See 1 below)	
Deferred discount		4,000
Cash		197,667

(1) $200,000 \times 10\% / 12$ months

The deferred discount is often grouped with the investment account on the balance sheet.

To accrue interest to interest pay date:
May 31, 2002

Accrued interest receivable	$8,333	
Interest revenues		8,333

$200,000 \times 10\% \times 5/12$ months

This interest could be accrued monthly.

To record receipt of interest:
June 1, 2002

Cash	$10,000	
Accrued interest receivable		10,000

$1,667 + $8,333

To accrue interest to November 30, 2002:

Accrued interest receivable	$10,000	
Interest revenues		10,000

$200,000 \times 10\% \times 6/12$

To record receipt of interest:
December 1, 2002

Cash	$10,000	
Accrued interest receivable		10,000

To accrue interest to year-end:
December 31, 2002

Accrued interest receivable	$1,667	
Interest revenues		1,667

To book bond discount amortization:

Deferred discount	400	
Interest revenues		400

$4,000/10$ years $= 400$

This results in interest revenues of $20,400, which is a 10.2% yield. This yield approximates the market interest rates since the bond was priced to achieve this yield.

5) To record the sale of the bond:

Cash	$197,500	(See 1 below)
Discount	3,600	(See 2 below)
Loss on disposal	2,267	(See 5 below)
Accrued interest receivable	1,667	
Interest income	33	(See 3 below)
Interest income	1,667	(See 4 below)
Long-term investments	200,000	

(1) $198,000 − $500 transactions costs
(2) $4,000 − $400 amortization booked to December 31, 2002
(3) Amortization of discount to January 31 = $4,000/10 years × 1/12 months (for January)
(4) $200,000 × 10% × 1/12 months
(5) Investment at NBV @ January 31, 2003 = $200,000

Discount at amortized value	=	(3,567)
Accrued interest to January 31, 2003	=	3,334
		199,767
Proceeds less costs		(197,500)
Loss		$2,267

The interest could have been accrued separately to January 31 and the discount could have also been amortized to this date (i.e., in separate entries). If these two entries had been booked separately prior to the disposal, the journal entry would have been:

Cash	$197,500	
Deferred discount	3,567	
Loss	2,267	
Accrued interest receivable		3,334
Long-term investment		200,000

CASES

1) ALUWAHLIA LIMITED

Aluwahlia Limited (AL) was a conservative company, run by conservative people. Being very profitable, the company often had excess cash. Normally, the cash was invested in low-risk bank term deposits until it was needed. This helped maximize returns on the funds.

In 2002, Nancy, the controller, suggested that a greater return could be earned by investing in equity shares. She had been watching the stock market for the last six months and knew of just the company to invest in. Company A's share price had doubled over the last two years and Nancy felt that this would be a good investment in which to place excess cash, at least in the short to mid-term. She convinced the other managers, who grudgingly accepted the idea after Nancy criticized their overly conservative style of running the company.

When the shares were purchased, at the beginning of January, management hoped to hold the shares for only six months since the money was needed for an expansion project. Twenty percent of the outstanding shares of Company A were purchased, entitling AL to appoint one out of four members of the Board of Directors. Nancy decided not to bother since the investment strategy was a short-term one.

During the year, the price of the stock plummeted well below the purchase price ($750,000 below) after Company A reported heavy losses of $5 million. These were the first losses reported by Company A in the past decade. Nancy was shocked since this company had previously been a stellar performer.

When it came time to sell, Nancy was not prepared to take the losses and decided to hang on to the shares. Reports indicated that the stock price would likely recover within the next two to five years since Company A was in the process of developing new products that would revolutionize the industry that they were in.

Nancy was not sure whether the other managers had been following the stock prices and was looking for some way to soften the blow. She had to present an income statement to them at the next management meeting.

REQUIRED:

Adopt the role of Nancy and determine how the investment should be accounted for.

2) BERKSHIRE HATHAWAY INC.—www.berkshirehathaway.com

Berkshire Hathaway Inc. (BHI) is a U.S. holding company with several subsidiaries that engage in a variety of business activities, the most prominent of which is the property and casualty insurance industry. The company was taken over in 1964 (when the share price was $19 U.S. per share) by Warren Buffet, now one of the richest men in the world. The shares now trade in the $60,000 range (per share U.S.$).

The company holds significant investments as is usual for the insurance industry. Premiums are collected from customers and the company insures these customers against future losses. Therefore, the company receives significant amounts of cash upfront, which it may or may not have to pay out later, should there be losses. The company invests these funds with the objective of saving sufficient funds to cover future losses and make a reasonable profit.

Through judicious investing, BHI has been able to make superior returns on these investments and thus increase the value of the company's shares. The debt on the balance sheet is not material to the company.

According to the notes to the statements, investments are recorded at market value and the unrealized gains and losses are recorded as a separate component of shareholders equity. For the year-ended 2000, the equity securities were carried at $37,619 million (out of $135,792 million total assets) and the unrealized gain on these investments was $27,217 million. The latter was booked as a separate component of shareholders' equity.

REQUIRED:

Adopt the role of a Canadian investor and comment on the accounting for the equity investments and unrealized gains.

SOLUTIONS TO CASES

1)ALUWAHLIA LIMITED

Overview

It is not clear whether GAAP is a constraint. The stakeholders of the financial statements will include the managers and they will want to objectively assess the investment performance. The investment was not a good decision and since Nancy effectively forced the others into making this investment, she might want to present the impact on the financial statements in the least negative manner.

Analysis and Recommendations

The issue is how to account for the investment, as a temporary investment or a long-term one.

Temporary:

The shares are readily marketable since they trade on the stock exchange and the investment was made to maximize the return on excess cash. Therefore, this would seem to support treating it as a temporary investment. However, this would mean that the company would have to take a write-down or loss on the investment of $750,000.

Long-term:

Although the shares were originally purchased with the intent of disposing of them in the short run, Nancy is now reluctant to dispose of them since then the loss will be realized. Reports show that the price of the stock will recover within the next two to five years indicating that in order to recover the investment, the strategy would be to hold on to the shares in the longer term. Nancy would have to convince the other managers first, however.

If the shares were treated as long-term investments, the issue arises as to whether the cost method or equity method should be used. The percentage ownership would indicate that either could be used and the issue would be whether there was significant influence. Since AL has the right to appoint a member to the board, this might indicate that significant influence is present; however, it has not exercised this right to date. There is no other evidence that AL has played an active role in the affairs of Company A, nor that it has influenced key investing, operating, or financing decisions.

If the equity method is used, AL will have to accrue its share of the losses incurred to date (i.e., 20% of $5 million). This would have a more negative impact on the income statement than writing the investment down.

Either way, an assessment would have to be made as to whether the decline in value is other than temporary. Because of the profitable history, the bright future, and the fact that the stock price has only recently been depressed, the decline would likely be considered temporary.

In conclusion, the least offensive presentation would result from treating the investment as a long-term investment using the cost method. Under this method, the operating losses need not be accrued and the investment need not be written down.

Since this happened in the same reporting period, this "unofficial" policy change would be allowed. If a year-end had occurred shortly after the acquisition, and the investment was accounted for as a temporary investment, the switch to long-term would be more complex.

2) BERKSHIRE HATHAWAY INC.

Overview

The company is basically in the insurance business, deriving revenues from insurance premiums. These premiums are invested to cover potential future losses. Because of judicious investing, the investments have appreciated in value significantly, such that market is far in excess of cost. The investments are a significant portion of total assets and the gain or appreciation is very material. U.S. GAAP is a constraint since the shares are publicly traded in the United States.

The statements are used primarily by the shareholders of the company that appear to be long-term investors. The debt on the books is not significant to the company. As a Canadian investor, I might be interested in Canadian GAAP and how it would affect the statements so that I could make comparisons between BHI and other Canadian companies.

Analysis

The issue is one of **measurement/valuation** of the investments and **recognition** of the gains. In Canada, long-term investments are generally carried **at cost** unless there is a **loss in value that is other than temporary.** Therefore, these investments would be left at cost.

However, the company's **primary operations** are in the insurance industry. CICA HB 4210 deals with the **life insurance** industry, which allows for valuation of investments at **market (moving average market)** and calls for recognition of gains and losses in income.

However, since BHI is in the **property and casualty** industry, HB section 4210 does not apply directly. Yet since there is no section of property and casualty insurance we could look to section 4210 for guidance. Furthermore, looking at **basic principles,** the market values are more **relevant** than the cost. The shares are equity securities and have readily available market prices and, therefore, the information is **objective** and **verifiable.**

In the U.S., all marketable securities are valued at market. This is a significant difference between U.S. and Canadian GAAP. Furthermore, if the securities are available for sale but not part of the trading securities, the unrealized gains are booked as a separate component of shareholders' equity ("Other Comprehensive Income"). This serves two purposes. Firstly, since the investments are usually more of a long-term type, then it makes sense to defer recognition of short-term gains. Secondly, the gains are as yet unrealized and could potentially never be realized if the shares subsequently decline in value. Therefore, the deferral of recognition until the gains are indeed realized is **conservative.**

Conclusion

The shares are appropriately valued according to U.S. GAAP and the gains are appropriately deferred. This treatment is a significant departure from Canadian GAAP and more information would be required to convert the statements for comparison purposes with Canadian companies since the amounts involved are so material.

SELECTED SOLUTIONS FROM THE TEXTBOOK

EXERCISE 10-6 (10–15 MINUTES)

(a) December 31, 2001

Loss on Temporary Investments	1,400	
Investment Allowance		1,400

(b) During 2002

Cash	9,400	
Loss on Sale of Securities	600	
Temporary Investments		10,000

(c) December 31, 2002

Securities	Cost	Fair Value	Unrealized Gain/(Loss)
Kelowna Corp. shares	$20,000	$19,100	$ (900)
Barrie Corp. shares	20,000	20,500	500
Total of portfolio	$40,000	$39,600	(400)
Allowance account, before adjustment			(1,400)
Adjustment needed			($1,000)

Investment Allowance   1,000
    Investment Income—Gain   1,000

EXERCISE 10-13 (15–20 MINUTES)

(a)   June 30, 2001
Cash   42,500
    Dividend Income (50,000 shares × $0.85)   42,500

                December 31, 2001
Cash   42,500
    Dividend Income   42,500

No entry. A write-down is usually not recorded unless the decline in value is other than temporary.

Carrying value of investment $1,200,000
Market value: 50,000 shares × $27   1,350,000

(b)   June 30, 2001
Cash   42,500
    Long-term Investment in Kulikowski Share   42,500

                December 31, 2001
Cash   42,500
    Long-term Investment in Kulikowski Inc.   42,500

Long-term Investment in Kulikowski Inc.   146,000
    Investment Income (20% × $730,000)   146,000

(c)

	Cost Method	Equity Method
Balance Sheet, December 31, 2001		
Long-term investment in Kulikowski Inc.		
(market value $1,350,000)	$1,200,000	$1,261,000*
Income statement, 2001		
Dividend income	$85,000	0
Investment income	0	$146,000

*$1,200,000 + $146,000 − $42,500 − $42,500

EXERCISE 10-14 (20–25 MINUTES)

(a)   Long-term Investment in Chow Corp.   400,000
          Cash   400,000

(b)   Cost $400,000
       Book values:
          Assets $800,000
          Liabilities   100,000
                                                  700,000
                                          ×   40%   280,000
          Excess $120,000

       Allocated
          Assets subject to amortization
          [($680,000 − $600,000 × 40%] $ 32,000
          Unrecorded intangible assets*   88,000
                                                              $120,000

*It is assumed that the purchase price difference is attributable to intangible assets with a useful life of 10 years. Alternatively, it could be assumed that the $88,000 represents unrecorded Goodwill which is no longer subject to amortization, but rather is tested on an annual basis for impairment.

          Cash   50,000
             Long-term Investment in Chow Corp.   50,000
                ($125,000 × .40)

          Long-term Investment in Chow Corp.   64,000
             Investment Income ($160,000 × .40)   64,000

          Investment Income   12,800
             Long-term Investment in Chow Corp.   12,800
                Undervalued amortizable assets
                   ($32,000 ÷ 8) $ 4,000
                Unrecorded intangible assets
                   ($88,000 ÷ 10)   8,800
                                                              $12,800

(c)   Loss from Investment (extraordinary)*   12,000
       Long-term Investment in Chow Corp   64,000
          Investment Income ($190,000 × .40)   76,000

       *$30,000 × .40 = $12,000

       Investment Income   12,800
          Long-term Investment in Chow Corp.   12,800

PROBLEM 10-6

(a)   February 1

Long-term Investment in Bonds	500,000	
Interest Income*	20,000	
Cash		520,000

*(4/12 × .12 × $500,000 = $20,000)

April 1

Cash	30,000	
Interest Income		30,000

($500,000 × .12 6/12)

July 1

Long-term Investment in Bonds	200,000	
Interest Income*	1,500	
Cash		201,500

*(1/12 × .09 × $200,000 = $1,500)

September 1

Cash	104,000	
[($100,000 × 99%) + ($100,000 × .12 × 5/12)]		
Loss on Sale of Securities	1,000	
Long-term Investment in Bonds		100,000
($500,000 × 1/5)		
Interest Income (5/12 × .12 × $100,000 = $5,000)		5,000

October 1

Cash	24,000	
[($500,000 − $100,000 × .12 × 6/12]		
Interest Income		24,000

December 1

Cash ($200,000 × 9% × 6/12)	9,000	
Interest Income		9,000

December 31

Interest Receivable	13,500	
Interest Income		13,500

     (3/12 × $400,000 × .12 = $12,000)
     (1/12 × $200,000 × .09 = $1,500)
     ($12,000 + $1,500 = $13,500)

(Note: Some may debit Interest Receivable at date of purchase instead of Interest Income. This procedure is correct, assuming that when the cash is received for the interest, an appropriate credit to Interest Receivable is recorded.)

(b)   All the entries would be the same except the account title Temporary Investments would be used instead of Long-term Investment in Bonds. In addition, temporary investments would be valued at LCM at year-end, so an adjusting entry would be made if cost exceeded the market value.

ACQUISITION AND DISPOSITION OF TANGIBLE CAPITAL ASSETS

Acquisition

- Acquisition costs: land, buildings, equipment
- Self-constructed assets
- Interest during construction

Other "Cost" Issues

- Cash discounts
- Deferred contracts
- Lump sum
- Share issuance
- Nonmonetary exchanges
- Exchanges considered monetary
- Contributions
- Investment tax credit
- Other valuation methods

Costs Subsequent to Acquisition

- Additions
- Improvements and replacements
- Rearrangement and reinstallation
- Repairs

Dispositions

- Sale
- Involuntary conversion
- Donations
- Miscellaneous problems

chapter 11

ACQUISITION AND DISPOSITION OF TANGIBLE CAPITAL ASSETS

PERSPECTIVE—ACQUISITION AND DISPOSAL OF PROPERTY, PLANT AND EQUIPMENT

Tangible capital assets (known as property, plant, and equipment) is a fairly straightforward topic, with the most contentious issues relating to subsequent additions, replacements, and repairs. The reason that these are the most controversial is that professional judgement must be applied in determining what to capitalize and what to expense. Amortization is covered separately in Chapter 12.

INSIGHTS

Capital intensive industries invest significant funds in capital assets and, therefore, recognition and measurement issues take on greater importance in these industries.

STUDY STEPS

1. Understanding Property, Plant, and Equipment within a Business Context

Property, plant, and equipment (PP&E) are **tangible assets** that are **used to generate income**. This latter factor differentiates property, plant and equipment from inventory, which is **held for resale in the ordinary course of business**. Generally, property, plant, and equipment are used up or wear out over time and must be replaced, except for land, which presumably retains its value over time and would not normally get "used up."

> **PP&E are used to generate income while inventory is held for resale in the ordinary course of business. This is a key distinction as PP&E are amortized, while inventory is not.**
> ***Tip!***

From time to time, money must be spent on maintaining the revenue-generating capacity of the assets, and they must be safeguarded to reduce risk of loss from fire, theft, etc. Even though certain assets may last a specific period of time (**economic life**), the company might choose only to use the asset for a shorter period (**useful life**). At the end of the asset's useful life, there may be a **residual value**, i.e., an amount that the company will realize through sale or disposition. This residual value is normally net of any additional costs that the company would have to incur to dispose of the asset.

> **Tip!** Life may be defined as either useful or economic. Economic life is the life of the asset, whereas useful life represents the period over which the company intends to use the asset. This will be equal to or less than the economic life.

> **Tip!** Residual value is the value of the asset at the end of its useful life. Therefore, there is a residual value at the end of the useful life and a salvage value at the end of the economic life

Barter transactions relating to PP&E

PP&E are considered to be nonmonetary assets since their value is not fixed in terms of dollars, i.e., the values will change over time. If a company trades another nonmonetary asset for some PP&E, a barter transaction occurs and the company faces the challenge of assigning a transaction cost to the transaction. This topic was discussed in Chapter 6 of the Study Guide and the accounting issues have already been analysed in Chapter 6. Included in the problems are two that deal with nonmonetary transactions that reinforce the material introduced in Chapter 6.

STUDY STEPS

2. Understanding How Property, Plant, and Equipment Related Issues Fit into the Financial Reporting Model and Conceptual Framework— Analysis and Critical Thinking

The main issues here are **what to include in the cost** of the asset, how to **measure** it and how to account for **subsequent repairs and maintenance.** Below is a chart to assist in this analysis. There is also an exhibit showing relevant criteria, definitions and issues.

Exhibit 11-1: Relevant criteria, definitions, and issues

Business perspective: Capital assets are often the largest asset on the balance sheet. They require ongoing expenditures to safeguard them, repair and maintain their capacity, and their cost must be recovered from future net cash flows for the business to be viable.

	How it relates to PP&E	Relevant criteria/ definitions/terms	Topic specific analysis— how it should be	What makes the analysis challenging—how it is
Measurement	• net book value • self-constructed assets	• **historical cost** • **betterments vs repairs and maintenance** • **lower of cost and net recoverable amount**	• include any cost incurred to **get the asset ready for intended use** • capitalize any costs incurred to **enhance or extend the capacity/life of the asset** • future cleanup costs and site restoration costs should be accrued if an **obligation exists due to law, contract or management policy** • only write down asset value if **unable to recover unam. cost from est. net future cash flows**	• PJ required for capitalization of indirect costs such as interest—allowable if company policy and asset not yet in use • very difficult to determine whether costs subsequently incurred are betterments or maintenance—key is whether asset enhanced beyond original estimates • for site restoration and cleanup costs management policy to cleanup establishes a liability and therefore this section is non neutral as it may induce some companies not to formalize any plans for cleanup

Presentation/ Disclosure	• how to present in balance sheet and note disclosures	• **full disclosure**
		• definition
		  - held for use
		  - continuing
		  - not intended
		    for sale
			• disclose cost, accumulated depreciation, and amortization method used; also, NBV of assets not being amortized, amount of amortization and any writedowns	

Prepared by Irene Wiecek
©2002 John Wiley & Sons Canada, Ltd

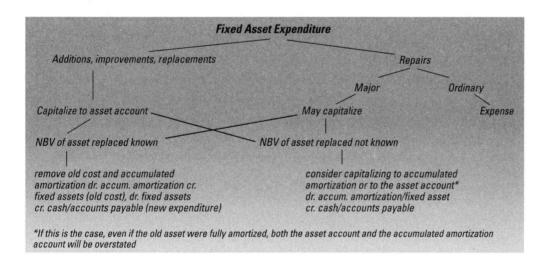

Fixed Asset Expenditure

Additions, improvements, replacements — Repairs (Major, Ordinary)

Capitalize to asset account — May capitalize — Expense

NBV of asset replaced known — NBV of asset replaced not known

remove old cost and accumulated amortization dr. accum. amortization cr. fixed assets (old cost), dr. fixed assets cr. cash/accounts payable (new expenditure)

consider capitalizing to accumulated amortization or to the asset account* dr. accum. amortization/fixed asset cr. cash/accounts payable

*If this is the case, even if the old asset were fully amortized, both the asset account and the accumulated amortization account will be overstated

Below are two decision trees to help with analysis of barter transactions and government assistance:

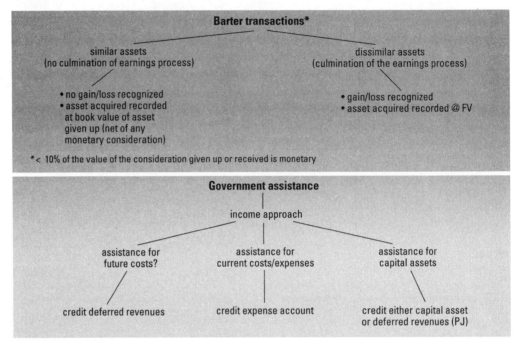

Barter transactions*

similar assets
(no culmination of earnings process)

- no gain/loss recognized
- asset acquired recorded at book value of asset given up (net of any monetary consideration)

dissimilar assets
(culmination of the earnings process)

- gain/loss recognized
- asset acquired recorded @ FV

* < 10% of the value of the consideration given up or received is monetary

Government assistance

income approach

assistance for future costs?

assistance for current costs/expenses

assistance for capital assets

credit deferred revenues

credit expense account

credit either capital asset or deferred revenues (PJ)

STUDY STEPS

3. Becoming Proficient in Calculations Relating to PP&E

There are few complex calculations or methods specific to this topic. One possible area relates to the potential capitalization of interest costs on self-constructed assets. There are several different ways to approach this and, in Canada, there are no set methods that are more acceptable than any others. Furthermore, the decision whether to capitalize interest or not is open to judgement. Therefore, this area is not dealt with in detail here. There are two problems included, however, that give examples of the calculations. See problems 4 (a) and (b).

MULTIPLE CHOICE QUESTIONS

1) Which of the following would not be charged to a capital asset account?
   a) cost which prolongs the service life of the asset
   b) cost of maintaining the normal operating condition of the assets
   c) cost which improves the quality of the asset's service
   d) cost which increases the useful life of the asset

(CGA adapted—FA1 Dec 1994)

2) Which of the following items would *not* be recorded as capital assets on the balance sheet?
   a) cars owned by IBM and used by senior executives
   b) used cars purchased by Turpin Motors and awaiting reconditioning before being assigned to their used car salespeople for use on company business
   c) old cars purchased by Mint Motors for parts in their automobile service department
   d) cars owned by Campbell Motors for lease on a daily, weekly or monthly basis

(CGA adapted—FA2 June 1995)

3) Which of the following should *not* be capitalized as capital assets?
   a) construction of an addition to the company's warehouse
   b) replacement of an old asphalt tile roof with a new clay tile roof, when the net book value of the old roof can be determined
   c) replacement of an old engine with a new engine of superior quality and performance potential, when the net book value of the old engine cannot be determined with any degree of reliability
   d) none of the above
   (CGA adapted—FA2 June 1995)

4) A capital asset should not be written down unless which of the following scenario exists: (Assume that the company intends to continue to use the asset in operations.)
   a) historical cost exceeds market value
   b) historical cost of the asset is no longer recoverable from future net cash flows
   c) the cost to replace the asset is significantly lower than the historical cost
   d) the market value of the asset has been below the historical cost for a number of years

5) Provision should be made for future removal and restoration costs where certain conditions exist. Which of the following choices would not mandate the accrual of a provision?
   a) the existence of a law that sets a standard for future restoration of a site
   b) the company has contracted with another party to provide for future restoration of the property
   c) company policy that states that the company is a good corporate citizen that plans to lean up any environmental problems that they create
   d) intent by corporate management to restore the site in the future

6) When assets are exchanged, no gain or loss would be recognized on the disposition of the asset given up under which of the following circumstances?
   a) the assets are dissimilar
   b) the assets are similar and cash consideration greater than 10% of the fair value of the total consideration is received
   c) the assets are dissimilar and no monetary consideration is received
   d) the assets are similar and cash consideration less than 10% of the fair value of the total consideration is given up

7) Interest costs are normally expensed as a period cost. There are certain situations in which the interest may be capitalized as part of the cost of an asset. Assuming that it was the company's policy to capitalize interest, which project below would not qualify for interest capitalization?
   a) interest on funds borrowed to complete income producing property where a substantial number of tenants have already moved in
   b) interest on funds borrowed to develop vacant land
   c) interest on funds borrowed for building being constructed for company's own use
   d) interest on funds borrowed to update obsolete manufacturing facility

8) Cormier Ltd. and Lafleur Ltd. exchanged equipment (deemed to be dissimilar for accounting purposes) with fair values in excess of carrying amounts. In addition, Cormier paid Lafleur to compensate for the difference in equipment value. As a consequence of the exchange, Cormier recognizes:
   a) a gain equal to the difference between the fair value and carrying amount of the equipment given up

b) a gain determined by the proportion of cash paid to the total consideration
c) a loss determined by the proportion of cash paid to the total consideration
d) neither a gain nor a loss

(CGA adapted FA2 March 1994)

9) For self-constructed assets, which of the following costs are generally not permitted by the *CICA Handbook* to be included as part of the cost? (Assume that funds to build the asset were taken out of excess cash.)
a) direct material costs and direct labour costs
b) cost of funds employed
c) insurance and property taxes on the asset being constructed
d) net revenue or expense derived from the asset prior to substantial completion

10) If the company's policy is to capitalize interest on self-constructed assets, the capitalization period is as follows:
a) from the date the funds are borrowed to the date that all aspects of the construction are complete
b) from the date the funds are borrowed to the date that the asset is substantially ready for use
c) from the date that construction begins to the date that all aspects of the construction are complete
d) from the date that construction begins to the date that the asset is substantially ready for use

SOLUTIONS TO MULTIPLE CHOICE QUESTIONS

1) b) The cost of maintaining the normal operating conditions are treated as repairs and maintenance expense since they do not contribute to any increase in value of the asset beyond its original life.

2) c) Since these are really part of inventory or supplies as opposed to capital assets it would not be recorded. They will be incorporated into other cars in the service department and sold for a profit or markup along with the service.

3) d) All of the choices from (a) to (c) should be capitalized, even where the old costs are not known. The latter may result in the capital asset account including an asset twice. However, the net book value would be properly stated assuming that the old asset was close to or fully amortized. The key factor is that all of the items do indeed add value to the asset beyond its original value. The clay tile roof would presumably prolong the useful life of the building. Replacements are generally capitalizable.

4) b) Historical cost is allocated to revenues through the process of amortization. Therefore, if future revenues are less than the depreciated historical cost, this will result in future losses. Accordingly, these losses should be recorded now as a write down of the asset. In all of the other cases, the market value is irrelevant since the company does not intend to sell the asset.

5) d) Company intent that is not part of a formal company policy would not mandate accrual of the costs. Many things could change in the future, including turnover of management. In the other cases, the costs would be accrued assuming that they were measurable since these conditions are stipulated in the *CICA Handbook* and since they either establish a legal, contractual, or formalized corporate obligation.

6) d) The asset received must either be dissimilar, or cash or monetary consideration greater than 10% of the total consideration must be received. Under (b), this is the case and therefore (b) would be considered a monetary transaction.

7) a) The key here is that the building is substantially ready for use and is being used by a number of tenants. Interest capitalization would cease when the asset is substantially ready for intended use.

8) a) Since the assets are dissimilar, there is a culmination of the earnings process and a gain is recognized. The cash paid is irrelevant to this analysis.

9) b) These costs were not incurred specifically for the project (*Handbook* Section 3061 par. .23 states that the costs should be "directly attributable"). This is an interpretation of the *Handbook* that is supported in general practice. Note that any incidental revenues and expenses prior to the asset being substantially ready for use are capitalized (*Handbook* Section 3061 par. .25).

10) d) Three conditions must be present for the capitalization to begin: the funds must be borrowed, the interest costs incurred and the funds must be spent on the construction process. Capitalization ceases on substantial completion.

SHORT PROBLEMS

1) *Purpose:* To demonstrate how cost is determined for purchased assets.

Penex Incorporated (PI) has recently purchased some vacant land and a building on another piece of land. The building will be used to house the head office and administration staff, whereas the land will be held for speculation purposes. A fair amount of work was performed on the land and building prior to the head office and administration staff moving in.

The following costs were incurred in connection with the two purchases, which were done separately.

Building and land:	
Purchase price	
Land	$5,000,000
Building	2,000,000
Legal costs	10,000
Commissions	500,908
New parking lot	975,000
Landscaping	50,000
New heating/air	
conditioning equipment	125,000
Demolition of parking garage	87,000
Land:	
Purchase price	$4,000,000
Property taxes	100,000
(incurred after the purchase)	

Required

Calculate how much should be in the following general ledger accounts and any other accounts that you think should be included in the general ledger relating to these transactions. Explain your allocations.

- Land
- Building

2) Purpose: To demonstrate accounting for barter or nonmonetary transactions.

The same year, PI purchased a new press for its manufacturing operations. Instead of paying cash, they were able to trade finished goods inventory for the new press. PI considered itself lucky to be able to barter since it would have had to borrow the funds at 15% if it had paid cash. Since the other company did not have the space for the inventory now, the inventory would be manufactured and delivered at the end of the year. The new press was delivered immediately. Production and raw material costs were expected to rise during the year and sales prices for the inventory would be set to increase correspondingly (i.e., 6% by the end of the year). Details of the transaction were as follows:

- Cost of inventory at date of transaction $236,000.
- FMV of inventory at date of transaction $435,678.

Required

Prepare the journal entries to record the transaction at the transaction date and at year-end. Show any calculations and explain your answer where necessary.

3) Purpose: To illustrate a non-monetary transaction where the earnings process is not culminated.

At the beginning of 2002, Tradex Limited (TL) decided to trade in its fleet of luxury cars that it had been using for its sales personnel. In return, TI purchased a fleet of mid-size economy models which were more in keeping with the times (recession). TI reasoned that the economy cars would make a better impression on TI's customers who were also cost cutting. Since TI had downscaled to cheaper models, it was a straight trade with no extra money required to purchase the new cars.

The net book value of the luxury cars was $130,000 whereas their fair value was higher, being $180,000.

Required

Prepare the journal entries to record the trade in. Explain.

4) Purpose: To demonstrate accounting for an asset built by a company for its own use.

Build-all Limited (BL) is in the construction industry and builds commercial buildings and warehouses. In 2002, BL was growing so quickly that they needed new premises for expansion. They decided to build a new warehouse for themselves. To that end, they obtained financing from the bank at 13%. The funds ($2 million) were advanced on February 28, 2002 and construction began March 20, 2002 after unanticipated delays. Excess funds were deposited in short-term deposits at 10%. The bulk of the material was purchased on March 20 and cost $1.2 million. Other expenditures were as follows: $250,000 June 30; $250,000 September 30. It is a policy of BL to capitalize interest.

Required

Calculate the amount of interest that should be capitalized as of December 31, 2002 under the following assumptions:

(a) Using the "avoidable interest concept."

(b) Assuming that BL takes the position that the entire loan was taken out specifically for this project and, therefore, all interest incurred (and interest revenue earned) is directly related to the asset and should be capitalized.

SOLUTIONS TO SHORT PROBLEMS

1) Building and land:		Building	Land	Other	
Purchase price					
Land	$5,000,000		$5,000,000		
Building	2,000,000	$2,000,000			
Legal costs	10,000	2,857	7,143		(See 1 below)
Commissions	500,908	143,115	357,793		(See 1 below)
New parking lot	975,000			$975,000	(See 2 below)
Landscaping	50,000			50,000	(See 2 below)
New heating/air conditioning equipment	125,000			125,000	(See 3 below)
Demolition of parking garage	87,000		87,000		(See 4 below)
Land:					
Purchase price	4,000,000		4,000,000		
Property taxes	100,000		100,000		(See 5 below)

Totals		
Building	$2,145,972	
Land		$9,551,936
Land improvements		$1,025,000
Equipment		$125,000

(1) Legal costs and commissions should be allocated between land and building since they apply to the entire purchase. The method of allocation is anything reasonable. Here, it has been done based on FV building/purchase price ($2 million/$7 million) and FV land/purchase price ($5 million/$7 million).

(2) These two should be segregated from land since both the parking lot and the land-scaping have limited lives and should therefore be amortized.

(3) The equipment should also be segregated from the building since it likely has a different life over which it should be amortized. Note that the original cost of the old equipment theoretically should be removed from the building account; since this cost is not known, this would not be possible. Chances are that if it needs replacing, it was fully amortized.

(4) The demolition is considered part of land since it is a cost incurred for the purposes of getting the land ready for use.

(5) The property taxes could be expensed as a period expense if they were incurred after the purchase. However, an argument may also be made for capitalization since the land is held for speculative purposes not yet generating revenues. Therefore, since the cost relates directly to the land, it might make sense to capitalize it until it starts producing revenues (perhaps not until sale) in order to match costs with revenues.

2) Normally, a barter transaction would be accounted for at the FV of the asset given up as consideration, provided that for the asset given up it could be considered that the earnings process had been culminated. In this case, inventory is given up or sold for equipment. Since the asset purchased or taken back is different in nature from the asset given up or sold, and since the corresponding risks and rewards of ownership are different, this would indicate that the earnings process had been culminated.

Therefore, FV would be appropriate for the cost base for the equipment, and the inventory would be considered sold at the FV resulting in a profit. However, the situation is complicated a bit since the consideration (i.e., the inventory) will not be given up until the end of the year. The question arises as to whether the amount should be discounted.

Furthermore, which FV do we use to record the transaction, FV at the date of the transaction or FV at the date that the inventory will be delivered (i.e., the end of the year)? This is not an executory contract since the other party has completed its obligation under the deal (i.e., to deliver the equipment immediately). Only PI has an outstanding obligation under the deal. Since PI has taken delivery of the asset it must now record an asset and an obligation to pay at the transaction date.

Assume that discounting is appropriate since the amount would be discounted if PI had given the other company a note to pay in cash at the end of the year. Also, assume that the relevant amounts are the actual production costs which have not yet been incurred (i.e., the future costs and the estimated future sales price). From a business perspective this would make sense as PI would be reluctant to give up the inventory at anything less than the sales price at the date of delivery of the inventory.

$435,678 \times 1.06 = \$461,819 =$ the sales price on the date of sale (year-end)

PV $461,819 for 1 year @ 15% = $401,582

To record the cost of the machine at delivery date (now):

Equipment	$401,582	
Accounts payable		401,582

To accrue interest at year-end on the accounts payable:

Interest expense	$60,237	
Accounts payable		60,237
($401,582 × 0.15)		

To record sale at year-end:

Accounts payable	461,819	
Sales		461,819
Cost of sales	250,160	
Inventory		250,160
($236,000 × 1.06)		

(This sale could not be recorded earlier since the risks and rewards of ownership would not pass until the goods were manufactured and delivered. Remember to treat these non-monetary transactions as two transactions, a sale and a purchase, and apply the corresponding principles to assist in determining the accounting treatment.)

Alternatively, the cost allocated to the equipment could be the FV of the equipment itself if it is decided that the FV of the consideration is too difficult to determine.

Note that a profit is recognized on the transaction of $461,819 − 250,160 − 60,237 = $151,422.

3) Since the luxury cars are being replaced by similar assets, (albeit cheaper models,) the earnings process has not been culminated with respect to the luxury cars traded in. The risks and rewards given up on the luxury cars are similar to the risks and rewards taken back on the economy models. Effectively there is no journal entry required since the new cost base for the economy models will be equal to the net book value of the luxury cars. No profit will be recognized on the disposal of the luxury cars either. Part of the reason for this is that FV cannot be objectively determined in this nonmonetary transaction.

4) (a) Using this concept, the amount of interest on the funds spent to date on the project should be calculated.

$1,200,000 × 286 days/365 days × 0.13	=	$122,235
250,000 × 184/365 × 0.13	=	16,384
250,000 × 92/365 × 0.13	=	8,192
Total		$146,811

Therefore, $146,811 would be capitalized and included as part of "Property, plant, and equipment under construction" on the balance sheet. The amount of interest capitalized should also be disclosed in the financial statement notes. The rest of the interest cost incurred and the interest revenues would likely be expensed under this concept.

(b) Under this assumption, all interest costs and revenues would be capitalized as follows:

Total interest expense $2,000,000 × 306/365 × 0.13   = $217,973
less: interest revenues on excess funds

$2,000,000 × 20/365 x 0.10 =	10,959	
800,000 × 102/365 x 0.10 =	22,356	
550,000 × 92/365 x 0.10 =	13,863	
300,000 × 92/365 x 0.10 =	7,562	
Total	$54,740	(54,740)
Net interest capitalized		$163,233

Note: Keep in mind that practice in Canada with respect to interest capitalization differs widely and that both of the above methods, and indeed perhaps others, are justifiable.

CASES

1) LAIDLE DISPOSAL LIMITED (PART 1)

Laidle Disposal Limited (LDL) is a small company that collects household garbage and disposes of it in a manner that is acceptable to the communities involved. The company has a fleet of trucks that pick up the garbage weekly. The garbage is then trucked to a local disposal site where it is dumped and then covered with topsoil. The disposal site is usually owned by LDL, having been purchased after the required permits for zoning have been obtained from government authorities.

This is the first year that LDL will be up and running and L.L. Laidle (L.L.), the president of the company, is deliberating on how he should account for the landfill sites (i.e., as inventory or fixed assets). The sites are purchased, filled with garbage, and ultimately sold as industrial land. The resale will be accompanied by a guarantee that no toxic materials are buried in the landfill.

Financial statements are used to obtain new contracts. Obtaining new contracts, as well as keeping old contracts, depends on competitive bidding, profile in the community, past work performance, financial stability, and adherence to strict environmental standards.

REQUIRED:

As an independent consultant to L.L., discuss the financial reporting issues and provide recommendations.

2) TELESAT CANADA—www.telesat.ca

Telesat is a national communications common carrier, providing telecommunications and broadcast distribution services throughout Canada and into the U.S. via its fifth generation Anik E satellites. In 1994, the company was owned by Alouette Telecommunications Inc., an alliance of provincial telephone companies and Spar Aerospace Limited. The Canadian radio-television and telecommunications commission, who, among other things, approves rate changes, regulates the company by the company for revenues.

Telesat is facing a great challenge in that the Canadian broadcasting industry is poised to enter a new technological era with the arrival of Digital Video Compression technology (DVC). With DVC, the amount of satellite capacity required to transmit information, is drastically reduced. Because of the capacity for DVC to erode Telesat's position in the market, Telesat has been closely monitoring the technology.

On January 20, 1994, two of the company's key income producing satellites, Anik E1 and Anik E2, experienced component failures, causing disruption in satellite transmissions to local television stations. As a result of the failures, most television sets in the transmitting area went black. Telesat was able to take corrective action and fully restore Anik E1 customer traffic the same day and by March 16, 1994, the date the 1993 financial statements were released, the company had restored nearly all of its customers' services back on satellite. This was done by using available capacity on Anik E1 and by accessing U.S. satellite capacity that was made available under restoral arrangements. However, although service had been restored, at the time of the statement issue, Anik E2 was still out of commission.

Telesat began developing a recovery plan for Anik E2 immediately after the disaster. Although not identified separately in the financial statements, the recovery plan would entail further expenditures. As a matter of fact, much of these would have already been expended by March 1994. Telesat stated that they were confident that the recovery plan would restore Anik E2 to operations within the year although this was by no means certain. Management stated that in the event that the satellite was restored, the operating life would be reduced by 10%.

According to the accounting policies, the satellites are amortized using an escalating charge method whereby amortization charges increase over time. The policy was put in place in 1993 and previously, the straight-line method had been used. According to the established accounting policies of the company, in the case of extraordinary failure of an operational satellite (like Anik E2), the unrecovered cost of the satellite (NBV) is still amortized over the estimated remaining life of the satellite immediately prior to the failure. This policy was discussed and accepted by the CRTC.

The balance sheet shows assets relating to satellites of $766 million gross ($615 million net of accumulated amortization) out of total assets of $1 billion. There were six satellites in operation in 1993. Loss before income taxes for 1993 was $34 million and included two significant charges:

- $12.9 million for employee severance packages resulting from restructuring
- $15.5 million write-down on loans receivable from another company

Without these two charges, the President noted in his report that although the company would still have a loss for 1993, the loss would be 25% less than the loss for 1992. He noted that he felt that the company had turned a corner and was on the road to recovery.

REQUIRED:

Adopt the role of the company controller. Analyse the financial reporting issues, noting alternative accounting and disclosure treatments.

SOLUTIONS TO CASES

1) LAIDLE DISPOSAL LIMITED (PART 1)

Overview

The financial statements will be used to obtain new contracts and users will focus on financial stability and adherence to environmental standards. Management will want the financial statements to show the company in the most favourable light (i.e., maximize profits and assets and minimize negative disclosures). The statements will likely be constrained by GAAP since the government will want reliable statements.

Analysis

Issue: Are the landfill sites inventory (in which case they do not have to be amortized) or are they fixed assets (in which case they must be amortized)?

Inventory vs. Fixed Assets:

To the extent that the land is purchased and always resold, likely at a profit, it could be deemed as inventory. On the other hand, the resale is incidental to the real reason for buying the land and that is to fill it up with waste. The process of filling it up with waste generates income, and, therefore, the land is purchased primarily to generate revenues. The resale is secondary. Many fixed assets are resold once their usefulness has ended.

Recommendation

It would therefore seem reasonable to treat the assets as fixed assets.

2) TELESAT CANADA

Overview

This case involves Telesat's main income producing assets—the satellites. Users would include (a) the alliance, who would be looking at Telesat's ongoing business potential, (b) the CRTC who would be looking at regulatory issues including the impact of a significant loss on the rates charged by Telesat for its services; and (c) competitors who may be looking for the monetary impact of the loss in net income and net assets. Investors would also be looking at these issues. GAAP would be a constraint in this case as the company has many users who would likely want GAAP statements for consistency and comparability.

Management might be biased towards presenting a picture where the problem has been resolved with little or no loss to the company. In his report to the shareholders, the president of the company had noted that the company had "turned a corner" and, therefore, he might not be anxious to record another heavy loss from the satellite.

Note also that there was significant exposure in the press; therefore, management might wish to downplay the issue or, alternatively, to counter any negative publicity. The business environment and the encroaching DVC technology might lead management to wish to present a strong front to users of the financial statements.

As the controller, the analysis should be critical and examine all potential alternatives. The impact of the accounting policies chosen on net income is also important.

Analysis and Recommendations

Valuation of the asset:

The satellite, as previously mentioned is a key asset, (satellite assets are >60% of total assets) and any loss in value would significantly increase the net loss perhaps resulting in a greater loss than in 1992.

The issue may be seen as a **subsequent event issue.** The event happened after year-end and, therefore, would likely be seen as a **type 2 event.** Since the asset is very **material** compared to total assets, and since it is a key income-producing asset, note disclosure would be important, focusing on the potential **impact on future earnings.**

This brings up a larger issue, that of the **valuation of** the asset. If the asset no longer has value, should it remain on the balance sheet, or, is this a **contingent loss?** The test for write-down of assets is a **recoverability test,** that is, the asset should only be written down if it can no longer be recovered from **future net cash flows** (HB Section 3061). The **market** value of the asset today does not factor into it. Interestingly, in this case, the accounting policy, which has been accepted by the CRTC and therefore may be considered to be typical **practice within the industry,** is that in the case of extraordinary failure, the asset would still continue to be amortized over the pre-existing remaining life. This would mean that the asset would not be written down. However, if the asset had **no value in terms of future**

revenue-producing capacity, it would not seem to make sense to leave it on the balance sheet since it would no longer meet the definition of an asset (**future value**, also, the company does not necessarily have **control** or access to the satellite).

The practice of continuing to amortize would make sense from the CRTC view since, generally, the CRTC allows revenues to be set to recover costs and, therefore, it might make sense from an accounting perspective if the test is a **recovery test.**

Also connected with this issue is the issue of how to treat the recovery costs. On the one hand, the costs may be seen as a **significant expenditure that would certainly add value** to the asset by making it useful and productive again. However, the HB states that for capitalization, the expenditure should **enhance the service potential beyond its original potential** (before the incident). In this case, it is difficult to see whether this is an enhancement. Furthermore, there is **uncertainty** surrounding whether the recovery would even be successful.

The choice of amortization method would appear to amortize less in the earlier years and, therefore, if this satellite is not old, further delay the expensing of the asset. The switch is appropriate if the new method provides better **matching** based on new information. Here, there is insufficient information to determine this, but presumably this is the case.

In conclusion, although the value of the asset is uncertain at this time, because of the accounting policies, accepted by the industry, a write-down would not be warranted. The key factor here is the ability to recover the cost even if the asset is no longer contributing to revenues. This presumably has the effect of smoothing the losses and dampens the impact on rates charged to customers. Management is confident at this point of restoring the service and, therefore, they do not perceive a loss to be likely; therefore, under contingency accounting, a loss would not yet be booked. Measurability might be an issue anyway since the costs to attempt to rescue would not be known but would likely be material. Note disclosure would be critical since the company would wish to get the facts straight and assure users that everything is fine. Any costs incurred to recover might be capitalizable if they enhanced the service potential beyond the original potential.

SELECTED SOLUTIONS FROM THE TEXTBOOK

BRIEF EXERCISE 11-11

Truck (new)	35,000	
Accumulated Amortization	17,000	
Loss on Disposal of Truck	1,000	
Truck (used)		20,000
Cash		33,000

EXERCISE 11-4 (20–25 MINUTES)

Purchase

Cash paid for equipment, including sales tax of $8,000	$108,000
Freight and insurance while in transit	2,000
Cost of moving equipment into place at factory	3,100
Wage cost for technicians to test equipment	4,000
Special plumbing fixtures required for new equipment	8,000
Total cost	$125,100

The GST of $7,000 paid on purchase of the equipment should be reported as GST Receivable, and not be capitalized. The insurance premium paid during the first year of operation of this equipment should be reported as insurance expense, and not be capitalized. Repaid cost incurred in the first year of operations related to this equipment should be reported as repair and maintenance expense, and not be capitalized. The insurance and repaid costs relate to periods subsequent to purchase.

Construction

Material and purchased parts ($200,000 × .98)	$196,000
Labour costs	190,000
Overhead Costs	50,000
Cost of installing equipment	4,400
Total cost	$440,400

Note that the cost of material and purchased parts is reduced by the amount of cash discount not taken because the equipment should be reported at its cash equivalent price. The imputed interest on funds used during construction related to share financing and should not be capitalized or expensed. This item is an opportunity cost that is not reported.

Profit on self-construction should not be reported. Profit should only be reported when the asset is sold.

EXERCISE 11-6 (15–25 MINUTES)

(a) 1.

Land	131,250	
Buildings	306,250	
Equipment	262,500	
Cash		700,000

$$\$700,000 \times \frac{\$150,000}{\$800,000} = \$131,250 \qquad \text{Land}$$

$$\$700,000 \times \frac{\$350,000}{\$800,000} = \$306,250 \qquad \text{Buildings}$$

$$\$700,000 \times \frac{\$300,000}{\$800,000} = \$262,500 \qquad \text{Equipment}$$

	2.	Store Equipment	25,000	
		Cash		2,000
		Note Payable		23,000
	3.	Office Equipment	19,600	
		Accounts Payable ($20,000 × .98)		19,600
	4.	Land	27,000	
		Donated Capital		27,000
	5.	Warehouse	600,000	
		Cash		600,000
(b)	1.	Buildings ($306,250 − $250,000)	56,250	
		Land ($150,000 − $131,250)		18,750
		Equipment ($300,000 − $262,500)		37,500
	2.	Interest Payable	2,300	
		Store Equipment		2,300
	3.	Purchase Discounts	400	
		Office Equipment		400
	4.	Land	27,000	
		Donated Capital		27,000
	5.	Profit on Construction	140,000	
		Warehouse		140,000

EXERCISE 11-12 (15–20 MINUTES)

(a)	Land	81,000	
	Donated Capital		81,000
(b)	Land	180,000	
	Buildings	630,000	
	Common Shares*		810,000

*Since the market value of the share is not determinable, the market value of the property is used as the basis for recording the asset and issuance of the shares.

(c)	Machinery	40,100	
	Materials		12,500
	Direct Labour		15,000
	Factory Overhead		12,600*

*[(60% × $15,000) + $2,700 + $900]
(Overhead applied, 60% of $15,000 plus $3,600)

EXERCISE 11-19 (15–20 MINUTES)

Carlos Company:

Equipment (New)	10,500	
Accumulated Amortization	19,000	
Equipment (Old)		28,000
Cash		1,500

Vacation of equpment:

Book value of equip. given	$ 9,000		Fair value received	$17,000
Fair value of boot given	1,500	OR	Less gain deferred	6,500*
New equip.	$10,500		New equipment	10,500

*Fair value of old	
equipment	$15,500
Book value of old	
equipment	(9,000)
Gain on disposal	$ 6,500

Note: Cash paid is less than 10%, the transaction is nonmonetary, so the gain is deferred.

Lo Bianco Company:

Cash	1,500	
Equipment (New)	15,500	
Accumulated Amortization	10,000	
Loss on Disposal of Plant Assets	1,000	
Equipment (Old)		28,000

Calculation of loss:

Book value of old equipment	$18,000
Fair value of old equipment	17,000
Loss on exchange	$ 1,000

EXERCISE 11-27 (20–25 MINUTES)

(a)	Income Tax Expense	250,495	
	Cash (Income Tax Payable)		220,895
	Machinery and Equipment		29,600

Amortization base, tax purposes =
    $296,000 − 10\% ($29,600) = $266,400
Income Tax Expense =
    ($749,000 − $266,400/8) × 35\% = $250,495
Cash paid (payable) for income tax =
    $250,495 − 10\% ($29,600) = $220,895

| Amortization Expense—Machinery and Equipment | 33,300 | |
| Accumulated Amortization Machinery and Equipment | | 33,300 |

($296,000 − 29,600) / 8 = $33,300

(b)

Income Tax Expense	250,495	
Cash (Income Tax Payable)		220,895
Deferred Investment Tax Credit		29,600

| Deferred Investment Tax Credit | 3,700 | |
| Income Tax Expense | | 3,700 |

($29,600 / 8)

| Amortization Expense—Machinery and Equipment | 37,000 | |
| Accumulated Amortization Machinery and Equipment | | 37,000 |

($296,000 / 8)

(c) The net income under each approach is shown below:

	Reduction in asset cost	Deferred and Amortized
Income before amortization and income tax	$749,000	$749,000
Amortization expense	33,300	37,000
Income before income tax	715,700	712,000
Income tax expense	250,495	246,795
Net income	$465,205	$465,205

The net income under the two approaches is the same. The amortization of the deferred tax credit is allocated to amortization expense under the reduction in asset cost method and to income tax expense under the deferral method.

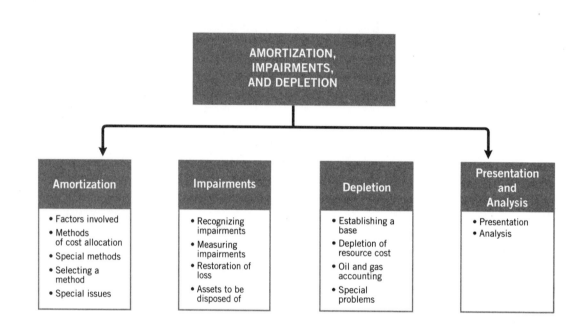

chapter 12

AMORTIZATION, IMPAIRMENTS AND DEPLETION

PERSPECTIVE—AMORTIZATION AND DEPLETION

This is an interesting topic because the choice of amortization method is often arbitrary. We all agree that assets with finite lives, usefulness, and limited ability to contribute to earning revenues should be amortized. Amortization takes the cost of the asset and matches it with the revenues, which the asset helps to generate. The objective is to select the method that best achieves this matching, and therein lies the problem. In most cases, it is impossible to prove that one method achieves this matching better than another does.

INSIGHTS

*There are numerous standard **methods of amortization,** e.g., the straight-line method, the declining balance method, units of production method and sinking fund method. Calculation of amortization under these methods should be mastered and the **impact on net income** of each method should be noted.*

In the resource industry, the depletion method helps allocate the cost of fixed assets to the periods in which it is contributing to revenues. This method should also be mastered.

STUDY STEPS

1. Understanding the Concept of Amortization Within a Business Context

STUDY STEPS

Amortization is a **cost allocation,** which is arbitrary at best. There is no cash flow impact of amortization. Having stated this, allocating the cost of the asset to the product that it is used to produce or the period in which the product will be produced or sold is very important from a business sense. It helps management get an idea of the **full cost** to produce a product or to run the business. This is important for pricing and for deciding whether or not to stay in business.

Tip! Even though amortization has no cash flow impact, it is important in pricing and profitability decisions.

Where amortizable assets are a significant portion of the balance sheet, the amortization expense can have a material impact on net income. Net income is a key number for management and users in decision making. Therefore, the choice of amortization method is very important.

Tip! The choice of amortization can impact significantly on net income and, hence, is very relevant to the decision-making process..

Capital cost allowance (CCA) is tax amortization according to the Income Tax Act. It is the amount that may be deducted for tax purposes in arriving at taxable income. CCA is calculated in a completely different manner than GAAP amortization since financial reporting objectives and Income Tax Act objectives are different. GAAP strives to match costs with revenues, whereas the Income Tax Act has different objectives and may be attempting, for instance, to encourage spending on certain types of assets in order to promote job creation. To that end, the government might allow assets to be charged to taxable income over a shorter period of time, thereby giving the company a greater tax break.

Tip! GAAP amortization allocates costs to revenues under the matching principle, whereas tax amortization is usually designed by the government to motivate certain types of behaviour.

Investment tax credits (ITC) are incentives offered under the Income Tax Act to taxpayers to encourage expenditures. ITCs are calculated by multiplying preset rates by the cost of the asset by present rates (e.g., the government might allow a 10% ITC for buildings). The resulting amount may be used to reduce taxes payable and, therefore, requires that ITCs be accounted for in the general ledger.

Tip! ITCs are further tax incentives offered by the government to motivate certain types of spending.

STUDY STEPS

2. Understanding How the Concept of Amortization and Depletion Fits into the Financial Reporting Model and Conceptual Framework—Analysis and Critical Thinking

Relevant criteria, definitions and issues

Business perspective: Although amortization is a non-cash item, and is generally viewed as a somewhat arbitrary allocation of costs, it is nonetheless important to decision making due to its often material impact on net income.

	How it relates to amortization	Relevant criteria/ definitions/terms	Topic specific analysis— how it should be	What makes the analysis challenging—how it is
Recognition	• when to recognize amortization or depletion expense	• **matching**	• since productive assets are used to generate revenues, costs should be allocated to periods in which revenues are generated in order to match costs with revenues • generally amortize over **useful life**	• difficult to determine **useful** or **economic life** • watch out for years where assets not in use
Measurement	• how much amortization to take	• **greater of a) cost less salvage over life; and b) cost less residual value over useful life** (HB 3061.28) • **recognize in a systematic and rational manner appropriate to asset and use** (HB 3061.31)	• look at revenue patterns to assist in determination of usage and contribution to revenues • to estimate useful life, consider effects of technological change, history of use, expected wear and tear • to estimate residual value, consider history, industry norms, etc.	
Presentation/ Disclosure	• what to disclose	• **full disclosure** (HB 3060.31)	• amortization method and amount	

3. Becoming Proficient in Calculating Amortization under the Various Generally Accepted Methods

STUDY STEPS

Any asset that has a limited life should be amortized in order to **match** the cost of the asset with the revenue that it helps to generate. The amount to be amortized should be the cost less any expected net residual value.

> For all methods, the residual value is deducted first, then the remaining amount is amortized. The exception to this rule is the declining balance method. Under this method, the residual value is not deducted first.

Problem 1 gives an example of how to calculate amortization under the various methods.

> Focus on the impact on net income of the various methods, i.e., does it increase net income or decrease it? What is the pattern over time? Below is a summary of the calculations from problem 1.

Amortization Method	Amount	Pattern over Time (Expense)
Straight-line	*$337,500*	*– constant*
Unit-of-Production	*$675,000*	*– varies with production levels*
Double declining balance	*$750,000*	*– decreasing*
Sinking fund	*$232,354*	*– increasing*

ITCs should be accounted for using the **cost reduction method** according to *CICA Handbook* Section 3805. This means that the ITC amounts should be booked as credits against the underlying costs to which they relate. For example, if the ITC relates to the purchase of a new building, the credit should be booked against the fixed asset account. If the ITC is for reducing payroll costs, the credit should be booked against payroll expense.

> **Tip!**
>
> **The cost reduction method should be used in accounting for ITCs (dr. taxes receivable cr. asset/expense that ITC is meant to offset).**

Problem 3 deals with calculation of ITCs using the cost reduction method.

Problem 4 deals with alternative methods of accounting for amortization of value of assets in the hotel industry.

MULTIPLE CHOICE QUESTIONS

1) Equipment with a four-year estimated useful life and a 10% salvage value was purchased on January 1, 2002. Calculate the amortization expense for 2004, using the double-declining balance method.
   a) original cost $\times$ .9 $\times$ .5 $\times$ .5 $\times$ .5
   b) original cost $\times$ .9 $\times$ .5 $\times$ .5
   c) (original cost less salvage value) $\times$ .5 $\times$ .5 $\times$ .5
   d) original cost $\times$ .5 $\times$ .5 $\times$ .5

(CGA adapted—FA1 Dec 1994)

2) Depletion expense:
   a) is usually part of cost of goods sold.
   b) includes tangible equipment costs in the depletion base.
   c) excludes intangible development costs from the depletion base.
   d) excludes restoration costs from the depletion base.

(CGA—FA2 December 1995)

3) Which of the following methods ignores residual value for depreciation calculation purposes?
   a) straight-line
   b) double declining balance
   c) units of production
   d) sum of the year's digits

4) When a company changes the expected remaining service life of an asset from seven years to five years because additional information has been obtained, the change should be accounted for:
   a) retroactively with restatement of prior years.
   b) retroactively without restatement of prior years.
   c) all in the year of the change.
   d) during the current and remaining periods.

(CGA—FA2 June 1996)

5) UVW Ltd. adopted an amortization policy by which the amortization method used each year would be selected in accordance with the company's ability to maintain and report a 20% rate of return on shareholders' equity. This is a violation of:
   a) the matching principle.
   b) the reliability characteristic.
   c) the consistency characteristic.
   d) all of the above.

(CGA adapted—FA2 June 1996)

6) The amount of amortization that should be charged to income is calculated as follows:
   a) the lesser of the cost less salvage value over life and cost less residual value over useful life.
   b) cost less salvage value over life.
   c) the greater of the cost less salvage value over life and cost less residual value over useful life.
   d) cost less residual value over useful life.

7) Jiang Ltd. purchased a machine for $3 million. The machine will last for 30 years (producing approx. 30 million units of product) and have a salvage value of $30,000 at the end of that time. In the first year, 600,000 units of product were produced. The company plans to use the machine for 30 years. Which of the following methods will result in the highest net income in year one?
   a) straight-line
   b) double declining balance
   c) units of production
   d) sum of the year's digits

8) An asset was purchased for $100,000 at the beginning of the year. The asset had a useful life of 10 years and an estimated salvage value of $10,000. Using the declining balance method, calculate the amortization expense for the second year.
   a) $9,000
   b) $8,100
   c) $1,600
   d) $10,000

9) A company switched from the sinking fund method to the straight-line method of amortizing its real estate properties based on a change in the extent that the assets were now being used. Net income for the current year in which the change is made would:
   a) increase by the difference in amortization expense as calculated under the different methods.
   b) decrease by the difference in amortization expense as calculated under the different methods.
   c) increase by the cumulative impact of the difference between the cumulative amortization expense under the two methods.
   d) decrease by the cumulative impact of the difference between the cumulative amortization expense under the two methods.

10) An oil and gas company uses the successful efforts approach for accounting for exploration and development costs. During the year, $300 million was spent on exploration and development of wells and potential well sites in the North Sea. Half of these expenditures led to dead ends. The remaining wells began production by the end of the year and produced 250,000 barrels. It is estimated that the total reserves prior to the production are at 250 million barrels. Calculate depletion for the year.
   a) $150,000
   b) $300,000
   c) $150,150
   d) $300,300

SOLUTIONS TO MULTIPLE CHOICE QUESTIONS

1) d) The double declining balance does not require that the salvage value be deducted in the calculation of amortization since the method will never theoretically reduce the net book value of the asset to zero anyway.

2) a) Since depletion represents a best estimate of the cost of the product being mined, it is recorded as cost of sales.

3) b) all other methods consider residual value

4) d) since the change is a change in estimate, it should be accounted for prospectively.

5) d) The policy violates the matching principle since no attempt has been made to match costs with revenues. The financial statements are not reliable if they are biased and if the depreciation is not calculated consistently from year to year on a systematic and rational basis.

6) c) This formula is identified as a recommendation in HB 3061.28. Since the greater amount of the two options must be chosen, this reduces any bias to minimize amortization expense.

7) c) units of production

$$\frac{600,000}{30,000,000} \times (\$3,000,000 - 30,000) = \$59,400$$

NB. Stright-line
   ($3,000,000 − 30,000) ÷ 30 years = $99,000

DDB
   $3,000,000 × .067* = $201,000
   (* 100% ÷ 30 years × 2)

SYD
   $$(\$3,000,000 - 30,000) = \frac{30}{465}** = \$191,613$$
   (** 1 + 2 + 3 + 4... + 30 = 465)

8) a) Amortization expense for the **second** year would be calculated as $100,000 × .9 × .1 = $9,000. Note that with the declining balance method, the residual value is ignored. Note also that this is **not** the double declining method.

9) b) The amortization expense under straight-line method is higher and therefore net income would be lower. The change would be accounted for prospectively since it is a change in estimate due to a change in circumstances. There would be no retroactive adjustment.

10) a) Under the successful efforts method, only those costs incurred to explore and develop successful wells would be part of the cost of the asset. Therefore, only half of the $300 million would be an asset. $150,000,000/250,000,000 barrels = $.6; $.6 × 250,000 barrels = $150,000.

SHORT PROBLEMS

1) Purpose: To illustrate the different methods of amortization and the impact on net income.

Capital Asset Corporation (CAC) recently purchased numerous pieces of machinery. The machinery cost $5 million and has an expected useful life of 10 years, at the end of which it will be worth $500,000. The equipment was acquired on March 1, 2002 and was first used in production on April 1, 2002. The sales representative who sold the equipment to CAC promised that it would produce 1 million units of inventory over its lifetime or CAC would get a rebate. By December 31, 2002, 150,000 units were produced.

Required

Calculate the amortization for the year ended December 31, 2002 using the following methods, noting the resulting amortization patterns over time, and giving an example where each method might be most appropriate.

(a) Straight-line.

(b) Units-of-production.

(c) Double-declining balance.

(d) Sinking fund method (10% interest rate assumed). For this item only, also calculate the amortization charges in years two and three.

2) Purpose: To review accounting for amortization in subsequent years when residual value and remaining life is reassessed.

Assume the same information as in 1 above, except that it is the following year. At the end of 2003, CAC reviewed the equipment and determined that the remaining useful life was only five years due to excessive wear and tear. They also determined that the residual value at the end of five years would be nil.

Required

Calculate the amortization charge using the straight-line method for 2003 and prepare the journal entry to record the amortization. Explain your answer.

3) Purpose: To illustrate the accounting for Investment Tax Credits (ITC).

Expansion Company Limited (ECL) was in the process of deciding where to locate a new facility that they were planning to build. At present, they were considering locating in Quebec since the government was offering a 10% ITC for new facilities located there. The government's objective was to stimulate investment in that province and to create jobs. By the end of 2000, the decision had been made and construction was underway. To date, $4,899,000 had been spent. The only way to obtain the ITC was to complete ECL's tax return for the year and to reduce taxes that would otherwise be paid by the ITC. Taxes payable before considering the ITC worked out to be $2,345,000.

Required

Prepare the journal entry to book the ITC and any amortization for the year.

4) Purpose: To illustrate the use of alternative amortization methods.

Hotel Company (HC) has a reasonably large investment in cutlery and fine china that is used in their food and beverage operations. The assets are considered to be fixed assets because they are used to produce food and beverage revenues (versus being sold). However, it is too difficult to depreciate the assets using conventional depreciation methods. Part of the problem is that breakage and theft are significant and traditional amortization accounting would neither capture nor reflect this. Therefore they take inventory annually to establish the quantity and value the inventory at 75% of laid-down cost to reflect that much of the cutlery and china is used.

On December 31, 2002, HC established the following after the physical inventory had been taken:

Value of cutlery at cost	$450,000
Value of china at cost	346,000
Value of cutlery and china December 31, 2001	600,980
Purchases during the year	134,000

Required

Calculate the amortization that should be booked on the cutlery and china.

SOLUTIONS TO SHORT PROBLEMS

1) (a) Straight-line:

($5,000,000 − 500,000) /10 years = $450,000
$450,000 × 9/12 = $337,500

The amortization has been prorated since the equipment has only contributed to revenues since April 1, 2002.

This method might be appropriate for a building where wear and tear is a function of the passage of time and where it contributes evenly to earnings over time (although it might just as easily be argued that it has greater value and earnings potential when it is new; consider a commercial rental building that attracts customers easily when new and generally loses tenants as it gets older and is perhaps less trendy or prestigious).

(b) Units-of-production:
$($5,000,000 - 500,000) \times 150,000/1,000,000$ units $= \$675,000$

This would be appropriate for an airplane whose engine is usually useable for a limited number of hours.

(c) Double-declining balance:
Ten years implies amortization of 10% per year. With double-declining balance, this is then doubled and the resulting percentage (i.e., 20%) is applied to the declining balance or net book value.

This might be applicable to a piece of machinery that is more productive when it is brand new, and has more down time and inefficiencies as it gets older. Therefore, it contributes more to earnings in the earlier years.

$\$5,000,000 \times 20\% = \$1,000,000$
$\$1,000,000 \times 9/12 = \quad \$750,000$

In 2003, amortization would be based on a book value of $\$5,000,000 - \$750,000 = \$4,250,000$.

(d) Sinking fund method:

$\$5,000,000$
$\quad = 15.93743x + 2.59374 \times \$500,000$
$\quad =$ future value of an annuity 10 yrs @ 10% + future value \$1 10 yrs @ 10%
$\quad x = \$232,354$

This would be prorated $232,354 × 9/12 = $174,265. Amortization for the first year would be $174,265. For the second year, it would be $232,354 plus interest on the $174,265 of 10% = $249,780. For the third year it would be $232,354 plus interest on the accumulated balance of ($174,265 + $17,426 + $232,354) @ 10% = $232,354 + $42,404 = $274,758. As you can see, the amortization increased each year, being the fixed amount plus interest on the cumulative amortization to date. This has sometimes been used in the real estate industry for property, to recognize that property values and earnings potential generally increase, and therefore support increasing amortization charges.

Tip! Amortization expenses increase over time. The sinking fund method is not widely used.

2) The net book value would be $5,000,000 − $337,500 = $4,662,500. Since there is no residual value and since the remaining life is now estimated at five years, the amortization for 2003 would be $4,662,500 / 5 = $932,500.

Amortization expense	932,500	
Accumulated amortization		932,500

This is treated as a change in estimate since it is part of management's ongoing review of accounts. It is therefore accounted for prospectively.

3) No amortization would be taken since the asset is not yet completed and is not contributing to revenues. The ITC would be calculated as 10% × $4,899,000 = $489,900. Since the ITC is given in order to assist in the financing of the asset, the credit should be matched against the cost of the asset and, therefore, used to reduce the cost (cost reduction method). In subsequent years, this would result in decreased amortization. The debit would be booked as a reduction of taxes otherwise payable.

Taxes payable	489,900	
Fixed assets		489,900

4) HC would use the inventory method. Their policy of valuing assets at 75% of cost is conservative and many companies value assets at 100% of cost. This is usually because, even though things like cutlery and china are subject to wear and tear, as long as they are useable, they have full value for the company. It is unlikely that they would wear out; Rather they are broken or stolen.

Opening balance	$600,980
Purchases	134,000
Less closing balance	
($450,000 + $346,000) × 75%	(597,000)
= amortization	$137,980

The amortization recognizes shrinkage through loss, theft, and breakage, and also recognizes wear and tear on remaining assets since they are valued at 75%.

CASES

1) LAIDLE DISPOSAL LIMITED (PART 2)

(See case in Chapter 11.)

If LDL's sites are accounted for as fixed assets, there is a further problem and that is which amortization method to use. L.L. has done some research and has noted that the following methods are used by a sample of companies:

> PepsiCo Inc. use straight-line on their property, plant, and equipment.
>
> Canadian Tire use declining balance on their property and equipment.
>
> Other companies use sinking fund for sum-of-the-year's-digits.

L.L. estimates that the sites will take, on average, 10 years to fill up and that the amount dumped will increase, at least initially (year 1, 3% of total capacity; year 2, 5% of total capacity; year 3, 10% of total capacity), as LDL picks up more contracts. On the other hand, most contracts are annual and the possibility exists that they may also lose some. The costs of most sites average $1 million and the financing has been obtained from various sources at an average rate of 10% which appears to be the best rate that they can get. Salvage values are not known at this time although land usually holds its value. L.L. is not sure what the difference is between these methods or what impact they might have on the financial statements. He is concerned that large amounts of amortization might make the financial statements look weak. On the other hand, the choice of amortization methods is probably arbitrary since one method is likely as good as another.

REQUIRED:

As an independent consultant to L.L., discuss the issues and provide recommendations.

2) CAMBRIDGE SHOPPING CENTRES LIMITED—www.cambridgemalls.com

Cambridge Shopping Centres Limited (CSCL) has as its largest asset on the balance sheet an item called Revenue Producing Properties. This item represents 85% of total assets on the balance sheet dated March 31, 1997. Amortization is taken on this balance using the sinking fund method (using a 5% interest rate in the calculations) so as to fully amortize these assets over their useful lives which range from 30 to 50 years. On the income statement, amortization for 1997 was $34 million ($31 million in 1996) and net loss for the year was $12 million ($105 million in 1996 after a write-down on the Revenue Producing Properties of $130 million pre-tax). The company has been in a loss position in four out of five of the most recent reporting years; however, it has had positive operating cash flows ranging from $43 million to $57 million.

The company has been operating since the 1960s and in the past decade, has doubled its Revenue Producing Properties balance on the balance sheet.

REQUIRED:

Adopt the role of a financial analyst and analyse the amortization policy adopted by CSCL.

SOLUTIONS TO CASES

1) LAIDLE DISPOSAL LIMITED (PART 2)

Overview

The financial statements will be used to obtain new contracts, and users will focus on financial stability and adherence to environmental standards. Management will therefore want the financial statements to show the company in the most favourable light (i.e., maximize profits and assets and minimize negative disclosures). The statements will likely be constrained by GAAP since the government will want reliable statements.

Analysis and Recommendations

Issues: Are the landfill sites inventory (in which case they do not have to be amortized) or are they fixed assets? If they are fixed assets, which amortization method is appropriate?

Inventory vs. Fixed Assets:

Dealt with in Part 1 to the case in Chapter 11

Amortization Method:

Since the assets generate income through use, it would make sense to amortize them, thereby **allocating the cost** to the periods in which the revenues are earned under the **matching** principle. The question arises as to which method to use. The straight-line method will result in equal amounts being booked to expense in each year and therefore will provide consistent net income. The declining balance will provide for decreasing amounts of expense and is best suited to revenues that decline over time or where the assets contribute less to revenues over time (i.e., as they wear out). The sum-of-the-years'-digits also results in decreasing charges to net income over time. The sinking fund method results in increasing charges and, therefore, is suited to assets that result in increases in revenues over time.

These methods are theoretically equally acceptable and to some extent the choice is arbitrary. However, true matching would attempt to **match the amortization pattern with the revenue pattern.** In this case, less revenues will be generated in the earlier years according to LDL estimates (yr 1, 3%, yr 2, 5%, etc.). The usage will not always be increasing, however, as contracts are annual and may be lost, therefore resulting in less capacity used. Based on this, the most appropriate choice may not be one of the methods presented, but rather one based on activity (e.g., if 3% is used in the first year, then 3% of the gross cost of the assets should be depreciated and 5% in the next year, etc.).

As a final note, the amount amortized should exclude salvage value according to the *Handbook*. In this case, the salvage value is not known, although land usually retains its value. Perhaps then, there is nothing to amortize. In the case, however, the land may not hold its value to the extent that it was used as a garbage dump and is likely not located in a primary location.

Therefore, assuming that the salvage value is not estimable, it would make sense to amortize based on the amount of the assets used up each year. This will result in more favourable income statements in the earlier years since the site will be used less initially. This will meet the financial reporting objective of making the financial statements look better, at least in the earlier years.

2) Cambridge Shopping Centres Limited

Overview

The financial statements will be used for investment purposes and, as a financial analyst, I would want to prepare a critical evaluation of the accounting policies and the impact on key financial statement ratios of the company. The real estate industry was hit hard in the middle 1990s in Canada with many companies going bankrupt. This is evidenced in the CSCL financial statements by the large write-down taken in 1996 and the fact that the company has suffered losses in four out of the past five years. On a positive note, the company has been able to maintain a positive cash flow from operations throughout this period.

Analysis and Recommendations

The company uses a sinking fund method of amortization, which generally provides for lower amortization in the earlier years. For a company that is expanding, this method would provide significantly less amortization and therefore higher net income than the use of the straight line method, for example. CSCL has almost doubled its Revenue Producing Property portfolio (in $) over the past decade and, therefore, choice of an amortization method would likely have a material impact on net income. This is true especially since these properties comprise 85% of the total assets and since amortization is more than twice the amount of the loss for the 1997 year-end.

Whether this method is appropriate or not depends on many things. This method is **often used in the real estate industry** and, therefore, it is supported by industry practice. It also is felt to better **match** the cost of the asset with the revenues generated by the properties. Since the value of these properties generally increases over the long-term and since revenues from these properties generally increase as well, then it may make more sense to charge greater amounts of amortization to match with the higher revenues.

Note that this particular argument might not hold true in Canada over the past decade or so when there have been two recessions that have sent real estate values and rentals spiralling. Of further interest is the crisis in the retail industry over the past few years that has seen many retail giants being forced to restructure. This will also affect CSCL if some of these giants are tenants of CSCL shopping centres (i.e., Eaton's).

In conclusion, the valuation and amortization of the Revenue Producing Properties is very significant and material in terms of impact on decisions. The practices adopted by CSCL have been accepted by the auditors of the company since the statements are audited and the practices appear to have industry backing. Both the method of amortization and the amortization period do have the impact of increasing net income or lowering net losses.

SELECTED SOLUTIONS FROM THE TEXTBOOK

BRIEF EXERCISE 12-10

(a)   Asset Turnover ratio:

$$\frac{\$143,011}{\dfrac{\$41,655 + \$59,007}{2}} = 2.84 \text{ times}$$

(b)   Profit margin:

$$\frac{\$10,710}{\$143,011} = 7.49\%$$

(c)   Rate of return on asset:

1. $2.84 \times 7.49\% = 21.3\%$

2. $$\frac{\$10,710}{\dfrac{\$41,655 + \$59,007}{2}} = 21.3\%$$

EXERCISE 12-2 (20–25 MINUTES)

(a)   If there is any residual value and the amount is unknown (as is the case here), the cost would have to be determined by looking at the data for the double-declining balance method.

$$\frac{100\%}{5} = 20\%; 20\% \times 2 = 40\%$$

Cost $\times$ 40% = \$20,000
\$20,000 $\div$ .40 = \$50,000 Cost of asset

(b)   \$50,000 cost [from (a)] − \$45,000 total amortization = \$5,000 residual value.

(c)   The lowest charge to income for Year 1 will be yielded by the straight-line method, and this will yield the higher net income.

(d)   The highest charge to income for Year 4 will be yielded by the straight-line method.

(e) The method that produces the highest book value at the end of Year 3 would be the method that yields the lowest accumulated amortization at the end of Year 3 which is the straight-line method.

Calculations:
St.-line = $50,000 − ($9,000 + $9,000 + $9,000) = $23,000
book value, end of Year 3.
D.D.B. = $50,000 − ($20,000 + $12,000 + $7,200) = $10,800
book value, end of Year 3.

(f) Since CCA must be used for fax purposes, neither the straight-line, or the double-declining balance method will impact cash flows in any of the years. Net income must be converted to taxable income by removing the accounting amortization and substituting capital cost allowance.

(g) The method that will yield the highest gain (or lowest loss) if the asset is sold at the end of Year 3 is the method which will yield the lowest book value (see part (e)) at the end of Year 3 which is the double-declining balance method in this case.

EXERCISE 12-12 (20–25 MINUTES)

(a) 1975–1984: ($2,000,000 − $60,000) ÷ 40 = $48,500/yr.

(b) 1985–2002:
Building ($2,000,000 − $60,000) ÷ 40 = $48,500/yr.
Addition ($500,000 − $20,000) ÷ 30 = $16,000/yr.
$64,500/yr.

(c) No entry required.

(d) Revised annual amortization
Building

Book value: ($2,000,000 − $1,358,000*)	$642,000
Residual value	60,000
	582,000
Remaining useful life	32 years
Annual amortization	$ 18,188

Addition

Book value: ($500,000 − $288,000**)	$212,000
Residual value	20,000
	192,000
Remaining useful life	32 years
Annual amortization	$ 6,000

* 48,500 × 28 years = $1,358,000
** $16,000 × 18 years = $288,000

Annual amortization expense:
building ($18,188 + $6,000) $24,188

PROBLEM 12-1

(a)   1.   Amortization Base Calculation:

Purchase price	$73,500
Less: Purchase discount (2%)	(1,470)
Freight-in	970
Installation	3,800
	76,800
Less: Residual value	1,200
Amortization base	$75,600

Straight line   2002: ($75,600 ÷ 8 years) × 2/3 year = $6,300
2003: ($75,600 ÷ 8 years) = $9,450

2.   Double-declining balance for 2002:
($76,800 × 25% × 2/3) = $12,800
DDB for 2003: ($76,800 − $12,800) × 25% = $16,000

(b)   CCA for 2002: $76,800 × 25% × _ = $9,600
CCA for 2003: ($76,800 − $9,600) × 25% = $16,800

(c)   An activity method. These methods allocate the amortization base based on actual usage of the asset over its estimated service life. In years where productivity is low, amortization expense will also be low and in years of high productivity, amortization will be high. This will provide better matching to the revenues generated from the use of the machine.

PROBLEM 12-11

(1) $82,000   Allocated in proportion to appraised values (1/10 × $820,000).

(2) $738,000   Allocated in proportion to appraised values (9/10 × $820,000).

(3)   Forty years   Cost less residual ($738,000 − $40,000) divided by annual amortization ($17,450).

(4) $17,450   Same as prior year since it is straight-line amortization.

(5) $91,000   [Number of shares (2,500) times fair value ($30)] plus demolition cost of existing building ($16,000).

(6)   None   No amortization before use.

(7) $30,000   Fair market value.

(8) $4,500   Cost ($30,000) times percentage (1/10 × 150%)

(9) $3,825 Cost ($30,000) less prior year's amortization ($4,500) equals $25,500. Multiply $25,500 times 15%.

(10) $150,000 Total cost ($164,900) less repairs and maintenance ($14,900).

(11) $37,500 Cost times 2/8 ($150,000 × 2/8).

(12) $9,375 Cost less prior year's amortization ($37,500) multiplied by 2/8 = $28,125 for the year. Multiply by 4/12 to get expense since was sold Feb. 1.

(13) $52,000 Annual payment ($6,000) times present value of annuity due at 8% for 11 years (7.710) plus down payment ($5,740). This can be found in an annuity due table since the payments are at the beginning of each year. Alternatively, to convert from an ordinary annuity to an annuity due factor, proceed as follows: For eleven payments use the present value of an ordinary annuity for 11 years (7.139) times 1.08. Multiply this factor (7.710) times $6,000 annual payment to obtain $46,260, and then add the $5,740 down payment.

(14) $2,600 Cost ($52,000) divided by estimated life (20 years).

```
                        ┌─────────────────┐
                        │   INTANGIBLE    │
                        │     ASSETS      │
                        └─────────────────┘
```

INTANGIBLE ASSETS

Intangible Asset Issues

- Characteristics
- Current standards
- Recognition and measurement at acquisition
- Valuation after acquisition

Specifically Identifiable Intangibles

- Patents
- Copyrights
- Trademarks
- Leaseholds
- Franchises

Goodwill

- Recognition
- Negative goodwill
- Valuation after acquisition
- Impairment

Intellectual Capital

Deferred Charges and Long-Term Prepayments

- Research and development costs
- Pre-operating costs
- Initial operating losses
- Organization costs
- Advertising costs
- Conceptual questions

Financial Statement Disclosure and Presentation

- Balance Sheet
- Income Statement
- Illustrative disclosures

chapter 13

INTANGIBLE ASSETS

PERSPECTIVE—INTANGIBLE ASSETS

Recognition and measurement of intangible assets is one of the most significant issues facing accountants. Often, the bulk of a company's intrinsic value is traceable to its management and employees, or goodwill due to other factors. This value is usually not recognized in the financial statements. The key problem is measurement of the transaction in an environment where there is bias to overstate the assets. The CICA has recently issued a new section (3062) dealing with intangible assets.

The text describes the basic types of intangibles normally encountered and discusses costing and valuation as they relate to each one.

INSIGHTS

- *Research and development costs, due to their size and significance, are dealt with separately in Section 3450 of the Handbook.*

STUDY STEPS

STUDY STEPS

1. Understanding the Nature of Intangible Assets and Deferred Costs

Goodwill

Goodwill represents the value attributable to a company (in excess of the value of net tangible assets) because it is a successful, functioning business with customers, established suppliers, trained employees, and a good management team.

If one company purchases another, and the latter company is successful, the purchaser will likely pay more than the recorded net assets are worth at fair value (FV). The excess is due to the factors mentioned above and represents either goodwill or other unrecorded intangibles.

Tip! Goodwill is never recognized unless it is purchased by the company, i.e., another company's goodwill. This is due to the difficulty and subjectiveness of measuring a company's own goodwill.

Research and development (R&D)

R&D costs pose other challenges. Many successful companies in today's business environment spend significant amounts of money on research and development. The research and development process is as follows:

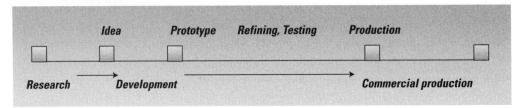

CICAHANDBOOK

R&D defined:

Research is planned investigation undertaken with the hope of gaining new scientific or technical knowledge and understanding. Such investigation may or may not be directed towards a specific practical aim or application

Tip! Research is a search for new knowledge.

CICAHANDBOOK

Development is the translation of research findings, or other knowledge, into a plan or design for new or substantially improved materials, devices, products, processes, systems or services prior to the commencement of commercial production or use.

Tip! Development activities centre on the development of a tangible idea to the commercial production stage.

Tip! Development activities usually begin with a tangible idea, often at the point when a prototype is developed. The cutoff between what is research and what is development is not obvious and requires professional judgement.

STUDY STEPS

2. Understanding How Intangible Assets and Deferred Costs Fit into the Financial Reporting Model and Conceptual Framework—Analysis and Critical Thinking

The following illustrates the decisions which must be considered in deciding how to account for **R&D**. The main thing to keep in mind is that research must be expensed and development costs may be capitalized if certain criteria are met.

Expense research, defer development if five criteria have been met. Once commercial production has begun, cease deferral and begin amortization. *Tip!*

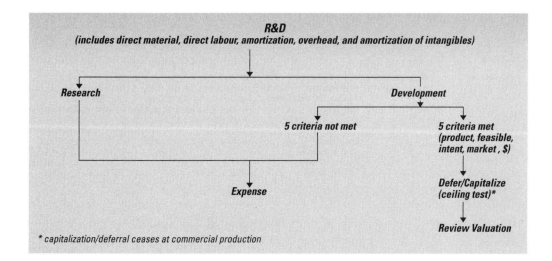

The following decision tree examines amortization and impairments of intangibles.

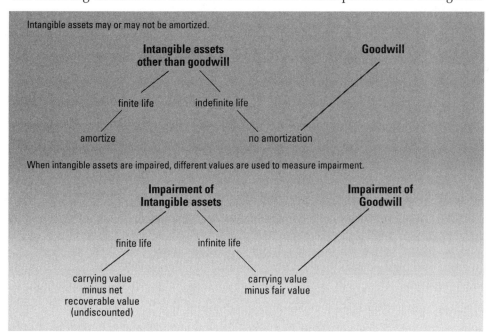

Note that goodwill and certain intangibles are no longer required to be amortized. It therefore becomes more important to assess these assets for impaiment.

Exhibit 13-1: Relevant criteria, definitions and issues

Business perspective: Intangible assets have no physical substance but have real value and contribute significantly to the value of the company. Intangible assets such as goodwill are very difficult to value and are often never reflected in the financial statements even though they continue to increase in value in successful companies.

	How it relates to intangible assets	Relevant criteria/ definitions/terms	Topic specific analysis— how it should be	What makes the analysis challenging—how it is
INTANGIBLES Recognition	• whether to reflect in balance sheet	• **definition of asset** • **future benefit** • **control over/access to** • **transaction has occurred**	• many intangibles meet the definition of an asset since they yield future benefit to the company and the company can control or has access to them (patents, copyrights, goodwill)	• complicated because whether there is future benefit and how much is very judgemental and management would tend to argue future value exists
Measurement	• what are these worth?—useful life? • when to write down	• **laid down cost** • **net recoverable value** • **recognize amortization in a systematic and rational manner for assets with finite lives** • **no amortization for assets with infinite lives**	• generally include any cost incurred to get assets ready for use such as registration and legal fees for patents, etc. (including fees to successfully defend) • capped at net recoverable amount, i.e., from future revenues (if finite life) • useful life must be re-estimated every reporting period • amortize to match cost with revenues (if finite life) • no amortization if infinite life • impairment – finite life – net recoverable value – infinite life – fair value	• biggest issue is uncertainty of future revenues and useful life–open to bias • must consider legal life and factors such as technological obsolescence when amortizing • judgement as to whether asset has finite or infinite life
Presentation/ Disclosure	• what to disclose	• **full disclosure**	• amortization method and amount • nature of measurement uncertainty (HB 1508.06) • disclose goodwill write downs	
DEFERRED DEVELOPMENT COSTS (in addition to issues above)				
Measurement Classification	• value of deferred costs	• **definition of research vs. development** • **dir. costs vs. indirect** • **5 capitalization criteria—product, feasible, intent, market, $**	• any cost to translate an idea and develop into commercial product— capitalized but due to uncertainty of future revenues must meet 5 criteria	• because of large amounts involved and tendency to defer costs, CICA has strict criteria that must be adhered to • **PJ required as to when research** becomes development and when development becomes commercial **production**

Prepared by Irene Wiecek
©2002 John Wiley & Sons Canada, Ltd

3. Becoming Proficient in Calculating Goodwill

Goodwill may be initially calculated by taking the fair market value of the assets and liabilities of the purchased company and deducting this number from the purchase price. This equation is called the purchase price equation.

Tip!   The concept of a purchase price equation was reviewed in the investments chapter when calculating investment income under the equity method. The equation looks at what was paid and what the company received in return.

Amount paid to buy the company	$xxxx
Less: fair market value of	
net assets purchased	(xxx)
Equals goodwill	$xxxx

Therefore, goodwill is easy to quantify in situations where a company is being purchased as long as the FV of the recorded assets and liabilities can be determined. It is simply a residual calculation. Problem 1 is another example of this.

MULTIPLE CHOICE QUESTIONS

1) Which of the following would not be included as research and development?
   a) routine or periodic alterations to existing products, production lines, manufacturing processes and other on-going operations
   b) depreciation of equipment being temporarily used for R&D
   c) laboratory research aimed at the discovery of new knowledge
   d) testing in search for, or evaluation of, product or process alternatives

2) Which of the following criteria is the overriding requirement for deferral?
   a) financing available
   b) product technically feasible
   c) product defined and related costs identifiable
   d) development costs do not exceed expected related net income from future commercial sale of product/process

3) Below is a list of things that may or may not be included as R&D. Identify the item that would be included as a development cost.
   a) engineering follow-through in an early phase of commercial production
   b) trouble-shooting in connection with breakdowns during commercial production
   c) design of tools, jigs, moulds and dies, including new technology
   d) quality control during commercial production, including routine testing of products

4) Deferral of development costs commences:
   a) from the date that the deferral criteria are met.
   b) in the year that the deferral criteria are met.
   c) in the year following the date when the deferral criteria are met.
   d) once the development process begins (retroactively deferred once the deferral criteria are met).

5) When purchasing shares of another company, goodwill is calculated as follows:
   a) FV of shares purchased minus NBV company purchased.
   b) FV of net assets purchased minus NBV of company purchased.
   c) FV of consideration given up minus FV of identifiable net assets purchased.
   d) FV of consideration given up minus NBV of identifiable net assets purchased.

6) The following is a list of expenditures that may or may not be capitalized as intangible assets/deferred costs. Which item is generally not capitalizable?
   a) organization costs
   b) one-time expenditures being paid to train employees during the pre-operating period of a new branch of an existing company
   c) operating losses incurred in development stages of a new company
   d) legal fees to successfully defend a patent infringement

7) Internally generated goodwill should not be recorded on an ongoing basis. Which of the following does not support this?
   a) Internally generated goodwill is too difficult to measure.
   b) There is no external transaction to value the goodwill.
   c) The future value may bear no relationship to the costs incurred to generate the goodwill today.
   d) The information is not relevant to users

8) The excess of the FV of identifiable assets purchased over the consideration paid is referred to as:
   a) goodwill
   b) negative goodwill
   c) negative badwill
   d) fair value increment

9) Purchased goodwill should be:
   a) amortized over its useful life.
   b) written off immediately due to the uncertainty as to future value and to ensure consistency with internally generated goodwill which is expensed.
   c) charged to shareholders' equity on the basis that, unlike other assets, goodwill is not separable from the business and cannot be sold separately.
   d) capitalized and not amortized.

10) Intangible assets with finite lives should be written down when:
   a) the carrying amount is no longer recoverable from expected future cash flows.
   b) FV is less than carrying value.
   c) FV is greater than expected future cash flows.
   d) it is subsequently felt that the amount allocated to the assets on acquisition was too high in retrospect.

SOLUTIONS TO MULTIPLE CHOICE QUESTIONS

1) a) These would not be included since the expenditures are **routine or periodic** adjustments/alterations to **existing** operations. Basically, R&D is focused on new technology or alternatives to existing technology.

2) d) The overriding factor would be the ceiling test which prohibits any non-recoverable development costs from being capitalized.

3) c) The significant word here is "new" technology. The other items deal with changes during commercial production. As a general rule, any changes during commercial production are not development costs.

4) b) According to *Handbook* Section 3450 par. .24, the costs would be deferred in the year that the criteria are met. There would be no retroactive reinstatement beyond the year.

5) c) Goodwill is the excess paid over the value of other identifiable net assets. The key here is that if the excess amount paid cannot be attributed to any identifiable asset (including intangible assets), then it must be due to goodwill.

6) c) The general consensus is that operating losses of **developing companies** should not be capitalized (*CICA Handbook* Accounting Guideline 11). The one related exception is the operating costs incurred during the pre-operating stages of a new division/branch of an **existing company** (EIC #27). Legal costs to successfully defend a patent infringement are generally capitalized. However, if the lawsuit is lost, generally, the costs would be expensed as the process would not add any value to the company.

7) d) The relevance argument supports capitalization. Users would find an internal assessment of the ongoing goodwill of the company very useful. The other points emphasize the fact that the information is not reliable and objective and, therefore, argue that reliability is more important than relevance.

8) b) When a purchaser pays less than the FV of a company, this is known as negative goodwill, or badwill, and means that the company is not even worth the sum of its parts, i.e., the FV of the individual identifiable assets. The fair value increment is the difference between the recorded value of identifiable assets and the FV of the recorded assets.

9) d) Goodwill should be capitalized as an asset and not amortized. It should be tested for impairment periodically

10) a) The impairment test is the same test used for tangible capital assets as identified in *Handbook* Section 3061—that of recoverability. The FV test is not relevant unless the asset has an infinite life. Subsequent adjustments to the purchase price equation are not normally made (EIC #14), except under rare circumstances. Because of the wording on this question, d) is also an acceptable answer.

SHORT PROBLEMS

1) Purpose: To identify and calculate purchased goodwill.

Buyitall Limited (BL) acquired the net assets of Sellitall (SL) for $4,567,000. At the time of purchase, the net book value of those assets was $2,908,000 and the fair market value of the net assets, which was established through an appraisal, was $3.2 million. At the date of purchase, SL was earning higher than average profits because they had sole distribution rights for state-of-the-art digital equipment (the "rights") that was expected to become obsolete within the next 10 years. The digital equipment was developed internally by the company, whose research and development activities were seen by the industry as being leading edge. As a matter of fact, SL had several new products in the testing stages at the time of purchase. The value of these rights is included in the $3.2 million.

Required

Calculate the amount of goodwill that should be recorded, and note the amortization period if any for the rights, explaining your choice. At what value would the net fixed assets be recorded?

2) Purpose: To illustrate decisions that must be made when accounting for research and development expenditures.

Discovery Limited (DL) invests heavily in research and development. They are in the electronics business and the pioneering of new technology is the key critical success factor. In 2003, DL worked on many new products; however, only one resulted in a product that was saleable. The product, product X, was now in production. Product X was one of a kind and heralded by the industry as a significant breakthrough. Competitors were already sniffing around, however, and DL felt that the competition would have similar products out within the next three years. DL hoped to gross $5 million by then. Commercial production began December 1, 2003.

The following expenditures were made during the year:

Ongoing search for new products including $2,000,000 for product X	$10,000,000
Development of product X prototype to establish feasibility	750,000
Marketing activities to determine market acceptance of product X prior to commercial production	250,000
Product X testing/refining	1,000,000
Rent for warehouse where testing activities took place	400,000
Assets purchased for manufacturing product X (used for testing for nine months and commercial production for one month-useful life five years)	4,000,000
Salary of manager in charge of all research and development	150,000

Required

Explain how each expenditure would be treated and why (i.e., research, development, etc.). How much would be capitalized in the development account and what would its value be on December 31, 2003?

SOLUTIONS TO SHORT PROBLEMS

1) Purchase price equation:

Price paid by BL	$4,567,000
Fair market value of net assets purchased	3,200,000
Difference	1,367,000

The difference reflects goodwill. Since the net assets of the company were purchased, and not shares, goodwill would be booked as an intangible asset at the date of acquisition and would not be amortized.

With respect to the amortization period for the rights, the period could be established as 10 years since the excess profits being earned now appear to be due to sales of the new state-of-the-art digital equipment. The net fixed assets would be recorded at fair market value, which would become the new cost base. Amortization would be booked based on the fair market value of the assets and the remaining useful lives, which would be reassessed at the time of purchase.

2) The expenditures would be classified as follows:

Ongoing search for new products including
$2,000,000 for product X $10,000,000
(see 1 below)

Development of product X prototype to establish feasibility 750,000
(see 2 below)

Marketing activities to determine market acceptance
prior to commercial production   250,000
(see 3 below)

Product testing/refining   1,000,000
(see 4 below)

Rent for warehouse where testing activities took place   400,000
(see 5 below)

Assets purchased for manufacturing (used for testing for
nine months and commercial production for one month
—useful life five years)   4,000,000
(see 6 below)

Salary of manager in charge of all research and development 150,000
(see 7 below)

1)   Clearly research since it meets the definition. Therefore, expense all of it, even though it includes research on product X.

2)   Development of the prototype would be a development cost as stipulated in the *Handbook* and, more generally, since it is the translation of research findings into a saleable product. It may not be capitalizable since technical feasibility is required as a prerequisite prior to capitalization. This is a judgement call. The *Handbook* states in Section 3450 par. .24 that the deferral of development costs would commence in the fiscal year in which all five criteria are met. Therefore, it might be argued that any development costs in 2003 are capitalizable since all five criteria are met before year-end. However, costs written off in prior years would not be eligible for deferral.

3)   Normal marketing activities are not considered to be either research or development. However, marketing activities undertaken to establish the existence of a market for the product could be considered development cost, and capitalization would depend on the five criteria being met. As above, established market is one of the criteria and is required as a prerequisite prior to capitalization. Therefore, this is also a judgement call. Since all five criteria are met in 2003, it could be argued that this is eligible for deferral.

4) Clearly a development cost and, therefore, it is eligible for deferral.

5) This is also a development cost since it is directly related to the development of the product.

6) Nine months' worth of amortization would be deferred as development cost since the machine was required for development activity. Therefore, $4,000,000/5 \times 9/12 =$ $600,000 would be deferred. The fixed assets would be recorded as fixed assets but the amortization expense for the nine months would be deferred as development. The amortization for the one month would be expensed as a period cost.

7) This could be seen as an indirect period cost and, therefore, expensed. Alternatively, part of it could be deferred. The *Handbook* allows a reasonable amount of overhead to be included as development costs. The key thing is the relationship between incurring the cost and the development activity. Here, if we could substantiate the amount of time that the manager spent on developing product X, this might be capitalizable. Since no information is given, expense the salary due to subjectivity.

Therefore, $3 million would be deferred assuming five criteria met ($750,000 + $250,000 + $1,000,000 + $400,000 + $600,000). Since production began December 1, deferral of any more costs would also cease beyond this point and amortization would begin. The amortization period is subjective and would be shorter due to the nature of the industry. Since it is believed that competitors will come out with a similar product within three years, this might be an appropriate period. Therefore, for the year ended December 31, 2003, the net amount deferred would be $3,000,000 - ($3,000,000/36 months) = $2,916,667.

As a final note, deferral of costs would not exceed the expected revenues. Since the latter is $5 million we are okay for 2003. This would be subsequently evaluated annually as revised estimates of forecasted revenues are determined.

CASES

1) RESEARCH AND DEVELOPMENT EXPENDITURES

The bulk of research and development expenditures are spent in industries which are highly competitive and where product/process innovation is critical to the continued success of the companies. Consistently high or increasing levels of expenditures are required each and every year as competitors are quick to copy the new technology. Even in poor economic times, these expenditures are considered non-discretionary.

Many of these companies, and indeed most companies in all industries, lean towards expensing the costs.

REQUIRED:

Discuss the above statement making reference to whether GAAP should be modified such that all R&D expenditures are expensed.

2) Mbanx—www.mbanx.com

Mbanx is the brainchild of the Bank of Montreal. The company was first launched in late 1996 and the concept is that of a "virtual bank." The company does not have the same heavy capital expenditures tied up in the traditional bank branches nor does it have the huge salary costs that go with the more traditional branch banking and teller approach. Mbanx, on the other hand, exists only on the Internet and is, of course, supported by the Bank of Montreal head office function. Customers log on to the company's web site and can do all of their banking from their computer terminal. There is no need to physically go into a branch. The concept is further supported by telephone access to consultants who will help in whatever way they can.

The concept required a very radical advertising campaign, which deluged the television airwaves and newspapers for several months prior to the launch of the bank. Significant funds were spent on designing this campaign and paying for the advertising time. Mbanx was set up as a separate subsidiary of the Bank of Montreal.

Required:

Discuss the accounting issues that must be dealt with in the first year of financial reporting for Mbanx. Focus on the up-front expenditures.

SOLUTIONS TO CASES

1) Research and Development Expenditures

Support for expensing:
- Generally prevalent practice
- Would remove much of the required judgement
- Simple, practical
- Since much of the development is done in industries where technology changes at a rapid pace, and due to competitors' copying practices, chances are that the life of the product/process is very short (i.e., perhaps one to two years)
- Continued expenditures means that impact on net income is likely not material if expensed versus if it were capitalized
- Would be more in line with U.S. practice
- Would lead to more comparability between companies
- Would result in less manipulation

Support for deferral:

- The expenditures provide a future benefit and therefore should be matched with future revenues

- Just because expensing is generally practised or because it is easy does not justify its use. The objective of financial reporting is to provide useful information.

- Just because other countries use it does not justify it either, since other countries have different reporting environments and their standard-setting processes may be more political

- In Canada, certain industries such as the pharmaceutical industry are protected from other companies copying new advancements

There are obviously trade-offs within our conceptual reporting framework. One objective is to have neutral standards that have representational faithfulness; however, standards cannot be set in an ivory tower. That is, accountants and standard setters must consider the real-life implications and consider the cost versus benefit of the information provided under a standard. It is too easy to say "every one does it and, therefore, it is acceptable." As professionals, standard setters must set their sights higher and consider whether everyone does it for the right reasons. As for reducing the chance of manipulation, mandating one alternative will eliminate manipulation, but it will also reduce freedom of choice.

Canadian accounting standards are intentionally not as rigid as others since the basic premise is that no one rule can fit every circumstance. If used properly, choice, and therefore the use of professional judgement, is a good thing.

2) Mbanx

Overview

The company is in a very competitive industry which has been achieving new heights in profitability in the last two years. Therefore, profit maximization for the Bank of Montreal would be important. Furthermore, the banking industry in Canada has always been very traditional and conservative and, therefore, while championing this radical new, concept, Bank of Montreal would likely not wish to show that the costs involved in launching this radical concept was in any way eating into its profits and traditional operations. GAAP would be a constraint since it is a subsidiary of Bank of Montreal, which is public.

Analysis and Recommendations

The main issue would be how to treat the start-up costs associated with this new venture. The costs would likely be significant. Generally speaking, **start-up enterprises follow the same principles as existing companies.** This is supported by US GAAP as well as Accounting Guideline 11.

This scenario could be seen to be analogous to **development costs** and, hence, expensing would be required unless the five development criteria are met. In this case, there is a **product**-internet banking, that has a **prototype**—it is already in use in the first year. Judging by the advertising, management clearly has the **funds** and the **intent** to follow through. The question arises as to whether the **market exists.** Judging by the startling rise in home computer purchases and internet usage, it is likely that the market is ready, at least on a tentative scale. One of the major issues, of course, is security of sensitive information transmitted over the Internet. However, companies are fast increasing and refining encryption codes which scramble the information.

Therefore, it could be argued that these costs are like development costs and since the criteria are met, this would allow capitalization.

Furthermore, there is an EIC on **pre-operating costs** that would seem to be applicable here (EIC #27). This EIC deals with companies such as Bank of Montreal who are starting up new operations such as Mbanx and, therefore, it is worth analysing from the EIC perspective. The EIC allows capitalization, or deferral of costs, if the costs are **directly related** to placing the new business into service; the costs are **incremental** and it is **likely** that the costs will be **recoverable.**

Certainly the marketing costs can be seen to be **incremental** and **directly related** since the campaign does not necessarily refer to traditional banking nor to the Bank of Montreal. The question is whether the costs are **recoverable.** Management would likely argue yes since they have brainstormed the idea and have committed significant funds to the project. The recoverability is, however, open to uncertainty and therefore PJ.

In conclusion, it would be in the best interest of the bottom line to defer the costs and it would be a supportable, albeit aggressive, position.

SELECTED SOLUTIONS FROM THE TEXTBOOK

BRIEF EXERCISE 13-7

(a)

Purchase price		$750,000
Fair value of assets	$800,000	
Fair value of liabilities	200,000	
Fair value of net assets		600,000
Value assigned to goodwill		$150,000

(b) Goodwill is not amortized. It is tested for impairment on an annual basis and any difference between the asset's carrying amount and its fair value is recorded as an impairment loss.

EXERCISE 13-5 (15–20 MINUTES)

Research and Development Expense	940,000	
Patents	75,000	
Rent Expense [(5 ÷ 7) × $91,000]	65,000	
Prepaid Rent [(2 ÷ 7) × $91,000]	26,000	
Advertising Summary	207,000	
Income Summary	241,000	
Discount on Bonds Payable	82,950*	
Interest Expense	1,050	
Common Shares		250,000
Intangible Assets		1,424,000

*84,000 ÷ 240 months = $350; $350 × 3 = $1,050; $84,000 − $1,050 = $82,950

Amortization Expense—Patent	3,750	
Patents (or Accumulated Amortization)		3,750
[($75,000 ÷ 10) × 1/2]		

EXERCISE 13-10 (15–20 MINUTES)

(a)

Carter Corp.
INTANGIBLES SECTION OF BALANCE SHEET
December 31, 2003

Patent, net of accumulated amortization	
of $560,000 (Schedule 1)	$1,440,000
Franchise, net of accumulated amortization	
of $48,000 (Schedule 2)	432,000
Total intangibles	$1,872,000

Schedule 1: Calculation of Patent from Gerald Inc.

Cost of patent at date of purchase	$2,000,000
Amortization of patent for 2002 ($2,000,000/10 years)	(200,000)
	1,800,000
Amortization of patent for 2003 ($1,800,000/5 yrs)	(360,000)
Patent balance	$1,440,000

Schedule 2: Calculation of Franchise from Reagan Ltd.

Cost of franchise at date of purchase	$ 480,000
Amortization of franchise for 2003 ($480,000 ÷ 10)	(48,000)
Franchise balance	432,000

(b)

Carter Corp.
INCOME STATEMENT EFFECT
For the year ended December 31, 2003

Patent from Gerald Inc.:		
Amortization of patent for 2003		
($1,800,000 ÷ 5 years)		$360,000
Franchise from Reagan Ltd.:		
Amortization of franchise for 2003		
($480,000 ÷ 10)	$ 48,000	
Payment to Reagan Ltd.		
($2,500,000 × 5%)	125,000	173,000
Research and development costs		433,000
Total charged against income		$966,000

EXERCISE 13-13 (15–20 MINUTES)

Net assets of Zweifel as reported		$225,000
Adjustments to fair value		
Increase in land value	30,000	
Decrease in equipment value	(5,000)	25,000
Net assets of Zweifel at fair value		250,000
Selling price		350,000
Amount of goodwill to be recorded		$100,000

The journal entry to record this transaction is as follows:

Cash	100,000	
Land	100,000	
Building	200,000	
Equipment	170,000	
Copyright	30,000	
Goodwill	100,000	
Accounts Payable		50,000
Long-term Notes Payable		300,000
Cash		350,000

Glossary

GLOSSARY OF KEY TERMS

accretion - the increase in value that results from natural growth or the ageing process

accrual accounting - the recording of events that change an entity's financial statements in the periods in which the events occur, not just the periods in which the entity receives or pays cash

basket purchase - a purchase of a group of varying units at a single lump sum price

benefit-cost relationship - the weighing of the benefits that can be derived from the information against the costs of providing it

capital asset - identifiable assets that are acquired for use in operations and not for resale and are long-term in nature and usually subject to amortization

capital maintenance approach - the measurement of income by the difference in captial values (net assets) at two points in time

cash equivalents - short-term, highly liquid investments that are both readily convertible to known amount of cash and so near to their maturity that they present insignificant risk of changes in interest rates

comparability - a characteristic of the relationship between two pieces of information - ie, information that is measured and reporting in a similar manner for different enterprises in a given year or for the same enterprise in different years

conceptual framework - a coherent system of interrelated objectives and fundamentals that can lead to consistent standards and that prescribes the nature, function, and limits of financial accounting and financial statements

conservatism - the convention of taking the solution, when faced with reasonable doubt in an accouting situation, that will be least likely to overstate net assets and income

consistency - the result of using the same accounting policies for similar events from period to period

consolidation - the process that reports the parent and subsidiary as one economic entity

contingency - existing condition involving uncertainty as to possible gain or loss

contra account - an item on a balance sheet that reduces either an asset, liability, or shareholders' equity account

control - the ability to direct the strategic policies of a corporation (usually by ownership of voting interest)

cost - the purchase price and incidental direct acquisition costs, such as brokerage commissions, legal fees, and taxes

current assets - cash or other assets that are expected to be converted into cash, sold, or consumed within either one year or on operating cycle, whichever is longer

current liabilities - obligations that are reasonably expected to be liquidated either through the use of current assets or the creation of other current liabilities

decision usefulness - the extent to which there is appropriate linking of decision makers and their capability to understand financial information with the primary and secondary qualities of information

deferred charges - a classification used to describe an number of different items that have debit balances

depletion - the term used to indicate that natural resources have declined in service potential

depletion base - the amortizable amount of a natural resource

development stage enterprise - an enterprise trying to establish a new business

discovery basis - the practice of recognizing revenue equal to the value of resources at the time of their discovery

dissimilar nonmonetary asset - assets that are not of the same general type, that may perform a different function or might be employed in different lines of business

earning process - all of the activities and events a company engages in to earn revenue

economic entity assumption - the assumption that economic activity can be identified with a particular unit of accountability

elements - parts of the financial statement (assets, liabilities, etc)

feedback value - the usefulness of information in confirming or correcting prior expectations

financing activities - activities that involve liability and shareholders' equity items

f.o.b. destination - the shipping of goods where the risks and rewards of ownership do not pass to the buyer until the goods reach the destination

f.o.b. shipping point - the shipping of goods where the risks and rewards of ownership pass to the buyer when the seller delivers the goods to the transporter who acts as an agent for the buyer

franchise - a contractual arrangement under which the franchiser grants the franchisee the right to sell certain products or services, to use certain trademarks or trade names, or to perform certain functions, usually within a designated geographical area

full disclosure principle - the provision of information that is of sufficient importance to influence the judgement and decisions of an informed user

future removal & site restorations costs - costs associated with dismantling, abandonning, and cleaning up a property

generally accepted accounting principles (GAAP) - rules, practices and procedures relating to particular circumstances as well as their application and the concepts on which they are based

going concern assumption - the assumption that the business enterprise will continue to operate in the foreseeable future and will be able to realize assets and discharge liabilities in the normal course of operations

goodwill - the residual or the excess of the cost over the fair value of the identifiable net assets acquired

historical cost - the basis for valuing property, plant, and equipment that measures the cash or cash equivalent price of obtaining the asset and bringing it the the location and condition necessary for its intended use

historical cost principle - the practice of recognizing transactions or events in financial statements at the amount of cash or cash equivalents paid or received or the fair value ascribed to them when they took place

improvements (betterments) - substitutions of one asset (a better one) for another

instalment sale - any type of sale for which payment is required in periodic instalments over an extended period of time

investing activities - activities that include making and collecting loans; and acquiring and disposing of investments as well as property, plant, and equipment

investment tax credit - a credit that allows an enterprise to reduce its taxes payable by a stipulated percentage of the cost of qualified depreciable assets purchased

leasehold improvements - improvements made to a leased property which normally become the property of the lessor when the lease expires

liquidating dividend - the amount by which dividends received by the investor exceed its share of the investee's earnings since acquisition

liquidity - the amount of time that is expected to elapse until an asset is realized or otherwise converted into cash or until a liability has to be paid

major repairs - expenditures that go beyond maintaining plant assets in operating condition

markdowns - decreases in price below the original selling price due to special sales, soiled and damaged goods, overstocking, or competition

markups - increases in price above the original selling price

matching principle - the understanding that expenses that are linked to revenue in a cause and effect relationship are normally matched with the revenue in the accounting period in which the revenue is recognized

materiality - the extent to which an item, or aggregate of items would influence or change a decision if it were omitted or misstated

minority interest - the noncontrolling interest owned by someone other than the parent company

monetary unit assumption - the assumption that money is the common denominator by which economic activity is conducted, and that the monetary unit provides an appropriate basis for accounting measurement and analysis

negative goodwill (badwill) - the excess of fair value over the cost of the assets acquired

neutrality - the quality of information that is free from bias that would lead users toward making decisions that are influenced by the way the information is measured or presented

nonmonetary transactions - transactions for property or services

nonreciprocal transfers - contributions (received or made) such as donations or gifts

obsolescence - a situation where an asset has reached the end of its useful life and where neither inadequacy nor supersession is involved

operating activities - activities that involve the cash effects of transactions that enter into the determination of net income at some point

parent - a corporation that owns more than 50% of another corporation

period costs - selling expenses and general and administration expenses that are not considered to be directly related to the acquisition or production of goods

periodic inventory system - a system whereby the cost of goods sold is determined by adding Net Purchases to Beginning Inventory and then subtracting Ending Inventory

periodicity assumption - the assumption that the economic activities of an enterprise can be divided into artificial time periods

perpetual inventory system - a system whereby purchases and sales of goods are recorded directly in an Inventory subaccount as they occur

predictive value - the usefulness of information in helping users predict the outcome of past (yet uncompleted), present, and future events

product costs - costs which are directly connected with the bringing of goods to the place of business of the buyer and converting such goods to a saleable condition

professional judgement - the process of reaching a decision in an analytical, objective, prudent and ethical manner and using one's experience and knowledge

purchase commitments - contracts for the purchase of inventory in advance

relevance - the degree to which information can influence the decisions of users

reliability - the quality that states that the information is in agreement with the actual underlying transactions and events, is capable of independent verification and is reasonably free from error and bias

replacement cost - the amount that would be needed to acquire an equivalent item, by purchase or production, as would be incurred in the normal course of business operations

representational faithfulness - the result of transactions and events affecting an entity being presented in financial statements in a manner that is in agreement with the actual underlying transactions and events

residual value - the estimated net realizable value of a capital asset at the end of its useful life to an enterprise

restricted cash - cash set aside for a particular purpose including compensating balances

revenue realization principle - a guideline as to when revenue should be recorded in the accounts

securization - the phenomenon in the sale of receivables which takes a pool of assets such as credit card receivables, mortgage receivables, or car loan receivables and sells shares in these pools

significantly influenced investment - an ownership interest in another company that is sufficient to allow management to significantly influence that company's strategic policies

similar nonmonetary assets - assets that of the same general type, that perform the same function, or are employed in the same line of business

subsequent events - events that materially affect the company's financial position or operating situation and occur between the balance sheet date and its distribution to shareholders and creditors

subsidiary - a corporation that has greater than 50% of voting interest held by another corporation

temporary investments - short-term paper and equity securities acquired with cash not immediately needed in operations

timeliness - the availability of information to decision makers before it loses its capacity to influence their decisions

transfer with recourse - the sales of receivables where the seller guarantees payment to the purchaser in the event the debtor fails to pay

transfer without recourse - the sale of receivables where the purchaser assumes the risk of collectibility and absorbs any credit losses

understandability - the connection between the infomation and its users which facilitates decision-making

uniformity - the application of the same accounting methods by different enterprises

unrealized gross profit - the gross profit under the instalment method that is deferred until the period of cash collection

useful life - the estimate of either the period over which a capital asset is expected to be used by an enterprise, or the number of production or similar units that can be obtained from the asset by the enterprise

verifiability - the quality which allows knowledgeable and independent observers to concur that the representation of a transaction or event in the financial statements is in agreement with the actual underlying transaction or event with a resonable degree of precision

working capital - the excess of total current assets over total current liabilities